Artaud on Theatre

Artaud on Theatre

edited by
CLAUDE SCHUMACHER

with
BRIAN SINGLETON

Methuen Drama

Methuen

2 4 6 8 10 9 7 5 3 1

First published in 1989 by Methuen Drama

This edition, with new material and a new cover,
was published in 2001 by Methuen Publishing Limited,
215 Vauxhall Bridge Road, London SW1V 1EJ

Selection, Introduction and Commentary
copyright © 1989, 2001 Claude Schumacher
'Artaud, East and West' © 2001 Brian Singleton
Translation copyright © 1989, 2001 Claude Schumacher and
Brian Singleton (except extracts from
Collected Works, Vols 1-4, copyright © Victor Corti, 1989)
The Cenci translation copyright © 1970 Simon Watson Taylor

Methuen Publishing Limited Reg. No. 3543167

A CIP catalogue record for this book is available from the British Library

ISBN 0 413 73770 5

Typeset by SX Composing DTP, Rayleigh, Essex
Printed and bound by
Mackays of Chatham plc, Chatham, Kent

Contents

Part Three: Cinema (1926–32)

Part Four: The NRF Theatre Project (1931–3)

Part Five: 'The Theatre and Its Double' (1931–7)

PART SIX: 'The Cenci' (1935)

PART SEVEN: Religion and Sexuality (Rodez 1943–6)

PART EIGHT: Return to Paris (1946–8)

*To Robin Slaughter and
Donald Watson, a small
token of my gratitude*

Illustrations

We are privileged to publish portraits that Madame Denise Colomb took of Artaud, in her own home in Paris and at the nursing home of Ivry where Artaud stayed after his return from Rodez. We are honoured by Madame Colomb's confidence in our work and we thank her most warmly.

This is how Madame Colomb describes the circumstances in which the pictures came to be taken:

> It was after his return from Rodez, in 1947. Antonin Artaud was studying a portrait of Pierre Loeb's daughter. 'I do need photographs, but I won't go to a photographer. I can't stand them.' 'Don't worry,' said Pierre, 'my sister took this picture, not a photographer.'
>
> So he came to sit in my flat, in a Directoire-style armchair. He was extremely nervous and his facial expression like his physical demeanour kept changing with astonishing mobility. He gave me a copy of his *Letters from Rodez* with a dedication wishing me all possible ills . . .

Madame Colomb's brother, Pierre Loeb, an artist and an influential art dealer, used to invite friends and colleagues to his house and Artaud sometimes read from his work on such occasions. Madame Colomb, after having taken the photographs, attended some of the gatherings when Artaud was also present. She recalls that he spoke 'avec violence, avec une véhémence extrême' (very violently and vehemently). 'Artaud gesticulated while speaking the texts. He acted them out most aggressively, to the point of indecency', adds Madame Colomb who can still remember her embarrassment at Artaud's exhibitionism. But she fondly recalls the memory of a young woman novelist, Colette Thomas, author of *Le Testament de la fille morte*, 'who spoke Artaud's texts beautifully, far more beautifully than Artaud himself'.

Introduction

> No one, in the whole history of theatre, has taken theatre as
> seriously as Artaud, to the extent that it became for him the
> nub and the act of life itself . . . This was the real nature of
> his madness. He expected from theatre far more than it
> could ever give: salvation.
>
> [A. Simon]

Antonin Artaud, the man who – perhaps more than any other –
theatricalized his life, loathed the theatre. Yet through theatre he
wanted to reform life, to attain some kind of salvation, not only for
himself but for all mankind.

As actor and director, he failed. As a theorist, his influence was
confined initially to a handful of Parisian intellectuals. Silenced
during his lifetime, his posthumous voice remained muffled for
many years thanks to the wrangles between his closest friends,
admirers and idolaters. But since the sixties and particularly since
May 1968, Artaud, his ideas and his example, have become, for
theatre people, a compulsory source of reference. For many
commentators, contemporary theatre which does not plunge its
roots into the world of Brecht stems from Artaud.

The list of those who claim to be his heirs, who define their
work in relation to his, who are perceived to be his followers is
endless. Among post-1945 theatre people one must mention the
authors of the 'theatre of the absurd' (Adamov, Genet, Arrabal,
even Beckett); political avant-garde dramatists like Weiss or Gatti;
directors like Roger Blin, Jean-Louis Barrault, Jean Vilar, Roger
Planchon, Brook, Marowitz, Grotowski, Kantor; companies like
the Living Theatre, the Open Theatre, the Bread and Puppet
Theatre, La Mama, the Théâtre du Soleil . . .; theatrical
happenings, modern dance companies (Cunningham, Béjart, Pina
Bausch . . .), performance art, and so on. In their infinite diversity
they all share an Artaudian common denominator. This
anthology, which contains all of Artaud's most important texts on

theatre published to date, should go some way towards illuminating that common denominator.

Artaud, who died in 1948, had agreed to the publication of his complete works during the last months of his life, but the first volume of his complete works did not appear until 1956.

All translations in this anthology are based on the *new* edition of the complete works begun in 1976: Antonin Artaud, *Œuvres complètes*, Nouvelle édition revue et augmentée, Paris: Gallimard, 1976–.

For easy identification of the texts and to allow readers to find the full documents (in French as well as in English) without difficulty, complete bibliographical details are given at the end of each text:

CW = *Complete Works*, translated by Victor Corti, London: Calder and Boyars, 1968–74, Volumes 1 to 4;

OC = *Œuvres complètes*, Nouvelle édition revue et augmentée, Paris: Gallimard, 1976–, Volumes I to XXVI.

Antonin Artaud: A biographical outline

1896   4 September. Born in Marseilles: Antoine-Marie-Joseph. Father (Antoine-Roi) was a sea captain; mother (Euphrasie Nalpas) was of Greek origin. First-born of nine children (only three were to survive).

1901   Meningitis, which was the origin of life-long nervous disorders.

1906–9   His sister Germaine dies, aged seven months. Lengthy visits to his maternal grandmother in Smyrna.

1910   Death of his grandmother to whom he was very close. First poems and drawings.

1913   First extant texts (poems influenced by Baudelaire and Poe).

1914   Suffers from depression. Declared unfit for military service.

1915   First short stay in a nursing home.

1916   Mobilized for about six months before being discharged on medical grounds. First poems published.

1917   Several stays in mental institutions. Meets Yvonne
       Gilles, a painter, with whom he corresponds for several
       years. Treated for syphilis. Writes poetry.

1918   Undergoes further spells of treatment. Is sent to
       Switzerland (Le Chanet, near Neuchâtel) where he stays
       until the end of 1919. First use of drugs (laudanum, i.e.
       opium). Dreams of a 'spontaneous theatre' in Marseilles.

1920   **March**. His father takes him to Paris to see a psychiatrist,
       Dr Edouard Toulouse. The doctor and his wife treat
       Artaud as a friend and their friendship was to prove
       unshakeable. **May**. Walk-on parts at the Théâtre de
       l'Œuvre. **August**. Dr Toulouses gives Artaud editorial
       responsibility for his journal *Demain* (1912–22).
       October. Texts by Artaud appear in *Demain* and in *La
       Criée*. Meets the poet Max Jacob.

1921   Theatrical début at l'Œuvre. Meets André Malraux.
       Writes in several publications. Brief encounter with
       Jacques Copeau. **Autumn**. After the summer break,
       Artaud auditions for Firmin Gémier who sends him to
       Charles Dullin. Joins the Théâtre de l'Atelier. Meets
       Génica Athanasiou, a Romanian actress, with whom he
       lives, on and off, until 1927.

1922   Very active in the theatre (actor and designer). Publishes
       numerous poems. **July**. First contact with oriental dance
       theatre (Cambodian) at the Exposition coloniale in
       Marseilles. Vain attempts to give up drugs. **20
       December**. Tirésias in Cocteau's *Antigone*. Small part in
       Pirandello's *La Volupté de l'honneur*.

1923   **March**. Plays for the last time in a production at the
       Atelier in Alexandre Arnoux's *Huon de Bordeaux*. **April**.
       Joins Pitoëff at the Comédie des Champs–Élysées in
       Pirandello's *Six personnages en quête d'auteur* (Six
       Characters in Search of an Author). **May**. Talks of
       collaboration with Lugné-Poe on Strindberg's *La Sonate
       des spectres* (The Ghost Sonata) without results.
       Autumn. Performs in two plays directed by
       Komisarjevski; further performances with Pitoëff. More
       texts published. Complains of severe physical pain.

1924   **April**. First screen performance in *Faits divers* (Claude

Autant-Lara) and publication of his first important text on the theatre: 'L'Évolution du décor' in *Comoedia* (19 April). **7 September**. Death of Artaud's father. **October**. Joins the Surrealists. Abel Gance offers him a role in *Napoléon*.

1925   **January**. Becomes director of the surrealist 'think-tank', 'la Centrale Surréaliste'. **February**. Abel Gance starts the shooting of *Napoléon*. **April**. Publication of the third issue of *La Révolution surréaliste*, written by Artaud, followed later that year by further surrealist manifestos, *L'Ombilic des limbes* and *Le Pèse-Nerfs*. Meets Roger Vitrac. Article on Vitrac's *Les Mystères de l'amour* which he plans to direct.

1926   Further involvement with cinema. Creation of the Théâtre Alfred Jarry with Vitrac and Robert Aron. Expulsion from the surrealist group.

1927   End of love affair with Génica Athanasiou. **April**. Scenario of *La Coquille et le clergyman* is finished. **1 and 2 June**. First performances of the Théâtre Alfred Jarry. **July–September**. Germaine Dulac directs *The Shell and the Clergyman*.

1928   **14 January**. Second performance of the Théâtre Alfred Jarry: Act III of Claudel's *Partage de midi* and screening of Pudovkin's banned *The Mother*. **February**. Public showing of *The Shell and the Clergyman*: the Surrealists rally round Artaud to defend him against Dulac's 'betrayal'. The reconciliation is short-lived. **2 and 9 June**. The Théâtre Alfred Jarry performs Strindberg's *Le Songe* (A Dream Play). Final break with the Surrealists who disrupt the first performance. **24 and 29 December** (and 5 January 1929). Fourth and final production of the Théâtre Alfred Jarry: Vitrac's *Victor ou les enfants au pouvoir* (Victor, or Power to the Children).

1929   Writes film scenarios and acts on screen. **22 June**. Lecture on 'talking pictures'. Publishes 'Le Théâtre Alfred Jarry'. Several theatrical projects come to nothing.

1930   Publishes 'Le Théâtre Alfred Jarry ou l'hostilité publique'. Writes two production plans for Strindberg's *La Sonate des spectres* (The Ghost Sonata) and Vitrac's *Le*

Coup de Trafalgar. Abandons all future plans for the Théâtre Alfred Jarry. Acts in several films.

1931   Publication of Artaud's adaptation of *The Monk*, by Lewis. First mention of Shelley's *The Cenci*. Offers his services to Louis Jouvet. **July**. Sees Balinese dancers at the Exposition coloniale in Paris. Treatment for drug addiction. **10 December**. Lecture at the Sorbonne: 'La Mise en scène et la métaphysique'.

1932   Applies, in vain, for the post of film critic of the *Nouvelle Revue Française* (NRF). Among many abortive projects, plans a production of Büchner's *Woyzeck* at the Atelier. First suggestions for a 'Théâtre NRF' which would be sponsored by the publishers of the journal (Gallimard) and by well-known authors. Writes and publishes several manifestos (later to be included in *Le Théâtre et son souble* [The Theatre and Its Double]) and acts in films. **September–October**. First manifesto for a Theatre of Cruelty (*NRF*, No. 229). **December**. Treatment for drug addiction, which becomes an annual occurrence. Reads Seneca.

1933   Prepares a second manifesto for a Theatre of Cruelty. **6 April**. Lecture, 'Le Théâtre et la peste' (Theatre and the Plague). **November–December**. Writes 'En finir avec les chefs-d'œuvre' (No More Masterpieces) and 'Il n'y a plus de firmament' (There Is No More Firmament).

1934   Artaud reads extracts from Shakespeare's *Richard II* and from his own *La Conquête du Mexique* (The Conquest of Mexico) to possible sponsors of the 'Theatre of Cruelty'. Meets the painter Balthus. Further, unrealized projects: a play adapted from the writings of Sade, Seneca's *Thyestes*. **Autumn**. Starts writing his adaptation of *The Cenci*.

1935   **February**. *The Cenci* is ready. Several private readings for friends. Start of rehearsals. Financial and organizational difficulties. **6–22 May**. 17 performances. Critical response is mixed. **June**. Artaud turns down an offer of collaboration made by the young Jean-Louis Barrault. Acts in several films. Plans his trip to Mexico. Discusses the possibility of publishing his various theatrical manifestos in book form.

By the end of 1935 Antonin Artaud ceases to have any practical involvement in theatre and in cinema. He is not yet 40.

1936 **10 January**. Leaves for Mexico. Decides on the title of the forthcoming book: *Le Théâtre et son double* (The Theatre and Its Double). **7 February**. Arrives in Mexico, almost penniless. **26, 27, 29 February**. Invited to lecture at the university: 'Le Théâtre et les dieux' (Theatre and the Gods), followed by other lectures and articles published in Spanish. **September**. Spends a month with the Tarahumara Indians and is introduced to the 'cult of the peyotl'. **12 November**. Back in France. Signs contract with Gallimard for the publication of *Le Théâtre et son double*.

1937 Successive treatments for drug addiction. **April–May**. Marriage plans with Cécile Schramme, abandoned almost immediately. **June–July**. Writes and publishes *Les Nouvelles Révélations de l'être* (New Revelations on Being). Preoccupation with esoteric subjects. Is seen with a walking stick which he claims belonged to Saint Patrick. Leads virtually the life of a tramp. **August–September**. Fateful journey to Ireland, the 'land of Saint Patrick', which ends in disaster. Artaud is arrested by the Irish police and sent back to France. Because of a further obscure but possibly violent incident on board ship, Artaud is put in a strait-jacket and immediately committed on his arrival at Le Havre (**30 September 1937**). [He will remain in mental institutions until **26 May 1946**.] Until December his whereabouts are ignored by family and friends.

1938 **7 February**. Publication of *Le Théâtre et son double* (400 copies). **April Fool's Day**. Transfer to the Hôpital Sainte-Anne, in Paris.

1939 **February**. Transfer to the asylum of Ville-Évrard (Seine-et-Marne), 10 miles east of Paris. Visited by a few friends and his mother who, after the outbreak of war, tried to see him twice a week, bringing food and tobacco which she sometimes had to buy on the black market. Writes many letters, often calling for help and for heroin.

1943   **22 January**. Artaud is transferred from Ville-Évrard, via Chezal-Benoît, to Rodez (Aveyron), some 600 km. south of Paris, in the unoccupied zone. In Rodez, where he remains until his discharge in 1946, he is cared for by Dr Ferdière. Undergoes electro-shock therapy. **March**. Resumes creative writing and drawing.

1944.   Is allowed to circulate freely in Rodez in the company of friends. **10 May**. Second edition of *Le Théâtre et son double* (1525 copies).

1945   **August**. Hopes of being discharged are dashed, but is authorized to go out alone. Publication of *Le Voyage au pays des Tarahumaras* (Journey to the Land of the Tarahumaras).

1946   First plans for the publication of his **Collected Works** *Œuvres complètes* [*OC*]). Dr Ferdière prepares Artaud for his return to Paris, where he arrives on the morning of **26 May**. Stays at Ivry, in the clinic of Dr Delmas where he enjoys complete freedom of movement. **7 June**. Gala 'in honour of Antonin Artaud' at the Théâtre Sarah-Bernhardt. Readings by Adamov, Barrault, Blin, Dullin, Jouvet, Vilar . . . **8 June**. Records a radio programme, *Les Malades et les médecins* (Patients and Doctors) which is broadcast on **9 June**. Later in June, an auction of paintings and manuscripts in aid of Artaud brings in one million francs, thus ensuring his livelihood. **16 July**. Recording of *Aliénation et magie noire* (Madness and Black Magic), broadcast on **17 July**. **31 July**. Reveals plans to direct *Les Bacchantes* (The Bacchae) by Euripides. Signs contract for the publication of his **Collected Works**.

1947   **13 January**. Lecture at the Vieux-Colombier. **February**. Writes *Van Gogh et le suicidé de la société* (Van Gogh or Society's Suicide). **May**. Writes several texts on theatre. Refuses to exhibit with the Surrealists and corresponds with Breton. **September**. Plans a broadcast of *Pour en finir avec le jugement de dieu* (To Put an End to the Judgement of God). Writes 'Le Rite du soleil' (The Rite of the Sun) for 'Pour en finir . . .' and a new text on 'Le Théâtre de la cruauté', not included in the broadcast.

22–29 November. Rehearsals and recordings of *Pour en finir avec le jugement de dieu*.

1948   **16 January**. Artaud receives the Prix Sainte-Beuve for *Van Gogh ou le suicidé de la société*. *Pour en finir avec le jugement de dieu* to be broadcast on **1 February** is banned 24 hours before the scheduled transmission. The doctors diagnose an inoperable cancer of the anus. **24 February**. Artaud writes: 'From now on I shall concentrate exclusively on theatre as I conceived it.' **3 March**. Lunches with Paule Thévenin to whom he entrusts forthwith the publication of all his writings. **4 March**. Antonin Artaud is found dead that morning, sitting at the foot of his bed.

Artaud's Artistic Activities

Theatre

1922–4 In the course of three short seasons, Antonin Artaud acted in some twenty plays directed by four of the most prominent and influential Parisian directors of the time. These productions were:

La Vie est un songe (Life Is A Dream), by Calderón, Vieux-Colombier, 1922: Basile, King of Poland. Directed by Dullin.

Antigone, by Cocteau, Théâtre Montmartre, 1922: Tirésias. Directed by Dullin.

Huon de Bordeaux, by Alexandre Arnoux, Théâtre de l'Atelier, 1923: Charlemagne. Directed by Dullin.

La petite baraque (The Fairground Booth), by Alexandr Blok, Comédie des Champs-Élysées, 1923. Directed by Pitoëff.

Androclès et le lion, by Shaw, Comédie des Champs-Élysées, 1923: Retiarus. Directed by Pitoëff.

Six personnages en quête d'auteur (Six Characters in Search of an Author), by Pirandello, Comédie des Champs-Élysées: the Prompter (?). Directed by Pitoëff.

R.U.R., by Karel Čapek, Comédie des Champs-Élysées, 1924: the robot Marius. Directed by Komisarjevski.

1927–9 Together with Robert Aron and Roger Vitrac, Artaud founded the Théâtre Alfred Jarry. He organized and directed four productions:

Les Mystères de l'amour (The Mysteries of Love), by Vitrac; *Ventre brûlé ou la mère folle* (The Burnt Womb or The Mad Mother), by Artaud (text lost); *Gigogne*, by Max Robur (pseudonym for Robert Aron, administrator of the theatre; text also lost). 1 and 2 June 1927, Théâtre de Grenelle

Third act of *Partage de midi* (Break of Noon), by Paul Claudel, without the author's permission; and the screening of the banned film *The Mother*, by Pudovkin, after Gorki. 14 January 1928, Comédie des Champs-Élysées

Le Songe (A Dream Play), by Strindberg. Artaud played the part of the Dean of Theology. 2 and 9 June 1928, Théâtre de l'Avenue

Victor ou les enfants au pouvoir (Victor, or Power to the Children), by Vitrac. 24 and 29 December 1928 and 5 January 1929, Comédie des Champs-Élysées

1935   *Les Cenci*, written and directed by Artaud. Théâtre des Folies-Wagram. Artaud played the part of Old Cenci. The production opened on 6 May 1935 and ran for 17 performances.

Cinema

1924–35 Artaud acted in some 21 films, notably in:

Napoléon, by Abel Gance, 1927. Marat.

La Passion de Jeanne d'Arc (The Passion of Joan of Arc), by Carl Dreyer, 1927/8. Brother Jean Massieu.

L'Argent (Money), by Marcel L'Herbier, after Zola's novel, 1928. Mazaud.

L'Opéra de quat' sous (The Threepenny Opera), by Pabst (French version), 1931. A beggar.

Les Croix de bois (Wooden Crosses), by Raymond Bernard, 1932. Vieublé, a soldier crazed by trench warfare.

Lucrèce Borgia, by Abel Gance, 1935. The monk Savonarola.

Artaud wrote a number of screenplays, but only one was filmed, and it turned out to be an unhappy experience since he was denied the opportunity to collaborate with the film's director:

1927   *La Coquille et le clergyman* (The Shell and the Clergyman), screenplay by Artaud, directed by Germaine Dulac.

Radio

Artaud took part in some minor broadcasts before the war, but after his return to Paris in 1946 he recorded three programmes:

Les Malades et les médecins (Patients and Doctors), broadcast on 9 June 1946

Aliénation et magie noire (Madness and Black Magic), broadcast on 17 July 1946

Pour en finir avec le jugement de dieu (To Put an End to the Judgement of God), rehearsed and recorded from 22 to 29 November 1947 and scheduled to be broadcast on 2 February 1948. The programme was banned on 1 February. Now available on cassette.

Artaud and Theatre

Just as Ionesco wrote an 'anti–play' with *The Bald Prima Donna*, so Artaud dreamed of an 'anti–theatre'. Indeed, his conception of what theatre should be goes against any accepted notion of the function and nature of theatre. In life as in art, Artaud negated the idea of theatre, although, ironically, it could be said that his own existence became a deadly existential tragedy.

Artaud was paradox made flesh. Throughout his life he was a compulsive writer. Writing was his *raison d'être* and yet, again and again, he declared that 'writing is filth' ('de la cochonnerie'), that he could no longer believe in poetry ('je ne crois plus aux mots des poèmes'), that 'style made his flesh creep', and so on. Having just put the finishing touches to the 'First Manifesto of the Theatre of Cruelty', he judged it to be a 'flop' because its overall tone was too literary:

> I have not become a poet or an actor in order to write or recite poems, but to live them. I read a poem not to milk applause but to feel the bodies of men and women – and I mean *their bodies* – throb and quiver in harmony with mine.

> [OC, IX,173]

According to Artaud, theatre is life lived with authenticity. Life without lies, life without pretence, life without hypocrisy. Life which is the opposite of role-playing. Theatre means absence of 'theatre':

> We are not appealing to the audience's minds or senses, but to their whole existence. To theirs and ours. We stake our lives on the show that is taking place on stage.

> [The Alfred Jarry Theatre, 1926]

In 1971, Jean-Louis Barrault declared in an interview: 'Tragedy on the stage was not enough for [Artaud], he had to bring it into his own life.' While I hesitate to suggest that Jean-Louis Barrault, whose collaboration with Artaud dates back to the production of *The Cenci*, does not really grasp Artaud's aims, his reaction reveals a conventional perception of the stage as a separate entity from everyday life. For most people, there is everyday life and there is theatre, a fictional world animated by actors at predetermined times, in a special building where actors and spectators arrange to meet on either side of the footlights or the proscenium arch. It is precisely this division, based on the notion of 'spectacle', of 'mimesis', of 'imitation of life *outside* life' that Artaud rejects. He assigns to the theatre no less a mission than to renew life itself. Strictly speaking, Artaud never meant to 'work in the theatre', but to renew life by revolutionizing the theatre.

The texts which we have chosen – and which are the

fundamental core of Artaud's writings on the subject – do not lend themselves as guides to dramatic technique, like the works of Brecht, Meyerhold and even Craig. Here, we are given an 'Art poétique', an artistic manifesto which is, in reality, an 'Art vital', a manifesto on how to live, on how to become, in Artaud's words, genuine and authentic men and women. This revolutionary zeal, which fires all his statements about theatre, leads Artaud constantly to challenge the traditional segregation of art and life, as the following randomly selected quotations make clear.

> The theatre would be greatly enhanced if we got rid of all those who currently make their living out of providing entertainment, and be it theatre, music-hall, cabaret or brothel, it's all the same stinking business.

> In life I don't feel myself living. But on the stage I feel that I exist.

> I cannot conceive any work of art as having a separate existence from life itself.

> The theatre is at one and the same time scaffold, gallows, trenches, crematorium, lunatic asylum.

Much has been written on Artaud by so-called authorities but there is no substitute for his own words. If, on first reading, the meaning appears to be elusive, I suggest a further reading of Artaud's text. His 'meaning' might not become much clearer, but his voice will grow familiar and the readers will learn to trust their own response.

The following snippets of conversations between Pierre Chaleix (a literary critic), Jean-Louis Barrault (the theatre director) and Gaston Ferdière, the psychiatrist who treated Artaud in Rodez, serve as a fitting conclusion to this brief introduction.

CHALEIX: What do you think the young people of today can learn from Artaud?

BARRAULT: They can learn a great deal, provided they do not misinterpret him.

FERDIÈRE: The most important thing is that they read his work and do not go by what the critics tell them.

[*La Tour de feu*, special issue, October 1971, 144]

CHALEIX: I wonder whether, through these struggles and these contradictions, the unity in Artaud did not reside in his thirst for purity, his inspired revolt, which was in all cases directed against society and its lies.

[*T.d.f.*, 122]

BARRAULT: Yes, of course.

Artaud and Madness

Was Artaud mad? The question is often raised, but it is not easy to provide a clear-cut, definitive answer. Artaud was committed to a lunatic asylum in September 1937 and was not released until May 1946. But, with one or two exceptions, the friends of Artaud were and are convinced – as he was himself – that the poet was the victim of a conspiracy in the psychiatric establishment and that his sanity was never in any doubt. Not surprisingly the psychiatrists who treated Artaud and those who analysed his case after his death (without the benefit of first-hand acquaintance) tend to see in him a clinical case.

It cannot be denied that Artaud suffered from nervous disorders throughout his life. His sister stated that at the age of five, 'he was miraculously cured from meningitis'. [*T.d.f.*, 112] Whatever the true nature of that early illness, Artaud affirmed that from the age of six, he suffered from stammering and 'unbearable nervous spasms in his face and tongue'. At the age of 18, he could not sit his final school exams (the 'baccalauréat') because he was suffering from nervous depression. A year later, he spent some time in a nursing home to cure what he himself called «troubles psychiques» (psychological problems). Between 1917 and 1937, he went into a number of nursing homes of his own free will for treatment for his nerves and to cure his addiction to the ever-increasing doses of laudanum (tincture of opium) which he was taking to alleviate his frequently recurring agonizing head-aches. During these twenty years, he enjoyed the constant friend-ship and professional expertise of two eminent psychiatrists: Drs Toulouse and Allendy and, as far as I know, Artaud never accused these two physicians of having mistreated him.

Because of Artaud's lack of mental 'stability', the various

theatre directors who had worked with him between 1922 and 1924 (and who praised his acting talents) soon ceased to offer him employment, despite Artaud's frequent requests that he should be given another chance. Cinema directors similarly exploited his extraordinary quality of screen presence, but no one ever offered him the star role which he so desperately wanted. The sad fact is that Artaud fell out with practically all his collaborators and sponsors. He insulted the Swedish colony in Paris who had enabled him to stage Strindberg's *A Dream Play* just as he insulted the artistic, literary and political personalities who had been invited to a fund-raising cocktail party to launch an avant-garde theatre to continue the work of the Théâtre Alfred Jarry. Both verbally and in writing, he viciously attacked Dullin, Pitoëff and Jouvet who had given him support and whose work he had previously admired. He quarrelled with his friends of the *Nouvelle Revue Française* and with Roger Vitrac. Jean Paulhan told him the cruel truth when he wrote: «Étonnez-vous d'avoir des amis, non des ennemis.» (You should be surprised that you have friends, not that you have enemies). Artaud's attitude towards other people used to swing from one extreme to the other, and he often apologized sincerely for his virulent outbursts. He was obviously unbalanced and his instability damaged both his relationships with other people and his career in the theatre.

Just how this instability and its attendant problems led to his being committed to a lunatic asylum in 1937, where he was to remain until 1946, has never been adequately explained, and probably never will. We know he was arrested by the French police on his return from his Irish trip, after being involved in a brawl on board ship. Exactly what happened on the ship is not clear but the police report said that 'he was in a frenzy' and, consequently, he was taken in a strait-jacket to an asylum near Le Havre.

The official medical records of the asylum in Sotteville-lès-Rouen were destroyed during the war and the first extant 'certificate' was drawn up at Sainte-Anne, after his transfer there on 1 April 1938. It reads:

Raving paranoia: police plotting to poison him, fixation that he is under a spell affecting his speech and thought . . . split personality . . .

[Maeder, 215]

From 1937 to 1943, life was a harrowing ordeal for Artaud. Apart from the regular visits from his mother, a woman much abused by the poet's latter-day friends, and the real concern shown by Robert Desnos who arranged for his transfer to a hospital in the unoccupied zone, he was left to rot among lunatics. The medical and living conditions were very poor owing to the shortage of staff and food during the darkest hours of the Second World War. During these years Artaud was not able to keep up his literary output: whether this was due to his illness or to lack of privacy is still a moot point. He did, however, write letters. And Artaud's epistolary record of his life constitutes a major part of his 'work'.

By January 1943, Artaud was in a desperate condition, both mentally and physically. His mother urged Desnos to visit him and to do something to save her son. He arranged a transfer to Rodez and went to prepare Artaud for the trip. This is the letter he wrote after his visit:

My dear Ferdière,

I went to Ville-Evrard on Thursday. Artaud was . . . raving in delirium, talking like Saint Jerome and not wanting to go, because he would be separated from favourable magical forces. I had not seen him for 5 years – his excited state and his madness were a painful sight. I have persuaded his mother not to pay any attention to what he says, to let him go, so sure am I that he will improve with you. But he seems well settled in his fantasies and difficult to cure.

Desnos

Artaud will certainly think of me as his persecutor!

[*T.d.f.*, No. 136, December 1977; translated in Charles Marowitz, *Artaud at Rodez*, Marion Boyars, London, 106]

When Artaud eventually arrived at Rodez, on 10 February 1943, Dr Ferdière took personal charge of his new patient, made him welcome in his own home, invited him to his table and gave him a private room. There was no doubt in Ferdière's mind that Artaud's mental health was impaired. In his autobiography, *Les Mauvaises Fréquentations*, he writes: 'After the initial period of routine observation, I was able to establish a preliminary diagnosis which, essentially, was not and could not be different from that made by colleagues: "chronic and extremely fertile delirium . . . obsessions with magic . . . split personality . . . persecution mania with periods of violent reaction".' [Ferdière, 176] Before any other treatment was used, the doctor made sure that Artaud had plenty of food and tobacco (which had been in short supply in the occupied zone). Physically Artaud's health was soon improving but, according to Ferdière, he 'always remains in a kind of stagnation, in a kind of inactivity which is deeply disturbing . . . he sits doing nothing, sunk in hidden thoughts'. He feared that his patient was sinking 'hopelessly into insanity' and decided to use 'seismotherapy' (i.e. electrotherapy). The first such treatment was applied to Artaud on 20 June 1943.

Electrotherapy, in the 1940s, was not only a very popular psychiatric treatment in France, but it was also thought to be safe and efficient. On Artaud it seems that it had two diametrically opposed effects: on the one hand, it caused him unspeakable pain (he injured a vertebral disc during one of the first sessions and the injury instilled in him an insuperable fear); on the other hand, it helped him to resume his creative activities, after years of letter writing, and it also allowed him to shed his assumed personality of 'Antonin Nalpas' (Nalpas was his mother's maiden name) and to reassume his true identity.

Fortunately for us, Artaud often communicated with his doctor in writing and, on 5 February 1944, he sent him the following message: 'You have not only helped me to live, you have *encouraged me to go on living* at a time when I was withering away' (Artaud's own emphasis). Already, five months previously he had written to a friend: 'After a six year gap in my work, I have begun to write again' (7 October 1943). In the case of Artaud, playing the quotation game is like juggling with statistics: you can always find something to support the wildest point of view. In effect, as early as April 1944, Artaud was to complain of being ill-treated and committed against his will [Maeder, 244], although he had recently taken up painting again and was now free to walk the streets of the small town of Rodez unaccompanied.

As his health improved, his relationships with the doctors of Rodez deteriorated. The same people who had hitherto been his saviours became devils guilty of the most heinous crimes against him. Ferdière, for instance, was accused of having raped a kind nurse who was taking opium to Artaud and of torturing Artaud with electrotherapy every time his patient asked for the drug, despite being a drug addict himself. (Artaud never considered himself an 'addict' since he merely used drugs as pain-killers). [Maeder, 255]

With the end of the war, communication lines were re-opened within the country and more and more people became aware of Artaud's plight. Authors like Adamov and Breton, together with younger people who knew Artaud only through his writing, joined forces to obtain his release. It eventually came about on 26 May 1946, when Artaud was allowed to return to Paris, on condition that his friends would ensure his financial well-being and that he take up lodgings, as an 'out-patient', in a psychiatric nursing home. He was placed in the caring hands of Dr Delmas, at Ivry, who greeted the poet with these words: 'Monsieur Artaud you are at home here; here are your keys.' The stay in this particular hospital was not cheap and Artaud needed money for his own expenses too. To raise the necessary capital, his friends organized an auction of paintings, drawings, sculptures and manuscripts donated, *inter alios*, by Arp, Balthus, Bataille, Simone de Beauvoir, Braque, Chagall, Duchamp, Eluard, Giacometti, Gide, Michaux, Picabia, Picasso, Sartre, Gertrude Stein and many others. Artaud's financial future was secure, for the few months which remained to him.

Was Artaud mad, mentally ill or a victim of the medical establishment? The debate goes on. Much scorn has been poured on the doctors who came into contact with the poet and who dared to affirm that he did not behave in a 'normal' manner and that they tried to help him to conform to more acceptable standards of behaviour. In 1971, Ferdière wrote: 'For I had certainly not "cured" Artaud and he was really incurable with the present resources of psychic therapy. And I don't understand what the words "cure" and "mental health" mean in relation to such an exceptional man.' [in Marowitz, *Artaud at Rodez*, 108] These are not the words of a dogmatic and unsympathetic man.

For the last word on this thorny subject, let us turn to a poet who knew Artaud well and who was very well disposed towards him when he returned to Paris, despite their youthful disagreements. In a beautiful text, written after Artaud's death,

André Breton asks – and the same could be asked of authors like Blake, Nietzsche, Strindberg and Jarry – whether Artaud could only find his inspiration through his suffering, or whether he was punished for being too lucid. He concludes that Artaud had 'gone over to the other side' ('passé de l'autre côté):

> Artaud's illness was not the kind of illness which, in psychiatric terms, results in decreased intellectual capacity . . . shortly before his death he was able to write his *Van Gogh*, which is a *hyperlucid* work and an indisputable masterpiece . . . Youth will always rally to the charred and battered flag that he waved.

Artaud, East and West

by Brian Singleton

In 'Oriental and Western Theatre' (pp. 135-6), Artaud suggests
an Orientalist dichotomizing of culture in the modernist tradition.
In fact, nothing could be further from the truth. His aim, rather
than distance further two opposing cultural traditions, was to
cause his own European civilization to self-destruct. In the
true sense of 'Orientalism' Artaud's geographical East/West
dichotomy of culture was not so clear cut. He was obsessed with
the cultures of many early civilizations, from African tribal
customs and Chinese medicine to Mexican mythology, whose
totems, engravings, songs and dance trances he saw as exemplary
manifestations of societies with a deep metaphysical awareness, if
not comprehension, of the human condition. In *The Theatre and
Its Double* he divides the world into primitive and advanced
civilizations, side-stepping the problematic political question of
how this division came about. In each of the essays the veneer of
civilization in advanced societies (the 'diaphanous' apparel of the
indolent bourgeois) is considered to be a veil masking true
primitive culture, suppressed by the 'civilized' West but which we
still have imprinted on our unconscious minds. Extant true
primitive cultures without the mask are collectively referred to as
'eastern'. Differences are elided to make a point. The 'western'
cultures which come under attack are grouped largely around the
idea of a psychologically realistic view of the world and are
characterized by Euro-American high-cultural phenomena. Thus
the terms 'oriental' and 'occidental' do not geographically locate
cultures but divide them up into the categories of 'primitive' and
'civilized'. Far from exotic and contrary to dominant cultural
trends, primitive culture is not only represented positively, it is
deemed to be vital to the survival of Euro-American societies
processing the human condition through ephemera.

Many and varied are the examples of his primitivist
Orientalism. A troupe of Balinese dancers performing at a

Colonial Exhibition in the Bois de Vincennes in the summer of
1931 was one of Artaud's rare direct experiences of oriental
culture and was most significant in the development of his
theories on theatre. But what of his other experiences? We know
that he had been exposed to the principles of Kabuki theatre while
working and training at Charles Dullin's Atelier in 1921 after
which he wrote that 'the Japanese are our masters' (p. 4). In 1922
he attended a performance of Cambodian dancing at a recon-
struction of the temple of Angkor in Marseilles. Numerous are his
references to Chinese acupuncture, and Chinese civilization in
general. His Gnosticism, a third-century heretical belief that the
whole of creation was essentially evil and beyond redemption,
rejects Christianity in favour of a pluralistic pantheon of
inspirational divinities, including the Hindu god Siva. His drug-
enhanced experiences in the Sierra Tarahumara in Mexico
invoked a similar enthusiasm for 'eastern' primitivism but so did
many other examples of pre-modern culture in his own European
heritage. He borrowed heavily from the Occultist Kabbala, and
from the Zohar, a second-century mystical commentary on the
first and third divisions of the Old Testament in Judaism. He was
influenced by the paintings of the early Dutch masters such as
Leyden and Brueghel, and by a wide variety of texts ranging from
Seneca and Ford to the Marquis de Sade. Crucially, his appetite
for primitivism led him to research the history and effects of
plague on civilization. Eclectic as these examples may appear, they
all share one common aim in his citation of them. They are keys to
unlocking the pre-structured unconscious, the metaphysical side
to the human condition. They are also keys, or – as he called them
– 'doubles', to free European theatre from the shackles of realism.

In the latter half of the twentieth century, intercultural performance, a practice inscribed in the history of Orientalism, has
become the postmodern discourse for the exploration both of
negative and positive aspects of cultural trade, appropriation,
colonization and hybridization. It is perhaps the most talked-
about of late twentieth-century theatrical trends, exemplified by
the work of Peter Brook and Ariane Mnouchkine who have sought
in the East a formalism to replace realism in the same vein as
Artaud. In fact, Artaud, by no means the first European to seek
inspiration in the East for the rejuvenation of theatre in Europe,

could be said to be the pioneer of this late twentieth-century practice. Politically innocent, interculturalism shares with postmodernism the same obsessions: cultural tourism, shopping, fragmentation, dislocation and 'bricolage'. It is a cultural condition made possible by the Boeing 747 and the World Wide Web. It operates in the hyperspace of virtual reality in a global village with no name, no indigenous population, no culture: a fabrication, a sham. It trades on the cultural futures market of recycling and many of its manifestations are culturally symptomatic of a dominant first-world capitalist economy. Its emergence was contemporaneous with mass cultural diffusion and rampant technological advances in telecommunications, and coincided with the breakdown of the Cold War dichotomies of capitalism/communism mirrored geographically by an East/West division of the territorial spoils. Its practice in performance has become the most talked-about and the most exciting development of late twentieth-century European theatre.

But it was not always thus. The discourse of representation of cultural border crossings in the first half of the twentieth century (in which we site Artaud) continued the practice and the dominant specularity of the French Orientalist painters, from Delacroix to Matisse, whose Orient began in the Moors' Spain, and whose exoticism was fuelled by the allure of a warm climate, a drug culture and a sense of the unknown. The Orient was a dark, mysterious 'extra-European Other', inexplicable and colonizable. According to the historian Edward Said, its representation was dominated by its positioning as subject to the greater glory of its creator; it could not speak for itself, but was spoken for. Even when rendered speechless, however, no attempt was made to make sense of it. Its exotic surface features were purloined to maintain the myth of its non-rational (and therefore inferior) mystery. This brand of representation reflected the colonial history of its European cultural creators and incorporated the multiple 'Orients' of Africa and Asia. The nineteenth-century practice of putting on display the cultural spoils of colonial mastery continued into the twentieth century in pseudo-folklorama known as Colonial Exhibitions in pavilions dislocated from their sociocultural contexts which were to provide Artaud with his only direct experiences of 'oriental' culture. By the 1920s, however, the spirituality, non-rationality, non-linearity, and non-verbal discourse of these once exotic performance practices became the inspirational force behind an avant-garde reaction against the stranglehold of realism in the European theatre.

Artaud's purpose in his investigation of so-called 'primitive' theatres of the East is to discover a practice which has not mistakenly attached itself to literature or does not see its function as a reading or staging of the literary text. The ideal performance language has two constituent parts; first, the visual and plastic realisation of the word and, second, a language independent of words altogether: a language in its pre-expressive or larval state before society has structured and layered it with connotations. The Artaudian ideal is a pre-linguistic 'making-sense' of the human condition. To achieve this in the western world it is necessary to disrupt the structuring of language, to dislocate signifier from signified. The resulting performance might be, not a display of pre-known certainties, but the presentation of a crucible of possibilities: a process, not a product.

The Balinese dancers whom Artaud saw at a Colonial Exhibition in Vincennes in 1931 appealed to him with their primal physicality, their mix of improvisatory skills and pre-determined gestural signs to narrate ancient myths and tales from the *Ramayana* to reveal metaphysical truths. In a letter to Louis Jouvet, the day after he saw the Balinese performance, Artaud wrote of the structuring of the unconscious, that true sub-(performance) text, 'in the hieroglyphics of gesture which are the disinterested and totally original constructions of the mind'. [*OC*, III, 217–18] Human emotions were replaced by states of mind. He read the automaton-like and codified movements of the body as representing the unconscious. The repetition of codified gestural patterns would liberate the unconscious: 'this double who, by his trembling, childish yelping and heels striking the ground in time with the very automatism of the unleashed subconscious, hides behind his own reality.' [*OC*, IV, 660] Artaud, through his analysis of Balinese dancing, presents us with a view of realism beyond our conception. In western theatre, realism, according to Artaud, reflects, describes and most importantly imitates. For the theatres of the East the representation of reality by heavily codified gestures reveals everything about reality which cannot be

imitated or described. Artaud refers to the irony in the fact that
the surface freedom and spontaneity offered by the western stage
is an illusion since it only provides for a material representation of
the world. He preferred to manufacture a formalism without the
raw sociocultural materials to support it. He talks of the potential
of eastern theatre to unleash demons through formalized gestural
language but does not point out that for a society to perform and
unleash them it must first believe in their existence and effect.
Crisis can only ever be achieved through belief and not through
the general *modus operandi* of western theatre spectating: the
suspension of disbelief. Artaud's charge is of western theatre
lacking in the spiritual through the rationality of the literary text.
Ironically it is the encrustation of civilization which has sanitized
and packaged spiritual awareness and the theatre event as social
commodities which prevent Artaud from even putting into place
a Balinese blueprint for western performance. Furthermore, the
post-colonial complicity with former European colonizers forces
the performance traditions of the East on cultural package tours,
transforming in the process their low cultural status of origin into
a product for the high cultural palate only interested in the
presentation of the fruits of labour and never understanding its
purpose, method and means of production. Only the aesthetic
surface of the travelling traditional culture is read and appreciated
at the expense of its sociocultural purpose or its religious base.

And what of the body of the actor? At this point his eastern
double must leave the equation as, since the *commedia*, the body of
the western actor has never been inscribed with the codes and
signs of formalistic training, and precedence has not been given to
corporeal narration. Artaud fails to point out the complexities of
simultaneous modes of narration in Asian theatres from *mudras*
(language of hand gestures) to footwork, facial or marked
expression, and rhythmic percussion. He was not calling for the
European body to impersonate the Asian other body since
inherited kinaesthetic training remains forever absent. He was
calling instead for the body's functions to be explored as a means
of communication. The body's communicative sign-system is not
simply that of gesture. A psycho-physicality of the body also
manufactures sounds (both linguistic and paralinguistic).
Furthermore, unconscious impulses of the muscular formation

not only communicate on a physical axis but on a vocal axis as well.
He calls for a total codification of the western actor similar to that
found in *The Natyashastra* and for an unconscious spasmodic
body. And therein lies the paradox: conscious learned behaviour
and an unconscious release from it. Trance hypnosis, which
Artaud used as a model for his desired form of acting, operates on
the same principle: an unconscious liberation from the structuring
of the mind through the repetitive pattern of a structured activity.
The breathing patterns advocated by him might achieve a trance-
like state but so, too, can hyperventilation. His acting practice was
based on the notion of exteriorization of an 'inner' truth: the
physicalization of unconscious mental activity. And this is where
the paradox is resolved: the outer truth, that is the motivation for
behaviour, is translated into the codified corporeal narration
which, by its very narration, provides for a material reality
through which an inner truth can be revealed. And this, similar to
the 'tai' and 'yu' of Japanese *Noh*, is a complete inversion of the
Stanislavskian model.

Artaud's actor suffers a similar paradox, being a signifier and a
signified at the same time. Many of the characters in Artaud's
favoured collection of theatrical texts speak both in a theatrical
reality and about it. The actor is also acknowledged as being a
system of signs amongst many others. He gives examples in *The
Theatre and Its Double* of how a sign can be signified by its very
physicality, but its unconscious Double can be liberated and
communicated through the simultaneous action of a separate sign
system. He gives the example of the movements of a plant being
communicated through the sound of an instrument. This
principle is at the very heart of many Asian performances and has
been used most widely in the West by Ariane Mnouchkine's
system of intercultural leitmotifs at the Théâtre du Soleil, such
as the connotative wail of an Indian *tampura* to signify a
Shakespearian character's sense of unrequited love. It is founded
on a belief in the essence of an object or character whose material
reality can only be expressed through transitory emotional
paradigms but whose liminality is best achieved theatrically by the
communication of a sign system separate from the 'essence' itself.
And thus Artaud's intercultural theatre begins to take shape: all
the sign-systems of the stage are accorded an equal validity but,

more importantly, by speaking for and as the sign of another system it not only fractures a pseudo-realism, it also signifies the separation of an exteriorized materiality from an unconscious reality. One sign signifying another: this is true Artaudian realism.

But where is the Orient in this European theatrical dislocation of signifiers from signifieds? The answer lies nowhere in actuality but everywhere in inspiration. The result is an imagined Orient, an Orient whose signs are transferred from their sociocultural base of origin to a purely theatrical European discourse. The resulting fabrication of extra-European but not quite Oriental signs has no communicative base in either source or target cultures. Artaud's theatre signs are the result of a process of hybridization of an imaginary Orient. The Orient in turn is an assembly of imaginary extra-European Others constituted by their shared features of a geographical, temporal and cultural remove from their European theatrical present. They are the result of a broad purloining of the surface of many Others and are predicated on the notion of distance. From the Aztecs to the Zohar, ancient civilizations and cultures, though not necessarily located geographically in the East, are plundered as source materials for his theatrical future. Although they are all pre-modern practices and artefacts, Artaud's use of them is without doubt an early manifestation of a postmodern condition having refracted and recycled the performance of his multiple selves. Artaud was revolutionarily cruel to be interculturally kind. His own body, ravaged by drugs and his own mental state, often tripping, delusional and wracked by electroshock therapy, was testimony to his envisioned theatrical future: an 'homme-théâtre' (man-theatre).

Artaud raids the larder of traditional cultures, ignoring their right to speak or not speak for themselves. His neo-colonial plundering, unintentionally blind to the consequences given his desire for a cultural revolution in his targeted Europe, denied the source cultures a voice. And it is this absence of a politicization which partly rendered his practice impotent. A naïveté, amateurism, and lack of a cultural base were also contributing factors. And yet his intercultural practice left a legacy in the late twentieth century: the acknowledgement of a lack, gap or absence in the home culture and inspiration to fill it in eastern traditional formalism. In a decolonizing Europe this practice remains in a

historical, political, religious and social vacuum untroubled by the
politics of culture. The exoticism of Artaud's intercultural
practice operates in a virtual space. The forms he borrows and
applies are a series of simulacra unhinged from their contexts.
Artaudian interculturalism may be a process whereby the
elimination of difference affected by a revolutionary cruelty leads
to an ownership of sameness in a post-cultural void. His
intercultural Orient of otherness is set up as a quasi-imaginary
paradigm for a not-as-yet postmodern re-vision of European
culture. His Orient is constituted by two distant cultures of
otherness: geographically distanced formalism (although giving
way to pre-cultural chaos) and temporally distanced textual relics
of ancient civilizations. And this is precisely what characterized
the work of Brook and Mnouchkine in the late twentieth century
who, to a large extent, appear to perform interculturally in a
political void. Intercultural Artaud, however, did not simply fill
his theatrical trolley in the global supermarket in similar fashion.
He visited the corner store, not to buy imported goods in place of
the home-produced, but to blow up the corner store itself and take
out the vestiges of cultural consumerism, in the hope of man's
need for cultural food overriding the habit of transaction. We
must separate, therefore, Artaudian shopping from Artaudian
sustenance and acknowledge the political in Artaud's interculturalism. Artaud looked to the East, not to borrow, colonize or
appropriate, but for cultural models by means of which he might
reform European theatre practice.

Part One

Early Writings (Paris 1921–5)

Charles Dullin's L'Atelier (*L'Atelier de Charles Dullin*)

In founding l'Atelier, Charles Dullin has undertaken the important business of purifying and regenerating the customs and spirit of French theatre, on whose present low state there is no need to dwell. Apart from the Vieux-Colombier, we have no theatre at the present time. One can only consider the Théâtre de l'Œuvre as commercially enhancing the fine Nordic tragedies.

First of all, it was essential to form a small group of perfectly disciplined actors who were completely aware of what their profession demands, who were perfectly *conscious*. This is the tendency of the new methods inaugurated by Dullin, the first to invent or use them in France. The most important of these methods is improvisation, which forces the actor to *think* his actions through his soul, instead of acting them. Perfect harmony in theory and practice characterizes this interesting group, and already distinctive personalities, actors and actresses, are emerging from it. These actors give us an ideal image of what the total actor could be in our time, approaching the eternal model of the Japanese actor who has developed his physical and psychic powers to a convulsive point.

Perfect purity of morals and beliefs. Above all, Dullin demands that his students respect their art. For l'Atelier is not a business, it is a research laboratory. Allowance is made for error. Love of the profession whips up their energy. And finally, the flash of an apt discovery is its own reward. Thus the condition of *surprise* is fulfilled, which, according to Edgar Allan Poe, is the basis of Art.

It is undeniable that Dullin, although avoiding excessive idiosyncrasy, will give us theatre that harmonizes best with his own taste and methods of expression. A theatre of latent barbarism in a Hoffmannesque mood. This is because there is not only the actor we know in him, but the stuff of a marvellous man of the theatre who is conscious and deliberate about his own aesthetic and even stage mystique. In Dullin, culture equals sensitivity, and serves as a jumping-off point. All of which makes l'Atelier more than an enterprise – it is an idea.

[*CW*, 2, 128–9; *OC*, II, 134–5]

First published in the literary journal *Action*, 2nd year, special issue, at the end of 1921 or at the beginning of 1922. Antonin Artaud had been recommended by Max Jacob and *Action* published several poems by Artaud in 1921 and 1922. See also *OC*, I*, 167–8.

To Max Jacob

[*c*. October 1921]

Dear Max Jacob,

Your influence has been a great help and you are largely responsible for the fortunate change taking place in my life. I recently managed to get an audition with Gémier who, after having heard me, thought that what I was doing might interest your friend Dullin. I had written to Dullin, mentioning you, but before I received a reply I went to see him and said that Gémier had sent me. So Dullin auditioned me and took me on immediately. I told him I had written the letter and, when your name was mentioned, we became friends, or rather we had yet another bond in common.

I am thrilled with what he is doing. It seems to me to be by far the most interesting experiment now being made in the theatre. It is all based on such a desire for moral *purity*, both in behaviour and in the acting profession, and on such highly developed artistic principles that it can really be considered an *innovation* of our time. Hearing Dullin teach, I feel that I am rediscovering ancient secrets and a whole forgotten mystique of production. It is both a theatre and a school. A few plays will be performed this season by a company trained by Dullin, with every actor his pupil. I need hardly say that some of these pupils have reached a point of development which would arouse the envy of thousands of well-known actors. We act with our hearts, our hands, our feet, every muscle, every limb. We feel the object, we smell it, we touch it, we see it, we hear it – and there is nothing, there are no props. The Japanese are our masters, together with Edgar Allan Poe. It is *admirable*. [. . .]

I am pleased to be able to be working with a friend of yours. As a man, I find him enchanting. Needless to say I have always admired him immensely as an actor.

My very best wishes, and thank you.

I hope to see you soon. Where?

Antonin Artaud

[*CW*, 3, 93–4; *OC*, III, 94–5]

To Mademoiselle Yvonne Gilles

[*c*. October 1921]

Mademoiselle,

All this week I have been very busy and *worried*. Gémier had given me an appointment for Monday afternoon to hear me in a scene and then put me off until Wednesday. The audition took place in ideal conditions, and he sent me to Charles Dullin, the actor who was with him last year at the Comédie Montaigne and whom you must have seen in *Le Simoun*, in which he played the lead brilliantly. This actor has founded a small theatre company in the tradition of the Œuvre and the Vieux-Colombier, but still more specialized, if that is possible. It is both a theatre and a school where he applies his own principles of instruction which aim at *interiorizing* the actor's performance. Because apart from purifying the stage, he wants to *renew* it, he is looking for its novelty. In other words he wants his performances to make a permanent impression of *jamais vu*. Everything takes place in the soul. The sets are still more stylized and simplified than those of the Vieux-Colombier. His ideal is the Japanese actor who acts without props. Brightly painted masks with black manes are hung on the walls, some in black leather or imitation wood. The gods of the school are not Tolstoy, Ibsen or Shakespeare, but Hoffmann and Edgar Allan Poe. The first play will be bitterly frantic, sharp and wild. Dullin himself will play the lead with his usual intensity.

It is strange, to say the least, that with my tastes I should have ended up in something so close to my way of thinking.

It is just beginning and is still very small. Hardly a third of the size of the Vieux-Colombier. It is almost a studio theatre. The auditorium can seat a hundred people at a squeeze.

After hearing me Gémier told me that what I was doing might interest Dullin and sent me to him. Dullin heard me on Thursday and I joined the company immediately after the audition. But it is hard work. Apart from the rehearsals, there are several hours of work a day: improvisation, rhythmical gymnastics, speech, etc. I will probably be in the second play since the first has been in rehearsal for a long time.

I will not be able to come for lunch since I am busy. I do not yet know when I shall be free, but I could come one afternoon. I shall write again.

Antonin Artaud

[*CW*, 3, 95–6; *OC*, III, 95–7]

Charles Dullin first performed *Le Simoun* by H. R. Lenormand at the Comédie Montaigne-Gémier on 21 December 1921 in which he played the part of the Prophet.

L'Atelier Theatre (*Le Théâtre de l'Atelier*)

There are those who go to the theatre as they would go to a brothel. Furtive pleasure. For them the theatre is only momentary excitement. It is like the dumping-ground of their need to experience pleasure through all their physical and mental senses. The hypertrophy of the theatre of entertainment has created, alongside and above the classic idea of theatre, a kind of game with easy rules which is now the norm in theatre and it masks the idea of theatre itself. So that one can say two theatres now exist: false theatre that is deceptive, easy, middle-class, a theatre for soldiers, bourgeois, businessmen, wine merchants, water-colour teachers, adventurers, whores and *Prix de Rome*, as put on by Sacha Guitry and the Boulevards and the Comédie-Française. But there is another sort of theatre that plays whenever it can, theatre conceived as the achievement of the purest human desires. Small companies of young actors gather here and there with ardent or simply sufficient faith, trying to revive Molière, Shakespeare or Calderón. Among them l'Atelier is the most ardent and has the soundest but also the strictest views. Founded a year ago by Charles Dullin from the Théâtre des Arts, the Vieux-Colombier, Gémier's studio and his own, this theatre has already presented Molière's *The Miser*, Mérimée's *Occasion*, Regnard's *Divorce*, and plays by Calderón, Lope de Ruenda, Francisco de Castro, Tristan Bernard, Courteline (why him?), Max Jacob and finally the impressive drama by Calderón, *Life Is a Dream*, which was a triumph.

L'Atelier does not claim to invent anything; it merely wants to try to serve theatre well. The achievements of Edward Gordon Craig and Appia, of all these liberators of the theatre will finally find a place where they can be presented in France. Accurately, yet without any concessions to old theatre, old tricks, old stage sets, without the sort of partisanship that emasculates. Even more than its percursors, l'Atelier will try to rediscover all of theatre, the theatre of the past and that of the future.

It would be unjust for the author of this piece, himself an actor associated with l'Atelier, to judge its productions, but he can analyse its trends. L'Atelier has it own way of working. For, outside rehearsals, the group continues to work; each actor becomes a student under Dullin's direction. The goal of the true actor should be to feel, live and think in a real way. For a long time now the Russians have been using a certain method of improvisation that forces the actor to work with his deepest sensibility, to exteriorize this real and personal sensibility through words, attitudes, and mental reactions that are improvised and invented on the spot. The search for intonations is a great danger to personality. These exercises of improvisation reveal and sharpen true personality. Intonation is found within oneself, and pushed out with the burning power of feeling, not achieved through imitation. Dullin has developed the method, and made it into a deep-rooted one. He improvises like the others. L'Atelier's artists have already taken part in performances of improvisation before very small, private audiences. With a few words, a few attitudes, a few facial expressions, they have shown themselves astonishingly able to portray the characters and mannerisms of human nature or even abstract feelings, or natural forces such as wind, fire, plants or pure creations of the mind, dreams, deformations, all of this on the spot without script, direction or preparation. [. . .]

[*CW*, 2, 130–2; *OC*, II, 138–40]

First published in *La Criée*, No. 17, October 1922.
In Dullin Antonin Artaud thought he had found a kindred spirit, as these early writings amply testify. Unfortunately the spiritual honeymoon was short-lived as Artaud's radicalism was soon disenchanted with Dullin's pragmatism. At the Atelier, Artaud acted in Molière's *L'Avare* (The Miser), Calderón's *La Vie est un songe* (Life Is a Dream)

and Arnoux's *Huon de Bordeaux*. He also designed the costumes for Calderón's tragedy.

'Six Characters in Search of an Author' (*'Six personnages en quête d'auteur'*)

At the start, life goes on as before. Without any show. We look upstage, right to the very back. The curtain has been flown. And the whole theatre is one vast stage where the audience is about to watch a rehearsal in progress. But a rehearsal of what? There is no play. The play will be created before our eyes. Everyone goes about his own little tasks. Little by little, however, the actors come together. Then a family in mourning steps out of the Comédie des Champs-Elysées' lift. Their faces are deathly white, as if aborted from a dream.

These are the Six Characters in Search of an Author. Now these Six Characters want to come alive. They want to take part in a dream. They are more real than you, director of the theatre, or you, disgusting hams. They are *real* and they'll prove it. What does your own reality entail, you are not imaginary characters, but characters of flesh and blood, having had a father and mother and a birth certificate. Besides your own uncertain physical reality, what are you in relation to yourselves, O, director, O, ham actors?

A picture, or at the very most the picture of your past desires, the fabric of your future illusions dashed, now turned to ashes, O, you who are alive. But we are what we are, a fixed idea, definite outlines, as you have always pictured us. Our own reality is eternally renewed, its rough shape constantly reviewed. Born in the mind, our established rule is to live unendingly, eternally incomplete. *Unleash us*, therefore, director.

Thus fiction and reality gradually merge, so interpenetrating one another that we, the audience, can no longer tell where one ends and the other begins. What are these phantasms doing in our world, on these boards, with stage hands walking about, with the players caught in the midst of their bickering? And the production heightens the play and promotes the illusion. The sky is a theatrical sky, those trees are canvas, no one is taken in, neither the rehearsing actors, nor us, nor these larvae in search of a mould. Then what is theatrical about it? THEM, they are alive, they assert they are real. They have made us believe it. But what are we? And yet these Six Characters are still personified by actors! In this the whole question of theatre is raised. Just as, when light plays on mirrors, the initial image is absorbed yet incessantly reflected, making every reflected image more real than the first and continually renewing the enigma. And the last image sweeps all the others away and cuts out all the mirrors. In the same way, all the Six ghostly-faced Characters, lined up like mummies, are seen leaving in the lift and disappearing up into the real flies until the next performance.

A lot of people have praised one actor or another. Yet Georges Pitoëff remains the only figure in the play. He endows the main character with a mask and visionary gestures. There was only one thing to be said about him, just that, nothing more. Ludmilla Pitoëff and Kalff are very beautiful yet stay human, I mean flesh and blood, in a word, I mean actresses. One plays the *ingénue* and the other plays the mother and they are very intense, but only physically, not mentally. And I leave the rest, the director and other lice, as pickings for the stupid critics to swoop down on.

[*CW*, 2, 134–5; *OC*, II, 142–3]

First published in *La Criée*, No. 24, May 1923.
Pirandello's play perfectly illustrates what was to become central to Artaud's thinking on theatre: theatre and life are indistinguishable from one another and if one human manifestation is more real than another it must be theatre because it is 'purer', because the imaginary characters are 'eternal', whereas the flesh-and-blood actors, being human, cannot attain perfection and are therefore of a lesser essence.

Six personnages en quête d'auteur, directed by Georges Pitoëff, was performed at the Comédie des Champs-Élysées on 10 April 1923. According to Jean Hort, a Swiss actor who was in Pitoëff's company at the time, Artaud rehearsed the part of the Prompter but failed to turn up for the first performance. Subsequently, however, Artaud was cast as an Actor in the same production. (See Jean Hort, *Antonin Artaud, Le Suicidé de la société*, Geneva, 1960.)

Maurice Maeterlinck

More than anything else, Maurice Maeterlinck's name evokes a certain mood. This would also be a good way of summing up his

contribution to the fields of literature and thought. We will not try
to establish that his birth at Ghent, 28 August 1862, bears any
relation to the intimate nature of his thought. Maeterlinck had a
Nordic soul, which is simply a fact, nothing more. We should
consider his talent rather as the result of his soul intensely aflame
in the particular tone of the period when he was born and which
his poems best define.

A deeply symbolist spirit truly exists in his little book, *Hothouse
Blooms* (1889). The other symbolists included and worked up a
sort of concrete bric-à-brac of objects and feelings their period
loved, but Maeterlinck brings out its very soul. Symbolism was not
just ornamentation to him, but a profound way of feeling.

In a similar way to the divine Max Elskamp in his *Praise of Life*,
all too neglected these days, but with a more *personal*, less
orthodox mysticism, Maeterlinck uses certain thought patterns
whose *relevance to the present day* is not remarked on enough. A
certain method of fusing – by virtue of whatever mysterious
similarities – things and feelings, and placing them on the same
mental level, while avoiding the metaphorical, is to be found on
the basis of ultra-modern poetic theory.

Jean Schlumberger used to ask flippantly how many of his
puppet plays still remained. Should we name them in order? In
any case some, like *Pelléas and Mélisande* and *The Death of Tintagel*
provide equivalents in the realm of the mind to the *puppazzi* of the
commedia dell'arte in the realm of movement, and produce an
unfamiliar note. Maeterlinck increased his circle of mystical
puppazzi. He added new faces to his delightful creations. His
theatre soon became a whole world where the theatre's traditional
characters reappear, evoked from within. With Maeterlinck, the
unconscious fatalism of ancient drama becomes the mainspring of
the action. The characters are puppets, moved by the fates.

But the intimate bent of his nature led him to seek food for
thought among the mystics. He translated Ruysbroek the
Superb's *The Spiritual Espousals* (1891) and Novalis's *Disciples at
Sais* (1895). Maeterlinck spoke in glowing terms of Novalis,
Ruysbroek and Boehme and his ideas make sense, they add new
depth to a subject.

In *The Treasures of the Humble* (1896), in the pages consecrated
to the thinkers, we discover his fondness for the guiding principle

of everyday drama. Maeterlinck had a splendid gift for language, but his thought cannot be analysed. The whole of his philosophy resides in his gift for revealing hidden feelings and unknown connections in thought by the use of imagery.

In 1898 he wrote *Wisdom and Destiny*; in 1902, *The Buried Temple*; in 1903, *The Double Garden*. Maeterlinck widened the field of our feelings, he made us sense the movements in the obscure life of plants, the occult laws of natural phenomena.

The Life of the Bees dates from 1901. The anguish, desires, repulsions and ecstasies of these splendid insects are extolled by a lyricist, probed by a philosopher.

Should we also say, like others, that as a philosopher, above all Maeterlinck served as a popularizer? No. Maeterlinck clarified a lot of obscure points and moreover he *brought them to life*.

He makes problems pass effortlessly from an imaginary state to reality. He lays them bare and shows them to us alive. First of all he frames them as problems, then isolates the data, giving us the impression of living them, for he evokes them with that modicum of positive sensuality which clings inalienably to our thoughts. Maeterlinck's whole philosophy should not be thought of as contained in the main theme of day to day drama. One would not be a major philosopher for having remarked that the whole of life was this immovable drama wherein the dark contacts between the forces of the fates is woven. Where Maeterlinck is truly great is in analysing these contacts and determining their conditions.

Maeterlinck evoked the figures of the mystics of old for us. He knew how to attune us to the stages of their thought. We really feel we are getting to the heart of the problem with him. 'God as a person is unknowable,' says the wisdom of the Talmud, 'but his ways are expressed in numbers and signs.' The majority of men are now insensitive to the nature of these *numbers*, which Maeterlinck set down in concise phrases.

Death, *The Unknown Guest* and *The Mountain Paths* contain the last stages of his great curiosity. In these later works the lofty thoughts of Boehme and Ruysbroek only remain as the echoes of a former doctrine. *The Great Secret* is like a concise breviary of man's conquests in the field of the Unknown.

Twelve Songs (1896) succeeded in melodically expanding his symbolic view of the world in ballad form.

Maeterlinck made his start in literature with a prose tale, *The Massacre of the Innocents* which was published in *La Pléiade* in 1886. Three years later he was famous. Mirbeau in a warm, enthusiastic article praised *Princess Maleine*. This was in 1889.

Maeterlinck translated *Annabelle* (*'Tis Pity She's a Whore*) by John Ford (1895) and more recently Shakespeare's *Macbeth* which, thanks to him, was produced at St. Wandrille Abbey with Séverin-Mars. Among other plays, he wrote *The Bluebird*, *The Engagement*, *Monna Vanna*, *Mary Magdalene*, *The Burgomaster of Stilmunde*, etc. [. . .]

Drama is the highest form of mental activity. The nature of the most profound things is to clash and combine, to infer. Movement is the principle of life itself. Maeterlinck endeavoured to give life to forms and states of pure thought. Pelléas, Tintagiles and Mélisande are like the perceptible figuration of these fair-seeming feelings. A philosophy emerged from these contacts and Maeterlinck attempted later to *express* it, to give form to the main thesis of everyday drama. Here fate unleashes its whims; here the rhythm is rarefied and spiritual. We are at the very eye of the storm, in circles as static as life.

Maeterlinck was the first to introduce the manifold richness of the subconscious into literature. The imagery in his poetry is arranged according to principles which do not occur in normal consciousness. But in Maeterlinck's poetry, things have not yet been restored to the state of being purely and simply things, handled by real hands, and feelings remained literary. This was the ransom of twelve centuries of French poetry. But the moderns stemmed the tide.

Maeterlinck appeared in literature at the right moment. He was a symbolist by nature, by definition. His poems, plays and essays are like the different states and shapes of one single thought. The intense feeling he had for the symbolic meaning of things, their secret communications and interferences, resulted in a preference for resurrecting them again, by clarifying them. Thus Maeterlinck interprets himself with the very ideas which serve as his sources.

[*CW*, I, 236–40; *OC*, I*, 213–17]

Foreword to *Douze chansons* (Twelve Songs) by Maurice Maeterlinck, Paris, Stock, 1923. Obviously Artaud recognized another kindred spirit in the Belgian symbolist author who could affirm that 'drama is the highest form of mental activity'. Artaud's own formula could have read 'theatre is the highest form of life'.

Macbeth, in Maeterlinck's own translation, was performed at the Abbaye de Saint-Wandrille on 28 August 1909. The play was staged in the courtyard, the refectory, the chapter-house and in the ruins of the church's chapels. Only fifty spectators were invited to attend and they were ushered from location to location by attendants dressed as Macbeth's servants. Richard Demarco's production of *Macbeth* at the 1988 Edinburgh Festival might well have been inspired by Maeterlinck's imaginative concept.

The Evolution of Set Design (*L'Évolution du décor*)

We must disregard *mise en scène,*[1] theatre.

All the great dramatists, the model dramatists, thought outside theatre.

Take Aeschylus, Sophocles, Shakespeare.

On another level, take Racine, Corneille, Molière. The latter, more or less, abolish external *mise en scène*, but they refine to the utmost the internal movements, the perpetual wavering of their heroes' souls.

Servility to the author, submission to the text, what a load of rubbish! But each text has an infinite number of possibilities. The spirit of the text, not the letter! But a text demands more than just analysis and insight.

There is a kind of magnetic intercommunication to be re-established between the mind of the author and the mind of the director. The director must even set aside his own logic and his own understanding. Those who have claimed up to now to relate exclusively to texts have managed perhaps to rid themselves of the blissful mimicry of certain traditions, they haven't been able to rid themselves of theatre and of their own understanding. They have replaced certain Molièresque and Odéon-like[2] traditions with some new-fangled traditions from Russia or the like. And while they were seeking to rid themselves of theatre, they were still thinking in terms of theatre. They compromised with the stage, with sets, with actors.

They think of each work in relation to theatre. Retheatricalize theatre. Such is their new frightful clarion call. But theatre must be thrown back into life.

That doesn't mean you have to make life in the theatre. As if one could imitate life. What is needed is to rediscover *the life of the theatre*, in all its freedom.

This life is completely bound up in the texts of the great tragedians, when they are heard in their true light, seen in their true dimensions, status, capacity, perspectives, particular density.

But we lack mysticism. What good is a director who is not accustomed to looking inside himself, first and foremost, and who wouldn't know, if he had to, how to detach and unleash himself? Such discipline is indispensable. More and more it is by purifying and by forgetting that we are able to rediscover the purity of our immediate responses and to restore to each gesture of the theatre its indispensable human meaning.

For the moment, let's look first for plays which are like a trans-substantiation of life. You go to the theatre to get away from yourself or, if you like, to rediscover not so much what is best, but what is most exceptional and most *vulnerable* in you. Everything is permissible in the theatre except dryness and ordinariness. Just look at painting. There are, today, young painters who have rediscovered the meaning of true painting. They paint chess or card players to look like gods.

What provokes this attraction to the circus and the music-hall of our whole modern world? I would happily use the word fantasy if I didn't feel it too prostituted, at least in the way it is meant today, and if it didn't inevitably lead towards that *retheatricaliz-ation* of theatre which is the very latest modish trend. No, I would rather say that one must intellectualize theatre, bring out from the feelings and the gestures of the characters their most unusual and most exceptional meaning. One must make the atmosphere of the theatre more subtle. That doesn't require any really highfalutin, metaphysical operation. Take the circus. But simply be aware of the values of the spirit. This abolishes and excludes from the theatre at least three quarters of the productions which take place there, but it forces theatre to return to its source and thereby saves it. To save theatre I would go as far as abolishing Ibsen, because of all his discussions on philosophical and moral points which don't sufficiently affect, *as far as we are concerned*, the soul of his heroes.

Sophocles, Aeschylus, Shakespeare rendered certain sufferings of the soul acceptable, though a little too much on an ordinary level, by a kind of divine terror which hung on the gestures of their heroes, and to which audiences then were more sensitive than today.

What we have lost on the strictly mystical side, we can make up for on the intellectual side.

But in order to achieve that we must learn to be mystical again at least in a certain kind of way: and by sticking close to a text, by forgetting ourselves, forgetting the theatre, wait for and hold on to images which will be born in us bare, natural and extreme, and taken to their limit.

Ridding ourselves not only of all reality, of all verisimilitude, but even of all logic, if at the end of all illogicality we still perceive life.

Practically speaking, and since we need principles in spite of everything, here are a few concrete ideas:

It is certain that everything which is visibly false in the theatre contributes to the creation of mistakes from which we are suffering. Take clowns. They construct the stage by the direction of a look. Thus on stage, nothing but the real. But all this has been said. We will not put up with three dimensional actors in motion in front of flat perspectives and with painted masks. Illusion does not exist for the front row of the stalls. We must either move the stage further back, or abolish the entire visual side of the show.

Furthermore, for the mental progression to be more perceptible, we must establish between Shakespeare and ourselves a kind of physical bridge. An actor, in some outfit which puts him beyond the realm of normal life, but without projecting him into the past, will supposedly attend the show, but without taking part in it. A kind of character in a top hat with no make-up who, by his appearance, would stand out from the crowd. The whole structure of the auditorium must be changed and the stage should be movable according to the needs of the action. Equally the strictly showy side of the show must be abolished. People would come not so much to see as to participate.

The audience must have the feeling that they can, without any special skill, do what the actors are doing.

With these few principles understood, it lies with the talent of the director to find the most suitable elements of suggestion and

style, the architecture or the essential line to evoke a work in its
proper mood and in its plausibility.

[OC, II, 9–12]

First published in the literary magazine *Comoedia* on 19 April 1924.
This essay was Artaud's contribution to a series of articles, letters and
interviews by designers, painters and directors published over a
period of some six months during 1923. Artaud completed his text by
October 1923. Two drawings accompanied the article.

In this, his first theoretical writing on theatre, Artaud takes issue
with Meyerhold and Evreinov, without naming them. Rather than
'theatricalize' theatre, he calls for the rejection of theatre altogether
and for the abolition of all illusionistic forms of representation. Not
only should theatre be *real*, it should be more real than life; in brief, it
should be ultimate reality.

1. There is no proper English equivalent for *mise en scène*. It means
'directing' and encompasses all the activities associated with staging a
play (casting, designing, stage management . . .) but it refers also to the
aesthetic conception of the production and the individual reading of
the director. (See particularly pp. 70 and 77.)
2. 'Odéon-like' translates *odéonien* and refers to the stilted, petrified,
old-fashioned style of acting prevalent at the Théâtre de l'Odéon, the
second house of the official Comédie-Française. The term is still in
use despite the new, modern image of the Odéon-Théâtre de l'Europe
which is one of the liveliest theatres in Paris and which regularly stages
plays and productions from all over Europe.

To the Director of the Comédie-Française

Paris, 21 February 1925

Sir,

You have infested the news long enough. Your brothel is too
greedy. It is time the representatives of a dead art stopped
deafening us. Tragedy does not need a Rolls Royce nor whoredom
jewellery.

Enough comings and goings in your official knocking-shop.

We aim beyond tragedy, the cornerstone of your poisonous old
shed, and your Molière is a twat.

But it is not only tragedy. We deny your alimentary organism
the right to perform any play, past, future or present.

With Piérat, Sorel, Segond-Weber, Alexandre and others, the Comédie-Française has been nothing but a sex house, and what sex! It has never had an inkling of an idea about theatre.

Chuck out Sylvain, chuck out Fenoux, chuck out Duflos, chuck out everybody, – the same buffoons, the same Alexandres, the same old wrecks, the same pantaloon tragedians always return to the top.

Do not renew yourself, Comédie-Française! Neither your 'Simouns' Porché, nor your 'railway' Poizat, those little strips of feeble tragedy, nor your latest Jean Coco can do anything to stop you creeping into the past.

All your hellish stew, your sauce-spoiling shareholders now need is some policeman's 'Knock' to show you where your Molière can lead you.

We refuse to go on supporting the cult of your blood-thirsty Corneille who sacrifices sons to their fathers and sets the tone for some patriotic myths about the supreme demands of the heart.

And as for Racine, cook him in Granval sauce, Sylvain sauce, Lambert sauce or caper sauce. He has not yet been performed by you.

You are twats. Your very existence is an insult. No base need, no manifestation, no mass rising of national idiocy have you failed to support. The power of feelings is strong enough not to allow it to be prostituted.

The theatre can do without you. It is made of a different matter to your wretched tissues. French Theatre, you say? You belong no more to France than to the land of the Kafirs. At best you belong to the Fourteenth of July.

The theatre is the land of Fire, the lagoons of Heaven, the battle of Dreams. The theatre is Solemnity.

You leave your droppings at the foot of Solemnity like the Arab at the foot of the Pyramids. Make way for the theatre, gentlemen, make way for the universal theatre which is content with the unlimited field of the mind.

[*CW*, 3, 102–3; *OC*, III, 116–18. First published in the literary magazine *84*, No. 13, March 1950]

Letter to the Chancellors of the European Universities (*Lettre aux recteurs des universités européennes*)

Sirs,

In the narrow tank you call 'Thought', the mind's rays rot like old straw.

Enough playing on words, syntactic stratagems and formula-juggling. We must now discover the Heart's great Law, the Law which is not a Law (a prison) but a guide for the Mind lost in its own labyrinth. Further away than anything science will ever reach, where reason's rays break against the clouds, this labyrinth exists, a focal point where all the forces of being and the ultimate Spiritual veins converge. In this maze of moving and ever-changing walls outside all known forms of thought, our Spirit stirs, watching for its most secret and spontaneous movements – those with the character of a revelation, an air of having come from elsewhere, of having fallen from the sky.

But the race of prophets is extinct. Europe is becoming set in its ways, slowly embalming itself beneath the wrappings of its borders, its factories, its law-courts and its universities. The frozen Mind cracks between the mineral staves which close upon it. The fault lies with your mouldy systems, your logic of $2 + 2 = 4$. The fault lies with you, Chancellors, caught in the net of syllogisms. You manufacture engineers, magistrates, doctors, who know nothing of the true mysteries of the body or the cosmic laws of existence, false scholars blind outside this world, philosophers who pretend to reconstruct the mind. The least act of spontaneous creation is a more complex and revealing world than any metaphysics.

So leave us alone, Sirs, you are only usurpers. By what right do you claim to channel human intelligence and award certificates of Mental merit? You know nothing of the Mind, you are unaware of its most secret and essential ramifications, those fossil imprints so close to our own origins, those tracks we are occasionally able to discover deep in the most unexplored deposits of our minds.

In the name of your own logic we say to you, Life stinks, Sirs. Look at yourselves for a moment, consider your products. A whole generation of gaunt and bewildered youth is passing through the sieve of your diplomas. You are a plague on the world,

Sirs, and so much the better for the world, but let it consider itself a little less in the vanguard of humanity.

We need confused adepts, more than active adepts.

[*CW*, 1, 178–80; *OC*, I**, 38–9]

The 'Letter to the Chancellors' first appeared in *La Révolution surréaliste*, No. 3, 15 April 1925. This was a special issue of the journal of the surrealist movement and had been edited by Artaud himself. The letter to the Director of the Comédie-Française was also written on that occasion but it was, unaccountably, left out.

Artaud had met the surrealist painter André Masson in 1923. Late in 1924 he joined the surrealist movement and he wrote several manifestos for *La Révolution surréaliste* (which were published in No. 2, 15 January 1925 and in No. 3). On 26 January 1925 Artaud became director of the 'Bureau de recherches surréalistes', but his intransigence, on the one hand, and his involvement in theatre, on the other, displeased his friends and, in November 1926, he was expelled. Despite this unhappy episode André Breton, in later years, proved himself an admirable friend.

'The Spurt of Blood' (*'Le Jet de sang'*)

YOUNG MAN: I love you and everything is beautiful.

GIRL [*in a quickened, throbbing voice*]: You love me and everything is beautiful.

YOUNG MAN [*lower*]: I love you and everything is beautiful.

GIRL [*lower still*]: I love you.

Silence.

YOUNG MAN: Face me.

GIRL [*same business, faces him*]: There.

YOUNG MAN [*in an exalted, high-pitched tone*]: I love you, I am great, I am lucid, I am full, I am solid.

GIRL [*same high-pitched tone*]: We love each other.

YOUNG MAN: We are intense. Ah, what a well-made world.

Silence. Noise like a huge wheel spinning, blowing out wind. A hurricane comes between them. At that moment two stars collide, and a succession of limbs of flesh fall. Then feet, hands, scalps, masks, colonnades, porticoes, temples and alembics, falling slower and slower as if through space, then three scorpions one after the other and finally a frog, and a scarab which lands with heart-breaking, nauseating slowness.

YOUNG MAN [*shouting at the top of his voice*]: Heaven's gone crazy. *Looks up at the sky.*

   Let's run off.

Pushes the GIRL *off ahead of him.*

A Medieval KNIGHT *in enormous armour enters, followed by a* WETNURSE *holding her bosom up with her hands and panting because of her swollen breasts.*

KNIGHT: Leave your teats alone. Hand me my papers.

WETNURSE [*giving a shrill cry*]: Oh! Oh! Oh!

KNIGHT: Shit, now what's the matter with you, dammit?

WETNURSE: Our girl there, with him.

KNIGHT: Shush, there's no girl there!

WETNURSE: I tell you they are fucking.

KNIGHT: And what the fuck if they are fucking.

WETNURSE: Incest.

KNIGHT: Midwife.

WETNURSE [*thrusting her hands in pockets as big as her breasts*]:
   Pimp.

She tosses his papers over hastily.

KNIGHT: Phiote, let me eat.

WETNURSE *runs off. He then gets up and pulls a huge slice of Gruyère cheese out of each paper. He suddenly coughs and chokes.*

KNIGHT [*mouth full*]: Ehp. Ehp. Bring your breasts over here, bring your breasts over here. Where's she gone?

He runs off. YOUNG MAN *returns.*

YOUNG MAN: I saw, I knew, I understood. Here is the main square, the priest, the cobbler, the vegetable stalls, the church portals, the red light, the scales of Justice. I can't go on!

A PRIEST, *a* COBBLER, *a* BEADLE, *a* WHORE, *a* JUDGE, *and a* BARROW-WOMAN *advance on to the stage like shadows.*

YOUNG MAN: I have lost her, bring her back.

ALL [*in a different tone*]: Who, who, who, who?

YOUNG MAN: My wife.

BEADLE [*very blustering*]: Your wife, huh, joker!

YOUNG MAN: Joker! She might be yours!

He runs off.

The PRIEST *steps forward next and puts his arm around the* YOUNG MAN's *shoulders.*

PRIEST [*as if hearing a confession*]: What part of her body did you refer to most often?

YOUNG MAN: To God.

The PRIEST, *disconcerted at this reply, immediately assumes a Swiss accent.*

PRIEST [*with a Swiss accent*]: But that's out of date. We don't look at it in that way. You'll have to ask the volcanoes and earthquakes about that. We gratify ourselves with man's minor indecencies in the confessional. There it is, that's all, that's life.

YOUNG MAN [*very impressed*]: Ah, that's it, that's life! Well, it's a mess.

PRIEST [*still with a Swiss accent*]: Of course.

It suddenly becomes night. The earth quakes. Thunder rages, lightning zig-zagging everywhere and its flashes light up the characters who run about, bump into one another, fall down, get up again and run like mad. At a given moment a huge hand seizes the WHORE'*s hair which catches fire and sprouts up visibly.*

A GIGANTIC VOICE: Bitch! Look at your body!

The WHORE'*S body appears completely naked and hideous under her blouse and skirt which turn transparent.*

WHORE: God, let go of me.

She bites God's wrist. A great spurt of blood slashes across the stage, while in the midst of the brightest lightning flash we see the PRIEST *making the sign of the cross.*

When the lights come up again, the characters are all dead and their corpses lie all over the ground. Only the WHORE *and* YOUNG MAN *are left, devouring each other with their eyes. The* WHORE *falls into the* YOUNG MAN'*s arms.*

The YOUNG MAN *hides his head in his hands.*

The WETNURSE *returns carrying the* GIRL *under her arms like a parcel.*

The GIRL *is dead. She drops her on the ground where she sprawls out and becomes as flat as a pancake.*

The WETNURSE'*s breasts are gone. Her chest is completely flat.*

At that moment, the KNIGHT *enters and throws himself on the* WETNURSE, *shaking her violently.*

KNIGHT [*in a terrible voice*]: Where did you put it? Give me my Gruyère.

WETNURSE [*brazenly*]: Here!

She lifts up her dress.

The YOUNG MAN *wants to run off but he freezes like a paralysed puppet.*

YOUNG MAN [*in a ventriloquist's voice and as if hovering in mid-air*]: Don't hurt Mummy.

KNIGHT: Damn her.

He hides his face in horror.

A host of scorpions crawl out from under the WETNURSE*'s dress and start swarming in her vagina which swells and splits, becomes transparent and shimmers like the sun.*

The YOUNG MAN *and* WHORE *fly off like mad.*

GIRL [*gets up, dazzled*]: TheVirgin! Ah, that's what he was looking for.

CURTAIN

[CW, I, 62–5;OC, I*, 70–6]

First published in *L'Ombilic des limbes* (The Umbilical Limbo, 1925) in the collection 'Une œuvre, un portrait' with a portrait of Artaud by André Masson.

   Le Jet de sang was Artaud's first dramatic text. The subtitle, *La Boule de verre*, refers to a play by Armand Salacrou which had been published a few months earlier. Yet it is neither the parodic element nor the very faint echoes of Apollinaire's *The Breasts of Tiresias* which should command our attention, but the visual and surrealist qualities of the text which is far closer to Buñuel's inspiration in *Le Chien andalou* (1928) than to any pre-existing literary text.

The Umbilical Limbo (*L'Ombilic des limbes*)

Here where others proffer their works, I claim to do nothing more than show my mind.

   Life consists of burning up questions.

   I do not consider any work apart from life.

   I do not like indifferent creativity. Nor do I consider the mind as unconcerned with itself. Each of my works, each outline of myself, each frozen flowering of my innermost soul oozes over me.

   I am as much myself in a letter written to explain the inner contraction of my being and the meaningless emasculation of my life, as in an essay outside me, which seems like an indifferent gestation of my mind.

I suffer because the Mind is not in life and life is not the Mind. I suffer because the Mind is an organ, the Mind is an interpreter or the Mind intimidates things to accept them in the Mind.

I hold this book up in life, I want it to be attacked by things outside, primarily by all the shearing jolts, all the twitching of *my future ego*.

These pages all float about like icicles in my mind. Thus excuse my complete freedom. I object to any differentiation between the moments of my ego. I do not acknowledge any plan in the mind.

We must get rid of the Mind, just as we must get rid of literature. I say the Mind and life interconnect at all levels. I would like to make a Book to disturb people, like an open door leading them where they would never have gone of their own free will. Simply a door communicating with reality.

This is no more a preface to a book than, say, the poems that stand out in it, or the enumeration of all the furores of soul-sickness.

This too is only an icicle stuck in my throat.

[CW, I, 49; *OC*–I* 49,50]

The short first text of this slim volume contains, in essence, Artaud's concept of the work of art: a human activity which is life itself.

All Writing Is filth (*Toute l'écriture est de la cochonnerie*)

All writing is filth.

People who leave the realm of the obscure in order to define whatever is going on in their minds, are filthy pigs.

The whole pack of literati are filth, particularly these days.

All those who fix landmarks in their minds, I mean in a certain part of their heads, in strictly localized areas of their brains, all those who are masters of their own language, all those for whom words mean something, all those for whom there are currents of thought and who think the soul can be sublime; those who are the spirit of the times, and who have named these currents of thought I am thinking of their specific tasks and the mechanical creaking their minds give out at every gust of wind,

– are filthy pigs.

Those for whom certain words and modes of being have only one meaning, those who are so fussy, those who classify feelings and who quibble over some degree or other of their laughable classifications, those who still believe in 'expressions', those who stir the ideological pots that are in vogue at the time, those about whom women speak so well and the same women who speak so well and speak about contemporary currents of thought, those who still believe in orientation of the mind, those who follow paths, who drop names, who have pages of books acclaimed,

– those are the worst pigs of all.

You are very free, young man!

No, I am thinking of bearded critics.

I told you; no language, no words, no mind, nothing.

Nothing, except a fine Nervometer.

A sort of impenetrable stop in the midst of everything in our minds.

Do not expect me to tell you what all this is called or into how many sections it is divided, or to tell you its value. Do not expect me to go along with it, or to begin to discuss all this, and in the process become confused and without realizing it, to start THINKING, – or to clarify it, or to bring it to life, to adorn it with a host of words, polished meanings, all different and clearly able to bring to light all the attitudes and shades of very sensitive and penetrating thought.

Ah, these unnamed states, these superior positions of the soul, ah, these periods in the mind, ah, these tiny failures which are the stuff of my days, ah, these masses teeming with facts! Still, I use the same words and yet my thoughts don't appear to advance much, but really I am advancing more than you, bearded asses, apposite swine, masters of the false word, despatchers of portraits, gutter writers, herbalists, entomologists and scabs on my tongue.

I told you my speech no longer existed, but this is no reason for you to persist, for you obstinately to go on speaking.

Come now, in ten years' time I will be understood by people who do what you are doing today. Then my eruptions will be understood, my crystals will be clear, they will have learnt how to adulterate my poisons and the play of my soul will be divulged.

By then all my hair, all my mental veins will be melted in quicklime, then my bestiary will be noted and my mystique will have become a cover. Then the joints in the stones will appear, fuming, and arboreal bunches of mind's eyes will set into glossaries and stone aeroliths will fall. Then lines will appear, then non-spatial geometry will be understood and people will learn what the configuration of mind means and they will understand how I lost my mind.

Then you will understand why my mind is not here, then you will see all language exhausted, all minds dry up, all tongues shrivel up, all human figures collapse, deflate, as if drawn up by shrivelling leeches. And this lubricating membrane will go on floating in the air, this lubricating, caustic membrane, this doubly-thick membrane, multi-levelled, infinitely fissured, this sad, translucent membrane. Yet it, too, so sensitive, so relevant, so capable of multiplying, splitting, turning inside out, with its shimmering fissures, senses, drugs and its penetrating, noxious irrigation.

Then all this will be considered all right.

And I will have no further need to speak.

[*CW*, I, 75–7; *OC*, I*, 100–2]

Text published in *Le Pèse-Nerfs* (The Nervometer), Leibowitz, 1 August 1925, in the collection 'Pour vos beaux yeux' edited by Louis Aragon. The cover was designed by André Masson.

All his life Artaud endeavoured to fight against 'style' and what he calls 'la trop belle littérature', because style and elegant prose came to him quite naturally, but he considered that such literary niceties that flowed from his pen only served to obfuscate the real purpose of his writing which was to communicate directly the pain and suffering of being. He will repeat the same points over and over again. (See his letter to Peter Watson, p. 194, and 'To Put an End to the Judgement of God', p. 220.)

Part Two

The Alfred Jarry Theatre (1926–30)

Alfred Jarry Theatre (1926–30)

The Théâtre Alfred Jarry was named after the author of *Ubu roi*, considered by the surrealists to be one of their most important forerunners. It was founded by Artaud, the playwright Roger Vitrac and the young publisher Robert Aron, with the active and financial support of Madame Yvonne Allendy and her husband, Artaud's psychiatrist. The Théâtre Alfred Jarry gave eight performances (i.e. four productions) in three different theatres.

1–2 June 1927, Théâtre de Grenelle

Les Mystères de l'amour (The Secrets of Love), by Vitrac. 'An ironic play, physically staging the misgivings, isolation, eroticism and criminal thoughts lurking in the minds of lovers. A *real dream* brought into being for the first time on stage.'

Le Ventre brûlé ou la mère folle (The Burnt Womb, or the Mad Mother), by Artaud (text lost). 'A lyrical piece, which exposed with humour the clash between theatre and the cinema.'

Gigogne, by Max Robur (alias Robert Aron; text also lost), 'Written and produced with the aim of systematic provocation.'

14 January 1928, Comédie des Champs-Élysées

Partage de midi (Break of Noon), by Paul Claudel (presentation of the third act, without the author's permission). 'This act was performed by virtue of the axiom that any published work is public property.' *The Mother*, by Pudovkin, after Gorki (the film had been banned by French censor). 'It was shown primarily for the ideas it contains, secondly for its own merits and finally as a protest against censorship.'

2 and 9 June 1928, Théâtre de l'Avenue

Le Songe (A Dream Play), by Strindberg. Production sponsored by the Swedish Embassy, but performances were disrupted by André Breton and other surrealists. 'This play was performed because of its exceptional nature, because oneirism plays a major part in it, because no one in Paris dared to put it on, because Strindberg had translated it into French himself, because of the difficulties involved in such an undertaking, and finally to apply a full-scale development of the techniques of *mise en scène* characteristic of the Théâtre Alfred Jarry.'

24 and 29 December 1928, and 5 January 1929, Comédie des Champs-Élysées

Victor ou les enfants au pouvoir (Victor, or Power to the Children), by Vitrac. 'This lyrical, ironic, outspoken play was attacking the middle-class family unit, featuring adultery, incest, scatology, anger, Surrealist poetry, patriotism, shame and death.'

Artaud directed all the plays and performed a small part in *A Dream Play* (Dean of Theology). 1926 to 1930 were his most productive years in terms of stage work. He concentrated all his energies on the Théâtre Alfred Jarry and not content with being a director, playwright, administrator and, on occasion, actor, he wrote numerous manifestos, programme notes and letters which chart the progress and decline of this venture.

The Théâtre Alfred Jarry was not strictly a 'surrealist' theatre, since Artaud and Vitrac had been expelled from the surrealist group before the launch of the venture. In any case, André Breton, the high priest of surrealism, considered any theatrical activity to be unworthy of true surrealists, because it could not really express the aims of surrealism and because it required financial backing and thus 'subordinated thought to money'. But Breton genuinely approved of the production of *Partage de midi* which was a serious attempt on the part of Artaud to bring to light a play disowned by Claudel, despite the generally held belief that Artaud had chosen the text to vilify it and its author.

Artaud himself, as usual, was responsible for the misunderstanding. At the end of a less than peaceful performance, he came forward to reveal the name of the author (even the actors were unaware of it). In his address to the audience, Artaud was supposed to denounce Claudel's 'intellectual betrayal', since the author exerted a kind of censorship on his own work. Instead of delivering the prepared speech, which he could not remember, Artaud improvised the following diatribe: 'Ladies and gentlemen, the play which the Théâtre Alfred Jarry was pleased to perform for you is *Partage de midi*, by Paul Claudel, French ambassador to the United States, who happens to be a notorious traitor.'

The temporary *rapprochement* between Artaud and his former literary associates was shattered when *A Dream Play* was performed. Breton accused Artaud of having accepted 'dirty money' from the Swedish Embassy (a fact which Artaud did not deny). Therefore Breton, with his surrealist friends, disrupted the first performance and threatened to do worse on the second and final showing of the play. Reluctantly the Théâtre Alfred Jarry (i.e. Robert Aron) called for police protection, thus ensuring a complete break between Artaud and the surrealist group. In terms of public relations the occasion was a complete disaster for, in order to salvage something of his former friendship, Artaud insulted the Swedes in a silly speech delivered from the stage during the interval of the first performance. To try and placate his friends, Artaud declared: 'We would like to stress that if we present *A Dream Play* by Strindberg, it is because Strindberg was a rebel, who loathed all homelands ('patries'), and especially his own Swedish homeland.' Breton was not impressed, the Swedes stormed out and Madame Allendy, who had wooed the generous sponsors, was placed in an impossible position.

Despite the critical success of Vitrac's *Victor ou les enfants au pouvoir*, the Théâtre Alfred Jarry was not financially viable. This and personal squabbles between the co-founders made its demise inevitable.

The Alfred Jarry Theatre (*Le Théâtre Alfred Jarry*)

First Year (1926–1927 Season)

Theatre conventions have had their day. As things stand now we are unable to accept theatre that tricks us. We need to believe in what we see. We can no longer subscribe to theatre which repeats itself every night according to the same, ever the same old rituals. The show we are watching must be unique and give us the impression of being as unexpected and as incapable of being repeated as any act in life, any occurrence whatsoever brought about by events.

In a word, with such theatre, we re-establish a connection with life, instead of cutting ourselves off from it. We can only take ourselves seriously and so can the audience if we have a very distinct impression that a heartfelt part of our lives is committed to a performance whose setting is the stage. Our sort of style, whether in tragedy or comedy, is one that makes you smile a rather sickly smile at a certain point. This is what we have undertaken to do.

This is the *human* anxiety the spectators must feel when they come out. They will be shaken and irritated by the inner dynamism of the production taking place before their eyes. The dynamism will be directly related to the anxiety and the pre-occupations of their entire lives.

Such is the inevitability we conjure up and the show will consist of this very inevitability. The illusion we are seeking to create has no bearing on the greater or lesser degree of verisimilitude of the action, but on the power of communication and reality of this action. By this very act, each show becomes a sort of event. The spectators must feel a scene in their lives being acted out in front of them, a truly vital scene. [. . .]

Most of the time, what gives the productions we put on their real, manifest value, is due to an imperceptible discovery, capable of creating the greatest illusion in the audience's mind. Suffice it to say that, as to production theory, we boldly leave it to chance. In the theatre we want to create, chance is our idol. We are not afraid of any failures or disasters. If we did not believe a miracle was possible, we would not even entertain such a risky course. But one miracle could repay us for our pains and patience. We are counting on that miracle.

A director who does not follow any rules but is guided by his own inspiration, may or may not find what we need. Depending on what play he is putting on, he may or may not discover anything, he may or may not make a strikingly clever discovery, he may or may not find *the necessary disturbing element to throw the audience into the sort of uneasiness he is aiming at*. Our success is wholly dependent on these alternatives.

Still, it is quite clear we will work with actual scripts. The plays we intend to perform are part of literature, of whatever type. Yet how can we manage to reconcile our desire for freedom and independence with the need to conform to a certain number of directions as laid down in the script?

The way we are trying to define theatre, only one thing seems sure to us, only one thing seems real. The script. But the script as a separate reality, existing as something self-sufficient in its own right, not for its spirit, for we are little inclined to respect that, but simply for the air breathed in enunciating it. That's all.

For the thing which seems to us most basically embarrassing in the theatre, and most basically destructible, is what distinguishes the art of theatre from the art of painting or literature, all those hateful trappings which clutter up a written play and turn it into a show, instead of it remaining within the limits of words, impressions and abstractions.

These trappings, this visual display are what we want to cut down to the bare minimum and immerse in a solemnity and a spirit of disturbing action.

The Alfred Jarry Theatre

[*CW*, 2, 18–20; *OC*, II, 18–20]

Eight page pamphlet published in 1926 expanding on the ideas put forward in a manifesto published by the *Nouvelle Revue Française*, No. 158, 1 November 1926 (*CW*, 2, 15–17; *OC*, II, 15–17). Over and over again Artaud repeats that theatre is the very opposite to game playing and that it must have a real and permanent impact on actors and spectators alike:

If theatre is a game, too many serious problems clamour for attention for us to be distracted from the tiniest part of them by something as ephemeral as this game. If theatre is not a game, if it is indeed a reality, the problem we must solve is how we can restore its standing as reality and how to make every show a kind of event. [. . .]

Is our goal now clear? It is this: with every production we are playing a very serious game and the significance of our efforts lies in the very nature of this seriousness. We are not appealing to the audience's mind or senses, but to their whole existence. To theirs and ours. We stake our lives on the show that is taking place on stage. If we did not have a very deep, distinct feeling that part of our intimate life was committed to that show, we would not think it necessary to pursue this experiment further. Audiences coming to our theatre know they are present at a real operation involving not only the mind but also the very senses and flesh. From then on they will go to the theatre as they would to a surgeon or dentist, in the same frame of mind, knowing, of course, that they will not die, but that all the same this is a serious business, and that they will not come out unscathed. If we were not convinced we were going to affect them as deeply as possible, we would think ourselves unworthy of this, our highest task. They must be thoroughly convinced we can make them scream.

Manifesto for an Abortive Theatre (*Manifeste pour un théâtre avorté*)

In the confused period in which we live, a period full of blasphemy and the dull glow of endless denials, when artistic as well as moral values seem to be disappearing into an abyss the like of which has never been seen in any other intellectual period, I was self-indulgent enough to think I could create a theatre, that I could at least do the groundwork for an attempt at resuscitating theatre's universally scorned values. But the stupidity of some people and the bad faith and viciousness of others have dissuaded me forever.

The following Manifesto is all that remains of that attempt:

On . . . January 1927, the A . . . theatre will present its first production. Its founders are very much aware of the kind of despair launching such a theatre implies. And it was not without a kind of remorse that they made up their minds to do it. Let there be no mistake. The A . . . Theatre is not a business; that goes without saying. But, that aside, it is an enterprise on which a certain number of individuals have staked everything. We do not believe, we no longer believe there is anything in the world that can be called theatre. We do not see how that name fits any reality. A terrible confusion weighs down our lives. We are undoubtedly in a very critical period from the spiritual point of view. We believe in all the threats of the invisible. We are fighting the invisible itself. We are whole-heartedly applying ourselves to unearthing a certain number of secrets. And what we want to expose is this

mass of desires, dreams, illusions and beliefs which have resulted
in this lie no one believes in any longer, called, probably
mockingly, the theatre. We would like to be able to revive a certain
number of images – obvious, palpable images that are not tainted
with continual disillusionment. We are not creating a theatre so as
to present plays, but to succeed in uncovering the mind's obscure,
hidden and unrevealed aspects, by a sort of real, physical
projection. We are not aiming to create an illusion of things which
do not exist, as was done heretofore, as has been done up to now
in the theatre. On the contrary, we aim to make a certain number
of scenes – indestructible, irrefutable images appealing directly to
the mind – appear on the stage. The very objects, props and
scenery on stage must be understood in an immediate sense,
without being transposed. They must not be taken for what they
represent, but for what they really are. Production as such, the
actors' movements, must be considered only as the visible signs of
an invisible or secret language. Not one theatrical gesture must be
devoid of the fatality of life and the mysterious happenings that
occur in dreams. Whatever has a prophetic sense in life, is like an
omen, is echoed in intuition, arises out of a fertile error in the
mind, will be found at any given moment on our stage.

Our efforts will be understood to be all the more dangerous in that
they are bristling with ambition. But we are not afraid of the void,
and this idea must sink into people's heads. There is no vacuum in
nature we believe the human mind incapable of filling, given the
right moment. One can see what a terrible task we have set ourselves.
We are aiming at nothing less than a return to the human or inhuman
sources of the theatre, thereby to resuscitate it completely.

What we would like to see sparkle and triumph on stage is
whatever is a part of the mystery and magnetic fascination of
dreams, the dark layers of consciousness, all that obsesses us
within our minds. And we are prepared to sink in the effort, to
expose ourselves to the ridicule of a colossal failure. Nor are we
afraid of the kind of tendency our efforts represent.

We consider theatre to be a true work of magic. We do not
intend to appeal to the eyes, nor to the direct emotions of 'soul'.
What we are attempting to create are *psychological* emotions of a
certain sort, where the heart's most secret movements will be
exposed.

We do not think life itself can be represented on stage, or that one should risk this.

We are groping blindly towards this ideal theatre. We partly know what we want to do and how we can accomplish this physically, but we believe that chance, a miracle, will occur and reveal to us all that we still do not know, that it will contribute all its profoundly superior life to this poor matter we insist on moulding.

Aside from the degree of success of our shows, those who come to our theatre must understand they are participating in a mystical pursuit, through which an important part of the mind and consciousness may finally be saved or lost.

Antonin Artaud, 13 November 1926

[*CW*, 2, 22–5; *OC*, II, 22–5]

First published in *Cahiers du Sud*, 13th year, No. 87, February 1927. At the proof stage Artaud added a post-script to his text in order to attack the surrealists who had recently excluded him from their group (November 1926) precisely because of his theatrical activities. At the time Artaud was going through a very difficult period. Because of personality clashes between the three directors (Artaud, Vitrac, Aron), the writing was already on the wall for the Alfred Jarry Theatre. As for Artaud's personal, financial and professional situation, a fragment of a letter, dated 14 February 1927, to the theatrical entrepreneur Jacques Hébertot is painfully revealing: 'I am a ghost and you a businessman. You are forever a theatre director and I am only a poor bloody actor who hasn't made it, whatever talent one might credit him with. Mr Jacques Hébertot, I need to earn my crust, I need to eat, that's how bad things are. I call upon the friendship you have shown me which has passed into the limbo of your most distant cares. I am only asking for work. Give me something to do, Mr Hébertot, anything: a role, a position in your offices, even a job as a road sweeper. I spurn my mind. [. . .] Worries, hunger perhaps, bring on bad dreams. [*OC*, III, 118]

To Jean Paulhan

[Paris] 2 July 1927

Dear Friend,

[. . .] without blowing my own trumpet, which I couldn't really give a damn about, I am surprised that Monsieur Benjamin Crémieux should be charting the theatrical movement in those blessed years of the theatre 1926-7 and should still cling to those doddering old corpses, those anti-representative phantoms of Jouvet, Pitoëff, Dullin, even Gémier, etc. When will people stop stirring up refuse.

Don't worry. I am not suggesting that there is nothing but the Jarry Theatre. Even the Jarry Theatre is ill, from lack of funds, and we do not know if we shall be able to keep it going. I am the first person to acknowledge the faults of our first experiment. We have excuses: time, money, but there is still *Les Mystères de l'amour* and whatever Monsieur Benjamin Crémieux thinks of it, it remains a play made for the stage.

Does the performance of a play such as this not contribute something to modern theatre, something which is lacking? Everything in *Les Mystères de l'amour* is pure objectivization. The lines adopt a weight and sound on the stage which they do not have on paper. Furthermore, the production must not be confused with that purely accessory element which consists of sets and lighting. The production is the scenic movement, the trepidation of the lines, the rhythm of the play. The cerebral subversions in a play like *Les Mystères de l'amour* are only of value once they are incarnated by living characters. A certain spiritual relentlessness is what counts and only comes to life once it is acted. Our aim is to materialize the most secret movements of the soul by the simplest and most naked means. To show an unexpected side of the most hackneyed, most banal situations.

In short, this play and its scenic conception contain a resistance, a density given to things of a moral order which were worth pointing out.

Ever yours,

Antonin Artaud

[*CW*, 3, 104–5; *OC*, III, 123–4]

Artaud here reacts violently against Crémieux's less than complimentary article on the first production of the Alfred Jarry Theatre and, carried away by his anger, he goes on to insult the best theatre practitioners of his generation, all men whom he once respected and admired and who had allowed him to get a foothold in the profession.

The Alfred Jarry Theatre (1928 Season)

The Alfred Jarry Theatre is intended for all those people who do not see theatre as a goal but as ways and means, for all those who are disturbed and anxious about the reality of which theatre is only a symbol. The Alfred Jarry Theatre will endeavour to rediscover this at random through its productions.

Starting with the Alfred Jarry Theatre, theatre will no longer be a straitjacketed thing, imprisoned in the restricted area of the stage, but will really aim at becoming *action*, subject to all the attractions and distortions of events, over which random happenings resume their rights. A production, a play, will always be unconfirmed or liable to revision in such a way that different audiences on different evenings would never see the same show in front of them. The Alfred Jarry Theatre will therefore make a break with theatre but, in addition, it will obey an inner *need* where the mind plays the main part. Not only are theatre's limitations now done away with, but so is its principal justification. A Jarry Theatre production will be as thrilling as a game, like a card game with the whole audience taking part. The Jarry Theatre will endeavour to express what life has forgotten, has *hidden*, or is incapable of stating. Everything which stems from the mind's *fertile* delusions, its sensory illusions, encounters between things and sensations which strike us primarily by their physical density, will be shown from an extraordinary angle, with the stench and the excreta of unadulterated brutality, just as they appear to the mind, *just as the mind remembered them*.

Everything which cannot be depicted as it is, or needs the illusion of artificial colouring, all this will be kept off the boards. Everything which appears on our stage will be taken in a direct, literal sense; nothing will look like a set in any sense whatsoever.

The Jarry Theatre does not cheat, does not ape life, does not represent it. It aims to extend it, to be a sort of *magical operation*, open to any development, and in this it answers a mental need which audiences feel is hidden deep down within themselves. This is not the place to lecture on present-day or practical magic, yet in fact we are dealing with magic.

How can a play be a magical operation, how can it answer

needs which go beyond it, how can the deepest part of the audience's soul be involved? This is what people will see if they trust us.

In any case, our aspirations alone would distinguish us. Our existence matters to all people who are concerned with mental anguish, who are sensitive to everything in the mood of today, who want to take part in the Revolutions that are afoot. They are the ones who will provide us with the means to stay alive. We are counting on them for it.

Besides, our programme exists and reveals what we intend to do better than any theories.

Last year we put on *The Secrets of Love* by Roger Vitrac. Among the plays to be presented this year, first mention should go to *Power to the Children*, by the same author, Roger Vitrac.

Before applying himself to ideas, Roger Vitrac, like any good dramatist, keeps the stage before him in his mind, while sticking to his own line of thought. This is the very thing that distinguishes him. In the least of his expressions we feel his mind, his grey matter, at work.

In *Power to the Children*, the pot has reached boiling point. The title alone indicates a basic lack of respect for established values. This play expresses the disintegration of modern thought in scathing and at the same time rigid actions, as well as its replacement by . . . by what? In any case, roughly speaking, here is the problem the play corresponds to: What do we think with? What's left? There are no longer any common yardsticks or scales of value. What remains? All this is expressed in a lively, tangible, but not at all philosophical way, as thrilling as a horse-race or a game of chess. [. . .]

The Alfred Jarry Theatre was formed to practise theatre, not to promote it. The writers associated with it have no respect either for authors or texts. They do not mean to keep to them, at any price or in any way.

If they receive any plays which are, originally and in the finality of their subject matter, significant of the state of mind they are seeking to express, these will be welcome in preference to others.

But if none show up, too bad for any Shakespeare, Hugo or

even Cyril Tourneur that comes their way or falls into their clutches.

[CW, 2, 26–9; OC, II, 26–9]

Eight page pamphlet published in 1928.

To Génica Athanasiou[1]

[Paris, 19 January 1928]

Génica,

You had the opportunity to be a marvellous success with a role to rank alongside the most beautiful you have ever played. This opportunity you would not grasp. Probably under the pretext that we were no longer living together you chose to listen to the advice of Berley[2] who is basically incapable by nature of understanding a text as sublime and as elevated as this. But because of its very nature, this text and play – which is nothing but text – could only be what the actors made it. This text could only achieve success through the *emphasis* which the actors placed on it. But such emphasis must be respected. And I had nothing more to do with it than what I did. But in this adventure and in the eyes of certain ill-intentioned people infected with the spirit of the so-called arts theatre, I appear an idiot and a bloody fool. How could you not have understood that you, much more than I, were responsible for the success of this play. If you had respected the timings and the interplay of emotions, you would have made this play the worthy success it should have been. But you had no faith in it, although you were dealing with one of today's masterpieces. No doubt this play wasn't theatrical in the usual sense of the word, but it's a mistake to believe that only plays considered theatrical can be staged. A work such as this, performed in the right conditions, would not just have been acceptable but exhilarating for an audience. Witness the reactions of the Surrealists who supported us throughout the show and with whom I made my peace after the show. They, unlike Gide and company and other denigrators of avant-garde theatre, considered that this interpretation and this translation of a known masterpiece improved on a straightforward reading of this very masterpiece and that, for me, is the most rewarding result I could have hoped for. But if *Partage de midi* had been played with the necessary movement and spirit then you would have seen the enthusiasm of a particular section if not the whole audience. I know you did all you could and that your moves, among other things, were splendid and have attracted considerable attention but you have let yourself be swayed by Berley's derisive attitude which such a work does not deserve, and that's how I appeared to have directed a flop.

Yours sincerely,

Antonin Artaud

[*Lettres à Génica Athanasiou*, Gallimard, 1969, 280–1]

It is generally (but wrongly) assumed that Artaud chose to include Claudel's *Partage de midi* (Act III) in the second production of the Alfred Jarry Theatre in order to ridicule the play and to make a vicious attack on its author. Nothing could be further from the truth. He and his erstwhile surrealist friends shared none of Claudel's religious, patriotic or moral convictions, but they recognized in him a great and powerful wordsmith of the French language. Not only have we Artaud's testimony that the production brought about a short-lived reconciliation with the surrealists, but we also know that Breton himself silenced the audience when there were attempts at disrupting the start of the performance.

1. Génica Athanasiou (1897–1966) was an actress of Romanian origin who joined Dullin's company in 1920. Artaud met her there in 1921. She was the first woman in Artaud's life and she remained the only woman with whom he ever lived. Their stormy affair lasted only from 1922 until 1927. Génica Athanasiou scored her greatest stage success in Cocteau's *Antigone* (1922). She played the female lead in *The Shell and the Clergyman*. In *Partage de midi* she played Yzé.
2. André Berley joined the Alfred Jarry Theatre for this single performance of *Partage de midi* (14 January 1928). He probably played the part of Mesa.

'A Dream Play' by Strindberg (*'Le Songe' de Strindberg*)

A Dream Play by Strindberg has a place in the repertoire of an ideal theatre, it constitutes one of the model plays whose production for a director is the pinnacle of his career. The range of feelings translated and assembled in this play is infinite. One rediscovers both the inside and the outside of a manifold and vibrant thought. The most eminent problems are presented, evoked in a concrete and, at the same time, mysterious form. It is truly the universality of the mind and life whose magnetic thrill is offered to us and grabs us at the point of our most precise and most fruitful humanity. The success of such a performance is inevitably the crowning of a director, a producer. The *raison d'être* and the theoretical basis of this new company are common knowledge. The Alfred Jarry Theatre would like to reintroduce to theatre the sense, not of life, but of a certain truth located in the recesses of the mind. There exists between real life and the life of dreams a certain game of mental associations, of gestural relationships, of events translatable into actions and which constitute very precisely this theatrical reality which the Alfred Jarry Theatre has taken upon itself to revive. The sense of the true reality of theatre is lost. The notion of theatre has been wiped out of human minds. It does exist, however, half-way between reality and dreams. But until it is found again in its most absolute and most fruitful integrity, theatre will not cease to be at risk. Present-day theatre represents life, seeks by way of more or less realistic setting and lighting to give back to us the ordinary reality of life, or else it cultivates *illusion* – and then it's worst of all. Nothing is less capable of deluding us than the illusion of the fake prop, of cardboard and painted cloths which the modern stage offers us. We must accept things as they are, and not seek to compete with life. In the simple exhibition of the objects of reality, in their associations, in their sequence, in the relationships between the human voice and lighting, there is a whole reality which is self-sufficient and doesn't need any other to come alive. It is this false reality which is theatre and which must be cultivated.

The *mise en scène* of *A Dream Play* thus complies with the necessity of offering the audience only what can be of immediate use, and which is used as such by the actors. Three-dimensional characters will move in the midst of properties, of objects, in the midst of a total reality equally three-dimensional. The fake in the midst of the real, that's the ideal definition of such a *mise en scène*. A meaning, a utilization of a new spiritual order given to the ordinary objects and substance of life.

[*OC*, II, 30–1]

Programme note for the production of Strindberg's play by the Alfred Jarry Theatre, directed by Artaud, on 2 and 9 June 1928 at the Théâtre de l'Avenue, Paris.

The Alfred Jarry Theatre (1929)

[. . .] The difficulties the Alfred Jarry Theatre has had to contend with since it was formed are not known widely enough. Each new play constituted a feat of willpower, a miracle of perseverance. Not to mention the positive outbursts of hatred and envy these performances unleashed.

The Secrets of Love had only one rehearsal on stage, the night before the performance. *A Dream Play* had only one rehearsal using costume and scenery. *Partage de midi* was only seen once on the boards, the morning before the show.

As to *Power to the Children*, things were even worse. We had no chance to see a run-through of the play on stage before the preview.

All these difficulties stemmed from the fact that the Alfred Jarry Theatre never had either a company or a venue. Such continuously repeated obstacles can only end up by ruining its efforts and simplest attempts. It cannot undertake more than one play at a time and must rid itself of the horrible difficulties which, up to now, have stood between it and complete success. To do this, it needs the security of its own premises and a company freely placed at its disposal, even for one single play. It needs these premises and this company for two months, that is, a month for rehearsals, then the premises and the company booked for a run of thirty performances. This is the minimum needed to allow it to progress and develop its success, if any, commercially.

In the course of this year the Alfred Jarry Theatre will stage a performance of *Ubu roi* adapted to present-day circumstances and acted without being stylized. It will also present a new play by Roger Vitrac entitled *Arcade* which does not mince matters.

The Alfred Jarry Theatre was founded as a reaction against theatre, as well as to restore to theatre all the freedom that music, poetry or painting have and from which it has been strangely cut off up to now.

What we want to do is to make a break with theatre regarded as a separate entity and bring back the old idea which, after all, was never put into effect, that of *integral theatre*. Without, of course, it being mistaken at any time for music, mime or dancing, and especially literature.

At a time when words are being substituted for pictures, under the guise of talking films alienating the best audiences from an art which has become a hybrid, there cannot help but be a revival of interest in the *total theatre* formula.

We steadfastly refuse to regard theatre as a museum for masterpieces, however fine and human they may be. Any work which does not obey the *principle of actuality* will be of no use to us whatsoever, or, we believe, to theatre either. Actuality of feelings and concerns, more than of events. Life taking shape anew through present-day sensitivity. Sensitivity to time as well as place. We will always maintain that any work is worthless if it does not belong to a certain *localized state of mind*, chosen not because of its virtues or defects, but purely because of its relativity. We do not want art or beauty. What we are looking for are INVOLVED *emotions*. A certain combustible power associated with words and gestures. Reality seen from both sides. Hallucination selected as the main dramatic method.

[*CW*, 2, 30–1; *OC*, II, 34–6]

First published as a four page pamphlet in 1929. The manifesto itself was accompanied by some fifteen extracts taken from the press reviews of the production of the Alfred Jarry Theatre (see *OC*, II, 276–8).

The Alfred Jarry Theatre and Public Hostility (*Le Théâtre Alfred Jarry et l'hostilité publique*)

The Alfred Jarry Theatre in 1930

STATEMENT. – The Alfred Jarry Theatre, conscious of theatre's collapse before the encroaching development of world-wide motion picture techniques, intends to contribute to the downfall of theatre as it exists in France today by specifically theatrical means, dragging all the literary and artistic ideas down with it in this destruction, along with the psychological conventions, all the plastic artificiality, etc., on which this theatre was built, by reconciling the idea of theatre, at least provisionally, with whatever is most feverish in life today. [. . .]

Free, candid undertakings of the Alfred Jarry Theatre's sort run up against all types of difficulties listed under this heading. These are: *raising capital, choosing the right location, difficulties over a company, censorship, the police, organized sabotage, competition, audiences and critics.*

Raising capital. Money is hard to find. Although enough may be found for one production, this is insufficient, since spasmodic undertakings are not properly speaking a going concern and do not benefit from the advantages of regular business exploitation. On the contrary they are bled by all sorts of suppliers who, not content with charging high prices, put them up as high as they can, reckoning it is fair to levy a surcharge on such *snob entertainment.*

The upshot is that all the subscriptions, subsidies and everything else are rapidly swallowed up, and despite the attempt, and the stir caused by the show, it has to close down after the second or third performance, that is, at the very moment when it could prove how effective it is.

The Alfred Jarry Theatre will do its utmost from now on to give regular evening performances.

Choosing the right location. It is just about impossible to perform in the evening with very little money. Either you have to be satisfied with a rudimentary, unequipped stage (lecture rooms, banqueting halls, etc.) or resign yourself to playing to matinées and only on slack days, or else during the off-season. In any case, the conditions are deplorable and are made worse by the fact that theatre managers categorically refuse, for reasons given below, to rent their theatres, or only at exorbitant rates.

Once again, therefore, the Alfred Jarry Theatre has found itself obliged to put on its productions at the end of the season.

Difficulties over a company. Actors cannot be found, since most of them have regular engagements which obviously prevent them working elsewhere in the evening. Furthermore, for a variety of reasons, theatre managers overstep their authority and stop actors joining up with the Alfred Jarry Theatre. Worse, they often grant permission then withdraw it later, thereby interrupting rehearsals and forcing us to look for a new cast. Not to mention the ill-will prevalent among junior staff at some theatres, over whom others, needless to say, are in charge.

But we must pay tribute to those performers who have taken part in our venture. They have all shown the utmost unselfishness and the greatest devotion, despite provocation and sniping. So much was this true that we always constituted a real ensemble, despite rehearsals carried on under preposterous conditions, and everyone acknowledged this homogeneity.

Censorship. We got around this problem by screening Gorki's *The Mother* at a private showing by invitation only. Touch wood, there is no theatre censorship yet. But we know the Chief of Police can insist on the show being cut as a result of a series of disturbances, or purely and simply suppress the show, or close the theatre. Unfortunately we have never had a long enough run to provoke such action. Nonetheless, long live freedom.

The police. As for the police, they always automatically step in with productions of this sort. Everyone knows this, even the right-wing Surrealists. For example, when S. M. Eisenstein delivered his lecture at the Sorbonne, there were a hundred or so policemen scattered about the building, not counting the Chief of Police. You can't do anything about that. You have to blame the Government.

Organized sabotage. This is generally the handiwork of malicious people or pranksters who methodically provoke the police to act against them, and in consequence against the audience and the show as well. Without them the police would quietly remain at the door. Having carried out their *coup*, these *agents provocateurs* have only to accuse the Alfred Jarry Theatre of being in league with the police and they've done the trick. They kill two birds with one stone. They stop the show and throw discredit on its promoters. Luckily, even if their little game sometimes comes off, the trick's played out now and does not hoodwink anyone any more.

Audiences. Here, we are only dealing with a prejudiced audience of the *I-was-there* or *flippant* sort. Those who find it disgraceful, or those who are full of very amusing jokes, for example imitating the sound of running water or a rooster crowing or declaring in a thunderous voice that M. Alfred Jarry invited him and he is at home here. In short, what is normally called a *typically French* audience. This is the very reason why we put on comedies and the audience's farcical reactions are something extra on the programme which another audience knows enough to appreciate.

Critics. Oh, the critics! First, let us thank them, then say no more about them.

[*CW*, 2, 33–62; *OC*, II, 39–66]

Jointly written by Artaud and Vitrac this manifesto was published in 1930 (48 pages with illustrations). This text not only signals the end of the Alfred Jarry Theatre but also the end of any collaboration between Artaud and Vitrac (see *OC*, II, 279–90).

To Roger Vitrac

[*c*. 24 February 1930]

My dear Vitrac,

I think that the wording of the initial declaration could be modified as follows:

from

by dragging to this destruction, etc.,

'dragging all the literary and artistic ideas down with it in this destruction, along with the psychological conventions, all the plastic artificiality, etc., on which this theatre was built, by reconciling the idea of theatre, at least provisionally, with whatever is most feverish in life today'.

I believe that with such a wording which you can *arrange anyway you please*, we will stay firmly in the essentially *theatrical* domain which is not your only concern, I know, but from which I don't want to disgress as far as the Alfred Jarry Theatre is concerned.

Should you wish to create a theatre to put across political or other ideas, I will not be a party to it. In the theatre only what is essentially theatrical is of interest to me; making use of the theatre to promote any revolutionary idea (except in the domain of the mind) seems to me to be of the basest and most repugnant opportunism.

A director's point of view if you like, but in the end everything which concerns *mise en scène* is theatre, and that's how one can act and *obtain concrete results*.

Besides, I think a conciliation is possible between our two conflicting points of view. That's why I accept a collaboration in everything concerning your plays but I don't want to limit myself by declarations which could be held against me later. My conscience will not allow me either.

As far as the address to be put in the brochure is concerned, I believe I am still capable of replying to a letter when it's necessary and important to do so. But it is first and foremost a point of principle.

In a theatre in which you are the only performed author and in which you are supposed to present everyone with ideas, especially after the publication of this brochure, I am unable to continue to let it be thought that you are the only one responsible for the Alfred Jarry Theatre. That's why I reacted so violently. But let me repeat to you once more, that as far as performing your play is concerned – which is admirable – I agree with you all the way. AFTER THAT WE SHALL SEE.

Affectionately yours,

Antonin Artaud

P.S. My disagreement with you over 'effectiveness' is such that if a man were to present to me in the form of a play such as yours, with character types like yours, a similar psychological atmos-phere, the same prominence of language, of situations, a play designed to uphold whatever reactionary or religious idea, and even though I may hate those very ideas, I would still perform it right away.

I think that this time you will understand me.

[*OC*, III, 174–5]

This letter, linked to the previous manifesto, shows that Artaud's idea of collaboration did not really allow for dialogue between partners (he dictates to Vitrac), that he is jealous of his position at the head of the enterprise and that, despite his protestations of conciliation, his views are totally incompatible with Vitrac's and with current theatrical practice.

Later in 1930, while working on a film in Berlin, Artaud wrote one of his last letters to Vitrac. The play which he says is being considered by a German theatre is *Le Coup de Trafalgar*. The project came to nothing and Artaud himself did not produce the play. Note the curious mixture of mundane details and peremptory aesthetic pronouncements:

Berlin, 5 November 1930

My dear Vitrac,

Your play will be performed in full without cutting a single word, and in the spirit appropriate to it and which it commands. For me, a play never admits 2 possible interpretations. You will be entitled to the same standard percentage as the authors here in Berlin. I can't say any more and I believe things are well on course. But no doubt everything hangs on the reading of your play and its reception. In this respect, moreover, I cannot urge you enough, if I may venture my opinion, to fill out the action a little. From the final tableau which you read to me I have kept an impression of *marking time*. All your characters are very odd, high in colour, in strangeness, so wonderfully alive, . . . all the same one would like to see them do something. They are too peculiar in their everyday aspect for one to be happy with this peculiarity. In fact a stage play is not a simple exhibition or even a simple development of characters around nothing. I say that to you impartially but I believe I am not mistaken.

Best wishes.

[*OC*, III, 189]

Three Letters to Louis Jouvet

Paris, 29 April 1931

Dear Sir,

I enclose the second project which I mentioned to you.

Some newspapers say – so I am not being indiscreet if I mention it to you – that you are thinking of taking over the Théâtre Pigalle in the next season.

I apologize for importuning you so often and at such length, but

I want to specify a certain number of points. You must realize that this instability, this irregularity which is held against me is only the result of the instability and irregularity of a life which has not accomplished its purpose. I am far less mad than people think; I will no longer be at all mad when I have some important responsibilities and find myself able to deploy all my activity in an interesting direction.

I felt, and I may be wrong, that you thought the idea of asking me to collaborate with you was faintly absurd. The few prejudices you may have would not survive the shortest test. I would work with you without any reservations, entirely on your side. Finally, I hope that you do not judge me by the improvised performances at the Alfred Jarry Theatre: you know better than I do how indirect the process of *mise en scène* is and how much one is betrayed

1. first by the actors
2. then by circumstances.

And I can say that I was betrayed as much as one can be. The theatre can stand improvisation less than anything else, unless it has trained improvisers ready for everything, which was certainly not the case.

Finally, whether it be good or bad, I am bringing to the theatre a new point of view. I have the impression that the spectators are fed up, that they need a change and that the only way to bring them back to the theatre is to invent plastically, physically and psychologically an unexpected form which grips them, but which is itself based on the oldest theatrical tradition.

I would like it to be you who enables me to find my way and I dare to say that it will be in your interest.

Very cordially yours,

Ant. Artaud

[*CW*, 3, 159–60; *OC*, III, 200–1]

[Around 15 October 1931]
Thursday evening

Dear friend,

When could you see me? I mean, let me have an hour of your time? I will not ask you that before the first night of *Judith*. But afterwards! I have a play which I would like to read to you, not to show you its beauty, which would be absurd, but so that you can *hear* my interpretation, to show you my personal note. Nothing which exists at present in the theatre seems to be more urgent than to *perform* this play. – Leave aside the perversion, the more or less advanced squalor of this age, just consider the painfully human sound of this play, the echoes like cries in a cavern or a dream. No man, at any period, is unaffected by the workings of his unconscious. Why not let me stage this play at the Théâtre Pigalle? Even if *Judith* is a success. That would make two of them if I am allowed the time to work as I wish. That would not raise the expenses of the Théâtre Pigalle excessively, since you have your own company. If there is a difference of a few thousand francs for the sets I may be able to find them.

Very cordially yours,

Antonin Artaud

[*CW*, 3, 175; *OC*, III, 225–6]

Tuesday evening
20 October 1931

Dear friend,

[. . .] I think you will agree that there is no performable play, however good, which cannot be improved and even remade by a skilful *mise en scène*. But I do not believe *mise en scène* to be a question of writing, which can be done on paper. The distinctive quality of the theatre is precisely that it cannot be contained in words or even in sketches. A *mise en scène* is achieved directly on the stage. And either one is a man of the theatre or one is not. It seems to me impossible to describe a movement, a gesture, or above all a theatrical *intonation* if one does not make them. To describe a *mise en scène* verbally or graphically is to try and make a sketch of a type of pain, for example. The plans for the *mise en scène* of *The Ghost Sonata* and *Le Coup de Trafalgar*, which seemed rather literary to you, seemed to me to be the maximum of what can be *written* and *described* if one limits oneself to the language of words. The same words trying to describe a gesture, the sound of a voice, can be seen and heard on the stage in ten thousand different ways. All this is incommunicable and has to be in the flesh. The idea of the theatrical apparatus which I could give you is only valid by the way in which it is furnished with movements, gestures, whispers and cries. I have an idea for a whole aural and visual technique which can only be described by volumes filled with verbal ratiocinations all revolving round the same point recaptured hundreds of times. All this would be useless if a single real intonation were to fulfil the same purpose instantaneously. Which means that the suggestions I could make would only be valid if I were enabled to direct the play materially, objectively. I see the production reduced to a few indispensable and significant objects and props, always with a certain number of floors or levels, the dimensions and perspectives of which form part of the architecture of the décor. I see these levels or floors as part of a *quality* of light which is for me the main element of the scenic world. But I also see the pitch of the voices and the extent of the intonations which also constitute types of floors, and in any case a concrete element as important as the décor or the luminous pitch. All this with movements, gestures, expressions regulated with the same precision as the movements of a ballet. For me it is this precision, attached to every possible form of expression on the stage, which is the theatre, while in European theatre only the text counts, if anything. As well as this truly paradoxical idea taken from Diderot, that the actor on the stage does not really feel what he says, that he retains complete control over his actions, and that he can act and think about something else at the same time: about his chicken and his soup. – I would have more to say about that, but I shall stop. All this will be the subject of a lecture on the theatre which I am going to give at the Sorbonne together with the reading of a play. I would like you to read my article on the Balinese Theatre in the *Nouvelle Revue Française* of October and discuss it with me. I am *honestly* at your disposal. I ask nothing better than to work at it very meticulously. I am no longer in a position to refuse work, since I no longer want to work in the cinema, as an actor, and I must even beg you to give me a chance to work.

Cordially yours.

Antonin Artaud
58, rue La Bruyère, Paris IX

[*CW*, 3, 176–8; *OC*, III, 227–9]

Between 1931 and 1934 Artaud wrote very often to Jouvet to propose projects, to ask for employment or to comment on Jouvet's work, but apart from a vague attempt at collaboration in early 1932 the two men were not to work together. (See also 'Production Plan for Strindberg's *The Ghost Sonata*', *CW*, 2, 97–105; *OC*, II, 101–10. That project was sent to Jouvet, then director of the Théâtre Pigalle, in April 1931.)

Judith, by Jean Giraudoux, Jouvet's favourite playwright, opened at the Théâtre Pigalle on 4 November 1931.

Part Three
Cinema (1926–32)

Cinema and Reality (*Cinéma et réalité*)

At present two courses seem to be open to the cinema, of which neither is the right one.

The pure or absolute cinema on the one hand, and on the other this sort of venial hybrid art. The latter persists in expressing, in more or less successful images, psychological situations which are perfectly suitable for the stage or the pages of a book, but not for the screen, and which only really exist as the reflection of a world which seeks its manner and its meaning elsewhere.

It is obvious that everything we have so far been able to see in the guise of abstract or pure cinema is far from satisfying what appears to be one of the essential demands of the cinema. Because, however capable of conceiving and adopting abstraction man's mind may be, we cannot help being irresponsive to purely geometric lines, of no valid significance on their own, which do not belong to any sensation which the eye of the screen can recognize and classify. However deep we may look into the mind we find, at the bottom of every emotion, even if it be intellectual, an effective sensation of a nervous order. This contains the susceptible, even if elementary recognition of something substantial, of a certain vibration which invariably recalls states, either known or imagined, clothed in one of the multiple forces of nature, in real life or in dreams. Pure cinema would therefore imply the restitution of a certain number of forms of this type moving according to a rhythm which is the specific contribution of this art.

Between purely linear visual abstraction (and a play of shadows and lights is like a play of lines) and the film with psychological undertones which might tell a dramatic story, there is room for an attempt at true cinema, of which neither the matter nor the meaning are indicated by any film so far produced.

In films telling stories the emotion and humour depend solely on the text, to the exclusion of the images. With a few exceptions the whole idea of a film is in its subtitles; the emotion is verbal: it calls for explanation, or the support of words, because the situations, images and acts revolve round a clear meaning. We must find a film with purely visual sensations the dramatic force of which springs from a shock on the eyes, drawn, one might say, from the very substance of the eye, and not from psychological circumlocutions of a discursive nature which are nothing but visual interpretations of a text. We are not trying to find an equivalent of the written language in the visual language, which is simply a bad interpretation of it. We are trying to bring out the very essence of the language and transport the action to a level where every interpretation would become useless and where this action would act almost intuitively on the brain.

In the following scenario I have tried to produce this visual cinema where psychology itself is devoured by the action. No doubt this scenario does not accomplish all that can be done in this direction, but at least it heralds it. Not that the cinema must be devoid of all human psychology, on the contrary; but it should give this psychology a far more live and active form, free from the connections which try to make our motives appear idiotic instead of flaunting them in their original and profound barbarity.

This scenario is not the reproduction of a dream and must not be regarded as such. I shall not try to excuse the apparent inconsistency by the facile subterfuge of dreams. Dreams have more than their logic. They have their life where nothing but a sombre truth appears. This script searches for the sombre truth of the mind in images which emerge exclusively from themselves, and do not draw their meaning from the situation in which they develop but from a sort of powerful inner necessity which projects them into the light of a merciless evidence.

The human skin of things, the derm of reality – this is the cinema's first toy. It exalts matter and makes it appear to us in its profound spirituality, in its relationship with the mind from which it emerges. The images are born, are deduced one from the other as images, impose an objective synthesis more penetrating than any abstraction, create worlds which ask nothing from anyone or anything. But from this mere game of appearance, from this sort of transubstantiation of elements, is born an inorganic language which moves the mind by osmosis and with no sort of transposition in words. And by the fact that it plays with matter itself the cinema creates situations which emerge from the simple collision of objects, forms, repulsions and attractions. It does not separate itself from life but returns to the primitive order of things. The most successful films of this type are those which are dominated by a certain humour, like the early Malec and the most inhuman Chaplin films. The cinema studded with dreams, which gives you the physical sensation of pure life, is fulfilled by excessive humour. A certain agitation of objects, shapes and expressions is only well interpreted by the convulsions and jerks of a reality which seems to destroy itself with an irony which makes the extremities of mind cry out.

[*CW*, 3, 19–21; *OC*, III, 18–20]

In the mid- and late twenties Artaud wrote several scenarios and texts about cinema. *La Coquille et le clergyman* (The Shell and the Clergyman) was the only one to be filmed, but the filming process and the result left Artaud dissatisfied. He had hoped to direct his scenario himself but it was given to Germaine Dulac who had the reputation of being a talented avant-garde film director. In the event Artaud was unable to attend the shooting of the film and Madame Dulac refused him access to the cutting room during editing. Artaud felt betrayed and, with the help of some friends (which included the poet Robert Desnos), he attempted to disrupt the first showing of the film and got himself thrown out of the cinema.

The scenario was finished in April 1927; the shooting took place during the early summer and the text was published in the *Nouvelle Revue Française*, No.170, 1 November 1927. The complete text can be found in *CW*, 3, 21–5 and *OC*, III, 20–5.

'Cinema and Reality' is more of a manifesto than a mere introduction to the text, and should be read as such.

'The Shell and the Clergyman' ('*La Coquille et le clergyman*')

The Shell and the Clergyman, before being a film, is an attempt or an *idea*.

When writing the scenario of *The Shell and the Clergyman*, I considered that the cinema possessed an element of its own, a truly magic and truly cinematographic element, which nobody had ever thought of isolating. This element, which differs from every sort of representation attached to images, has the characteristics of the very vibration, the profound, unconscious source of thought.

It surreptitiously breaks away from the images and emerges from their association, their vibration and their impact, not from their logical connected meaning. I thought it was possible to write a scenario which ignored knowledge and the logical connection of facts, and would search beyond, in the occult and in the tracks of feeling and thought for the profound motives, the active and obscure impulses of our so-called lucid acts, which always *maintain* their evolutions in the domain of sources and apparitions. It is to show how far the scenario can resemble and ally itself with the *mechanics of a dream* without really being a dream itself, for example. It is to show how far it restores the pure work of thought. So the mind, left to itself and the images, infinitely sensitized, determined to lose nothing of the inspirations of subtle thought, is all prepared to return to its original functions, its antennae pointed towards the invisible, to begin another resurrection from death.

This, at least, is the ambitious idea behind this scenario which, at any rate, goes beyond the structure of straightforward narrative, or problems of music, rhythm or aesthetics current in the cinema, to present the problem of *expression* in every domain and to its full extent.

[*CW*, 3, 63–4; *OC*, III, 71–2]

Published in *Cahiers de Belgique*, No. 8, October 1928. It might be worth mentioning that in this short theoretical text Artaud does not refer to the filming of the scenario nor does he mention Germaine Dulac's name.

To Madame Yvonne Allendy

Nice, 26 March 1929

Dear friend,

To make a talking picture now, or at any time, seems wrong to me. The Americans who have staked everything on it are preparing a very sinister future for themselves, as are all companies which produce bad films on the pretext that they are more saleable; the talking picture is idiotic, absurd. The very negation of the cinema. I admit that the sound of a landscape, the noises of a scene chosen for its pure visual quality, may *eventually* be synchronized, and I can well see what can be done in this direction. But there is no difference between this and the imitative sounds of an orchestra. The sound is produced by a loudspeaker, a record, instead of an orchestra, but it is not a different *value*. Because however well *synchronized* it may be, it does not come from the screen, from this virtual, absolute space which the screen spreads before us. Whatever we do, our ears will always hear it *in the auditorium*, instead of our eye seeing, *outside the auditorium*, what is happening on the screen.

An all-talking screen should be invented which manages to create perspectives of sound in three *dimensions*, in the same way as the visual screen creates perspectives for the eye. But that is science and does not interest me.

If I have an idea for a film with sonorous or musical possibilities I shall let you know. BUT I SHALL NOT USE ANY WORDS. [. . .]

You know that if I were to write a commercial scenario I would destroy myself. Worse than that: I would be setting a low standard. The sinister thing about these concessions is that they diminish and devalue a man, *primarily* because this man is doing something contrary to his nature and consequently contrary to his mind. The great American successes like *Solitude* and *Chicago Nights* are not what is usually known as commercial.

FINALLY

I cannot do anything until I have recovered.

I no longer thought myself ill, but PERFECTLY LUCID, the horrible compression in my head and the top of my spine, the convulsions in my chest, my obsession with blood and murder, the torpor, the inexpressible weakness, the general horror in which I am plunged with a mind which is basically intact, make this mind useless.

You understand that I would long ago have given myself satisfaction and would have stopped boring the pants off people if that had not all constituted an absolute obstacle in its miserable and ridiculous RELATIVITY.

Best wishes,

Artaud

[*CW*, 3, 121–2; *OC*, III, 144–5]

To René Daumal (draft of a letter)

Paris, 14 July 1931

Dear friend,

I am still wondering about the point of your objection concerning the intervention of the notion of duality in [   ].

And yet you agree with me in thinking that the sort of manifesto which we must draw up together to explain the aims of the theatre should be based on absolutely concrete objectives, should depart from the present situation of the theatre in France and Europe, and should say, for instance, that:

to the state of organic degeneration in which the French theatre has been struggling since the war, a sort of industrial crisis has been added of late which has just forced a large number of theatres in Paris to close prematurely.

However, the fact that a certain number of cinemas should continue to play to full houses is most significant for the future of French theatre. We do not believe that the relatively low prices of the cinema are enough to explain this sudden lapse of public interest in the theatre and sudden dislike of a form of expression for which the public once felt, especially in moments of crisis, a need comparable to that for provisions of prime necessity. It seems, however, that the taste for the theatre of that part of the public which only went to a theatrical performance in search of relaxation of a purely digestive order, finds the requisite satisfaction in the cinema. Because if we can see that the theatre, as it is practised in France today, is inferior to any film, however banal, we cannot see how it can manifest its superiority either in the intellectual sphere or from the point of view of the spectacle. Besides, the audience which walks out of all theatres where literary, pretentious plays of dubious psychological merit survive, does justice to something which has long been out of date.

If the theatre is made to condense a system of life, if it has to constitute the heroic synthesis of the epoch in which it was conceived, if it can be defined as the concrete residue and the reflection of the customs and habits of an epoch, it is certain that the cinema gives us a dynamic and complete image of modern life in its most varied aspects which the theatre comes nowhere near.

The stage as it has been used not only in France, but in the whole of Europe for over a century is limited to the psychological and spoken depiction of the individual. All the specifically theatrical means of expression have gradually made way for the text which absorbed the action to such an extent that one finally saw the entire theatrical spectacle reduced to a single person soliloquizing in front of a screen.

The concept, however valid it may be in itself consecrates, for the western mind, the supremacy of the articulated language which is more precise and more abstract, over every other. And its unexpected result was to make that art of images, the cinema, a substitute for the spoken theatre!

If the cinema won the first round in its competition with the theatre, it seems to have lost the second. But it is not as if the theatre, now become irremediably passive, had drawn from this state of affairs a life which it had long lost.

And yet, while French theatre seems unable to escape from a stuffy room and never exceed the interest of a court session, an effort was made in certain European countries before the war (particularly in Germany) and in Russia since the war to restore a lost lustre to theatrical production. The Ballets Russes have returned the feeling of colour to the stage. And from now on, when we stage a play, we will have to reckon with the necessity of visual harmony, just as, after Piscator, we have to reckon with the dynamic and plastic necessity of movement, just as, after Meyerhold and Appia, we have to reckon with an architectural concept of décor used not only in depth but also in height, and employing masses and volumes instead of flat surfaces and *trompe-l'œil*.

According to the psychological concept, the old classical concept of the comedy of manners and the comedy of characters, man was studied inertly, almost photographically, he was dead from the start, anti-heroic by definition, and was observed with his passions in an everyday setting so that every play was like a game of chess or psychological construction and only managed to give us a desolate and flat image of reality; and when, through some innovation, the usual concept of man cast in a simple mould, acting by thrusts and jerks, was succeeded by a scattered and multiform concept of man divided into a gallery or mirrors, as in the masterpieces of Pirandello, we left the court of summary justice, or at least the criminal court, for the psychoanalyst's consulting room and descended a step in our psychological and demoralizing experience of man, who remained the man of everyday, whatever monsters he produced and kept company with. Since then the only really theatrical experiment was performed in Russia, during the Revolution, in an attempt to make a theatre of action and of the masses succeed to this concept of man in ecstasy before his personal monstrosities.

An epoch of the theatre is closed, and we do [not] think we should waste our time condemning a tradition already condemned by events.

[*CW*, 3, 164–7; *OC*, III, 214–17]

To Jean Paulhan

Paris, 23 September 1931

Very dear friend,

One of these days I hope to open a school of dramatic and cinematographic art. I shall teach in the lecture room of the publishing house Denoël et Steele, 19 rue Amélie.

Do you think you can send me students?

In any case, I hope you can mention it to your acquaintances and print a short note about it in the *NRF*. It is enough to say that Antonin Artaud is going to give lessons in dramatic and cinematographic art. This is part of a whole plan of action. So you see that these lessons will have more than a merely didactic interest and I think they will interest many beginners.

Could this note appear in the next no.? I shall go on my own to the publicity department of the *NRF* to see if they can give me a small space for the same purpose, at a cheap rate.

If you are back I shall come to see you soon. I am longing to see you again.

Your devoted friend,

Antonin Artaud
58, rue La Bruyère

P.S. It will be enough for the prospective students to send me a note at 19 rue Amélie, care of Denoël & Steele, or at my address. Thank you and forgive me.

[*CW*, 3, 174; *OC*, III, 223–4]

The creation of a school and the necessity for a new method of training for actors always preoccupied Artaud. But this is the only instance when he considered training actors for the stage *and* the screen. His true feelings towards the cinema at that time are more accurately expressed in a note to Jouvet, sent from Berlin where he was working on a film: 'I am more and more convinced that the cinema is and will remain the artform of the past. It is only with shame that one can work in it.' (20 May 1932; *OC*, III, 283.)

Part Four

The NRF Theatre Project (1931–3)

To Jean-Richard Bloch

23 April 1931

Dear Sir,

Could you not see a way, thinking seriously for a moment, of getting a project off the ground which would assist the creation of a new kind of theatre. Careful reading of your book *Le Destin du théâtre* (Destiny of the Theatre) reveals that we are very close to one another on quite a few essential points, and you mustn't judge me on the hurried and improvised performances with the rough-and-ready resources of the 'Alfred Jarry Theatre'. These performances were not terribly precise in conveying either my true inclinations or my scope for production from a purely technical and professional point of view. My inclinations urge me on to 'Interior Theatre', theatre of dreams incarnate, of thoughts projected on the stage in a pure and unhindered state. I mean without an indication of their source!!! A theatre which turns its back on life, on reality, which allows no bounds, no visible transformation. A theatre not based on human, ordinary psychology of characters, which takes any stage, any scenic location, where psychology is divided between men and objects, where conflicts are resolved in a simultaneous collision of physical forces, of emotions elevated to the status of real people, of organic and objectivized hallucinations battling with men. In short a theatre in which the freedom of the mind attains its absolute expansion in all its possible forms: did the ancient theatre enjoy determining conclusively the psychology of its gods??? This theatre will restore for its audience the concept of absolute spectacle, it will offer the equivalent of a kind of intellectual music-hall in which all the senses and all the faculties will achieve fulfilment simultaneously. I cannot elaborate further in a simple letter, but still my mind is fully taken up with the idea of seeing this project succeed. The most difficult thing will be to find plays: in the programme, *Empedocles* by Hölderlin, *The Cenci* by Shelley, in spite of their human and brutish nature, in which would be restored, *plastically*, the complete idea of Shelley the poet, a play by Jean-Richard Bloch, a drama by Byron, *The Revenger's Tragedy* by Cyril Tourneur, etc., etc.

Nothing is being done for true theatre in France.

It seems to me that it should be easy to motivate certain circles, certain groups, perhaps certain wealthy people by proposing to them the idea of creating a theatre perhaps national in its outcome, with European dimensions, and with worldwide repercussions. A theatre which would fix the notion of a style of *mise en scène* invented *here*. For as far as I am concerned, the point of departure and the touchstone of true theatre is the *mise en scène*, as I understand the word in its deeper sense of visual and acoustic effectiveness, and in place of the theatrical style of a written work.

I am still trying to find my way with the greatest difficulty, and like a man trapped by life, getting such a project off the ground would permit me to find it.

Sincerely yours,

Antonin Artaud

[*OC*, V, 53–4]

With the demise of the Alfred Jarry Theatre and given the lack of response from the theatrical 'establishment', Artaud was already thinking of the creation of a new theatre and he wrote numerous letters to friends and acquaintances to sound them out and to enlist their support. At the same time Artaud was also busy giving lectures and writing manifestos (many of which will be included in the next section). His goal, on this occasion, was to secure the patronage, moral and financial, of the *Nouvelle Revue Française* and of its most prominent authors.

To Marcel Dalio

[Paris] 27 June 1932, Monday

My dear friend,

You will have seen from the interview and my letter in *L'Intransigeant* that my plans are in good shape. I telephoned you on Saturday to arrange a meeting. Either my message was not passed on to you or it came too late. Yet I must see you *urgently*. I asked you the other day, *face to face*, if you believed in this business, and either you commit yourself to the hilt or you don't commit yourself at all. The thing to do, in short, is to make a clean sweep. And I found it rather funny when you asked me if I intended to create an arts theatre, since it appears to me that by its very *definition*, this risk is ruled out: an arts theatre can only be a fringe theatre. But a theatre which aims at demolishing everything in order to get down to the essence, to seek by specifically theatrical means to achieve the essence, cannot be an arts theatre, and cannot be so *by definition*. To produce art, to produce aestheticism, is to aim at amusement, at furtive effect, external, transitory effect, but to seek to exteriorize serious feelings, to identify the fundamental attitudes of the mind, to wish to give the audience the impression that they are *running the risk* of something, by coming to our plays, and to make them responsive to a new concept of *Danger*, I believe that that is not to produce art.

I waited longer than I had intended before telephoning you, because I wanted to be fully prepared. Now I believe I am.

I know what I want to say to you and I am in a position to tell you objectively what I want to do.

As we wait for new writers to bring us plays in accordance with the essence, and which are capable of expressing scenically, orally and plastically what I am advocating, I have a programme.

The point which I must stress is that the plays I have chosen are not, as far as I am concerned, an end in themselves, nor a goal, but a means: 'Such plays cannot impede the use of the methods of *mise en scène* which I envisage.'

And likewise, it must be fully understood that, however dramatic they may be, these methods of *mise en scène* which aim at establishing a particular notion of a complete production will not, of course, make the production the ultimate goal of the theatre.

In short, I do not want to be blamed for creating an arts theatre, and those from the archaeological theatre who might criticize me, will not have understood what I am looking for. There is nothing secret about it, and I do not fear that my ideas will be wrested from me for I count on developing them to the full in a clear manifesto to be published.

From a practical point of view, the question which faces me is this:

'Once the productions are chosen, I will need a company of actors who can lend themselves to these methods of *mise en scène*, who will interpret *meticulously* the directions I will give them; for, of course, we will only be able to reach the mathematical precision we are attempting in these productions if the actors are prepared to follow scrupulously the directions I will give them.'

In other words, it is under my direction that these actors will be called upon to create these *living* productions based on personal approaches to *mise en scène*.

But I need a man, a remarkable man, who will be able, in the practical and financial fields, to take truly revolutionary initiatives, as revolutionary as you and I have admitted might be possible, and even necessary, in the field of art, of the plastic arts and of ideas. I am saying that these initiatives will have to be revolutionary not out of liking or out of a mad desire to mess everything up, but because I believe that in the present climate only new concepts in matters of finance will stand a chance of creating a sound business which will survive. There is nothing to hinder you being such a man, and I'm asking you, even with the support I'm giving you, the weight of the NRF, its name, and the names of writers who have promised to bring their authority to bear for me, to take charge of creating a sound business, in other words of procuring all kinds of credit which might enable us to acquire an auditorium, settings, publicity and a little cash to enable us to begin.

Ant. Artaud

[*OC*, V, 72–4]

The Theatre I'm About to Set Up (*Le théâtre que je vais fonder*)

I have a theatre project which I'm hoping to realize with the support of the NRF. They are giving me space to allow me to define the direction of this theatre objectively and from an ideological point of view. The article in which I will set out my programme and define my terms will constitute a kind of manifesto which several writers of the NRF will sign. What is more, André Gide, Julien Benda, Albert Thibaudet and Jean Paulhan will be the patrons of this theatre. And being members of the committee, they will take part in all the discussions concerning the productions which will be performed in this theatre.

I haven't yet considered the auditorium of this theatre, but it is possible I'll opt for a hangar which I will arrange and modify according to the principles which led to the architecture of certain churches, or even better, certain holy places and certain temples of Upper Tibet. I will turn theatre into a religious and metaphysical idea but in the sense of magical, real and absolutely effective action. And it must be understood that I'm using the words 'religious' and 'metaphysical' in a sense which has nothing to do with religion or metaphysics as they are normally understood. So you see to what extent the theatre intends to break with all the ideas on which European theatre in 1932 is feeding.

I believe in the true effectiveness of theatre, but not on the level of everyday life. Needless to say I consider futile all the attempts made in Germany, in Russia or in America in recent times to *make theatre serve* immediate revolutionary ends. However new the methods of *mise en scène* may be, these methods, given that they agree to, and indeed, are *willing to* adhere to the strictest of fundamental ideas of dialectical materialism, given that they turn their back on metaphysics in contempt, they remain simply *mise en scène* in the grossest sense of the word. I have neither the time nor the space to develop the debate here to the full. You can see that here are two conceptions of life and poetry which confront one another. Conceptions with which theatre is bound up in its direction.

In any case, speaking from an objective point of view, this is what I am able to say. I have considered performing *Woyzeck* by Büchner, and several works by Elizabethan dramatists: *The Revenger's Tragedy* by Cyril Tourneur, *The Duchess of Malfi* and *The White Devil* by Webster, the works of Ford, etc., but my aim is not to provide a programme, or to perform written texts. I believe that theatre can only become itself again when the playwrights completely change their inspiration and particularly their writing *methods*. For me the question we are faced with is of allowing theatre to rediscover its true language, a spatial language, a language of gestures, a language of cries and onomatopoeia, an acoustic language, where all the objective elements will end up as either visual or aural signs, but which have as much intellectual weight and palpable meaning as the language of words. Words being no longer used except in the parts of life which are *fixed* and discursive, like a more precise and objective lucidity appearing at the culmination of an idea.

And I hope to try to make around a well-known, popular or holy theme one or more attempts at theatrical creation where gestures, attitudes and signs *invent themselves* as they are being thought up, *directly* on stage, where words will appear to culminate and bring to a conclusion these lyrical discourses made by music, gesture and potent signs. And we must find a way of marking, like on a musical stave, with a notation of a new kind, everything that will be composed.

[*OC*, V, 28–30]

This text, published in *Paris-Soir*, 14 July 1932, is part of an orchestrated campaign to get his 'NRF Arts Theatre' off the ground. On 29 June 1932 Artaud wrote to Marcel Dalio, and announced:

I have a programme,
   a doctrine,
   support.
What I need now is to find the man who will bring it all to life, effectively and practically, and set up the business on a commercial footing.
But it must be clearly understood that those who lend me their support, and the entire NRF, will only keep doing so if the theatre which I envisage remains faithful to the principles laid down in my article in the NRF:
   Mise en scène and Metaphysics,
   and if from a theatrical point of view, I alone am responsible for making them concrete.
In other words, if the productions, the choice of which will be discussed by us all, are directed exclusively by me from the point of view of settings, lighting, movement, action, direction of the actors, etc., etc.
The manifesto we are about to publish will stress the fact that this theatre will propose to express all imminent changes in the spirit of the age, in its innermost recesses, in the recognition of the necessity to return to the essence to have the right to live, and it will offer the objective means of getting back to the essence of theatricality.

[*OC*, V, 74–5]

This was followed on 6 July 1932 with a letter to M. van Caulaert in which Artaud stated anew and even more forcefully some of the points made in '*Mise en scène* and Metaphysics' (see pp. 102–8) which belongs to the same campaign. The crucial paragraph of the letter reads as follows:

I was expecting to present a programme, but it's not important and it's not my aim to perform written plays. Theatre will only become itself again once the playwrights command new disciplines, change their source of inspiration and their writing methods. The question we are faced with is of allowing theatre to discover its true language, spatial language, gestural language, language of attitudes, expressions and mime, language of cries and onomatopoeia, an acoustic language where all the objective elements will end up either as visual or aural signs, but which have as much intellectual weight and palpable meaning as the language of words. Words being no longer used except in the parts of life which are fixed and discursive, like a more precise and objective lucidity appearing at the culmination of an idea.

[*OC*, V, 77–8]

On 8 July Artaud penned yet another draft which should have formed the basis for a circular letter and initially intended for M. van Caulaert or M. Fouilloux:

As you know, I have a plan for a theatre in accordance with my article, but practically, and at the point of cultural development we have reached, all the effort of such a theatre must lie in concretizing and objectivizing similar theories and finding an analogous expression for them. The entire originality of this theatre is the search for a new scenic language based on active and dynamic signs or gestures and not on words. Be that as it may, if theatre wants to survive it cannot continue to present itself as a kind of aid to digestion, and be at best, when excellent, the amusement of an intelligent and cultivated scholar. I believe that the aim of true theatre is to reconcile us with a certain idea of action, of immediate effectiveness which some think ought to be developed on a utilitarian level both of life and actuality, and which seems to me to concur with the ideas of certain great thinkers of this century, that it ought to seek to reach the deep-seated regions of the individual and create in him a real trans-formation, although hidden, and the consequences of which he will only perceive later. This is putting theatre on the level of magic, and that brings us close to certain rites, certain practices in Ancient Greece, and in India through the ages. Yet we must come to an understanding, and must not believe that theatre according to this conception should be reserved for an élite of religious and mystical minds and of initiates.

There are degrees. I have tried to depict for you the funda-mental aim of this attempt, but practically we must look for the elementary, simple, visible, external means of bringing about such effects, and objectively it is only a question of broadening the means of expression of theatre which may well resemble at first a kind of music-hall, teeming with expressions, solid images, a resonant and *spoken* pantomime, a series of tableaux and images in music – for music conceived in a new spirit will be of great importance in this theatre, and these games of expressions, intonations and words will be centred around simple, clear, and well-known themes when they are not centred around dramatic works of repute: *Woyzeck*, Webster and the best melodrama in the Romantic vein which will be its pretext and its object.

[*OC*, V, 79–81]

To André Gide

Paris, Sunday, 7 August 1932

Dear Mr Gide,

[. . .] I believe, in effect, that the organic field of the stage is the favoured place of a particular poetry, and it is through all it encompasses that it must reveal itself rather than through the Spoken Word, taking this in the restricted Western sense normally ascribed to it, in other words in the sense of being intellectually beneficial, turned to the inner meaning of words, to what, in them, is limited, constricted, and pigeonholed by the mind, without any possibility of expansion, in other words with-out any real effectiveness. This being so, I have drafted another text which now seems to me fully to live up to its intention. But I

won't ask you, or anyone else, to sign this text. This is what I
intend to do: I hope to publish this text in the September issue of
NRF and I will sign it myself, personally. – Once I have pointed
out the spiritual directives which this theatre will follow, I will set
out my programme. In this programme there will be no plays. So
no one will be able to accuse me of inadequacy, poverty or of
inopportunity. I will say that my aim is to unleash a certain
theatrical reality which belongs to the stage, in the physical and
organic domain of the stage, exclusively. This reality must be
unleashed through the performance, and thus the *mise en scène*,
taking this word in its broadest sense, regarding it as the language
of everything which can be 'put-on-the-stage', and not as the
secondary reality of a text, the more or less active and objective
means of expanding a text. So the director here becomes author,
i.e. creator. And the interest aroused by the performances I will
produce will be linked to the trust I will command, to the credit I
will procure, as creator, inventor of an absolute theatrical reality
which is self-contained. And why should I not command complete
trust, why should I not be thought capable of invention, of
revealing a scenic and amazingly attractive reality, which will
speak like the most beautiful of languages. Why should we not see
these productions develop as if through a kind of magic prism,
whose particular historical or sacred themes, or even plays which,
disregarding the text yet retaining the themes, will provide me
with my pretext and my subject.
   [. . .]
   Besides, since you spoke to me about an adaptation of an
apocryphal play by Shakespeare which you and I will produce *on
stage*, I'm asking you to permit me to give notice of this adaptation,
and as I haven't yet decided around which theme I intend to begin
to unleash this theatrical reality of which I spoke to you, I intend
to say that it is with this adaptation that this theatre will be
launched. Whether the circumstances at the time of the launch be
favourable or not, whether you are free at the time or not, I believe
that what is important in the presence of possible sponsors is to
have a definite and concrete promise to make to them for the
moment, and I believe that the promise of this adaptation will be
sufficient. I'll just say this; and in the manifesto I will adhere to the
text below:

As a first production we shall attempt an experiment in direct *mise en scène* around an apocryphal play by Shakespeare. André Gide, whose initiative this is, will be the author of the adaptation, but he will adapt it from the stage, using the objective language of the stage, in other words in close liaison with the *mise en scène* which will emanate from it. In this attempt, in which the spectacular element will be of prime importance, we shall try to unleash the notion of a production which does not appeal to the eye or to the ear, but to the mind. Gestures will be equivalent to signs, signs to words. The spoken word, when psychological circumstances permit, will be performed in an incantatory way. There will be no set in the proper sense: objects will make up the set, they will aim to create scenic landscapes, and for that purpose the sense of a particular objective humour will be used, created by changing positions, unforeseen groupings of objects. Movements, poses, bodies of characters will form or dissolve like hieroglyphs. This language will spread from one organ to another, establishing analogies, unforeseen associations between series of objects, series of sounds, series of intonations. The lighting will not be restricted to illumination but will have a life of its own, it will be considered as a state of mind. In short, we will attempt in this play a first application of this physical and objective stage language which will seek to reach the mind by way of the organs, of all the organs, in all degrees of intensity, and in all directions. But above all, the humour emanating from the spoken words will try to bring into question all the known relationships between objects, and taking the consequences of this dissociation to the extreme, it will render perceptible a physical poetry, in space, the meaning of which has long since been lost by theatre.

[*OC*, V, 87–91]

Gide sent a favourable reply on 16 August (see *OC*, V, 265), although he clearly stated that he did not want to be officially associated with the new venture as he professed to have no faith in theatre in general or even in Artaud's ability to bring this particular project to fruition. In fact by the time Gide had submitted the complete manuscript of his translation of *Arden of Faversham* to Artaud – and it took him only three short months to complete the work – the idea of a 'NRF theatre' was dead and Artaud was promoting a 'Société anonyme du Théâtre de la Cruauté' (Theatre of Cruelty Ltd, see *OC*, IV, 316, n. 1 and 319, n. 24).

Three Letters to Jean Paulhan

It is deliberate that these three letters are not presented in strict chronological order. The first letter must have been written on receipt of Gide's adaptation of *Arden of Faversham*. It would appear that the three months that elapsed since Artaud's enthusiastic letter of 7 August have all but killed his interest in the Elizabethan play. The second letter confirms that Seneca is now crowned 'the greatest tragic author in history' and the Roman playwright is even praised for having written the best examples of 'theatre of cruelty'. The final letter, written days after the request to Gide, is evidence that Artaud was already abandoning the idea of a 'NRF Arts Theatre' at the time he approached Gide.

[Paris] 27 November 1932

My very dear friend,

I have read *Arden of Faversham*.

It is, to be sure, a work far from lacking in merit, taking it at face value. But I don't think it should be read literally. There is an evident desire to parody Shakespeare, just as *Harnali*, a grotesque Romantic melodrama, was a parody of *Hernani*. Although this tendency to parody is at times not very pronounced. _____ Taking it at face value, it is worth neither more nor less than many other plays of the same period, in the same vein, and in the same spiritual mode. It contains virtually every tried and tested situation, every character, every feature that appears in Shakespeare or elsewhere. And apart from the story of the poisoned Crucifix, I fail to see how it can command our attention. It seems to me to be, in particular, of some archaeological and retrospective interest. But I cannot see its compelling qualities, and why its performance, in *present circumstances*, should be a necessity. How could it be considered *reactive*. It possesses the same qualities as fifty other similar plays, and were it not for the rich and perfect language with which André Gide has adorned it, especially grammatical richness and perfection, which must all but totally disappear for the production, there is nothing to distinguish it from those fifty other plays. If we were to perform *Arden of Faversham* I can't see why we don't then perform a Shakespeare play itself.

With this reservation, however, that there is in the language of the characters, in the exposition of the situations, something pure, something purified, which doesn't exist in Shakespeare and which makes *Arden of Faversham* a work of taste, on the one hand, a timeless and not too literary work, in which the action seems bare, is removed from any suspect contingency, without anything too verbal or too literary which locates it; all of this makes the drama seem pure and unlaboured, which means that we can isolate it, that it is self-sufficient and that criticism, if there is any, can only be directed at the action.

On the other hand, what definitely locates it and is literary in the piece, what can date it, appears in a parodic and humorous light. In the sections in which the play is not bare or *exposed*, it has the ring of the burlesque, of falseness, of jesting, of wilful distortion, although this is not very noticeable. I don't know the ending, but I have the impression that this ending can save the whole, can set off these attempts at parody, these vague hints at humour on a frenetic and jarring level where the play would take on a virulence which is somewhat lacking. In short I don't think it is mad enough for its incisive and spasmodic qualities, not mad enough for its overall classical nature, and its occasional meticulousness, not liberated enough for its desire to be free and non-conformist, not spasmodic enough for its abruptness and over-simplification, and I think that with the elements it possesses, the real play is yet to be created, or recreated, and it would be the purpose of the *mise en scène* to transform it in spirit and in intention, while leaving it materially as it stands. _____

The conclusion of all this is that I think we could attempt to put on a production with *Arden of Faversham* and I would be prepared to put it on if I were given the material means to do so. I would put it on in preference to creating my own show from scratch, if having a play by André Gide could inspire investors with more confidence, than a show of my own. _____ Even though I don't believe that the novelty and the urgency of THIS show is such to overstimulate the interest of the sponsors.

Whatever happens, I will direct *Arden of Faversham*, but I will ask André Gide to translate the title into French, and to find one which is true to the English original, but more stunning. Furthermore, I will endeavour to respect rigorously André Gide's text without editing one iota, it will be spoken by the actors as it is written and played in sequence; but I must be left free to pursue its *interpretation* in whatever way I consider necessary and to *add to it* whatever inventions of form inspired by the text, and thus not contrary to its spirit, but developed to the extreme, which I deem indispensable.

The text will not be performed literally, but parodied three quarters of the time, and the concrete images demanded by this parody: exaggeration and physical enlargement of the characters, affectation of gestures, group movement etc. etc., will be left to my choosing and to my unbridled imagination!!! _____

This will constitute MORE than *mise en scène*, a true theatrical adaptation of which I will be sole author. A new play specific in every detail will show through André Gide's text and from under the web of the action. And it is this new play punctuated by André Gide's spoken text which will be performed.

I actually don't see any other way of remaining true to my word. In other words there is important work which I must do prior to the *mise en scène* proper of the play, and when it goes into rehearsal.

It would really surprise me if André Gide did not go along with my way of thinking and in fact I believe that it is exactly what he expects of me. Just one more thing. I don't want to be denied the rewards of my work of invention and interpretation and we must find a way of defining what exactly falls to André Gide and what falls to me. I will write personally to André Gide to let him know my feelings on *Arden of Faversham* but you can already inform him of all this. In any case, be good enough to ask him to translate the last act as well, that is if there is only one left. And I think one shouldn't be afraid of pushing still further the virulence of the language, its coarseness, its bareness. Shakespeare and the Elizabethans have gone much further in this direction than any of us could possibly go.

Remaining yours faithfully,

Antonin Artaud

[*OC*, V, 130–3]

16 December 1932

Dear friend,

At the moment I am reading *Seneca*, and it seems crazy to me
that he could be confused with the moralist Tutor of some tyrant
of decadence – or else he was the Tutor, but he had grown old and
was despairing of magic. Whatever the case, he seems to me to be
the greatest tragic author in history, an initiate in the secrets who
knew better than Aeschylus how to put them into words. I cry as
I read his inspired theatre, and underneath the sound of syllables,
I sense the transparent seething of the forces of chaos frothing at
the mouth. And this reminds me of something: once I am cured I
intend to organize play readings – and for a man who denies the
text in the theatre that's no mean thing –, public readings at which
I will read the Tragedies of Seneca, and all the potential angels of
the Theatre of Cruelty will be summoned. You can't find a better
written example of what is meant by cruelty in the theatre than in
all the Tragedies of Seneca, but especially in Atreus and Thyestes.
Visible in the Blood, it is even more so in the mind. These
monsters are wicked as only blind forces can be, and theatre only
exists, I believe, on a level which is not yet human. Tell me what
you think of this plan.

A word from you would be appreciated. I hope to get out in ten
days – renewed.

Your friend,

Antonin Artaud

In Seneca the primordial forces resound in the spasmodic
vibration of the words. And the names which denote secrets and
forces do so in the *path* of these forces and with their wrenching
and crushing power.

[*OC*, III, 286–7]

Sunday, 29 August 1932, Paris

[. . .]

I have chosen the title 'Theatre of Cruelty', in spite of the
limitations it may have, and for the following reasons: The true title
would be too comprehensive; and it would miss the mark if it were
used. What it should be called, in actual fact, is 'Alchemical' or

'Metaphysical Theatre'. That would be one big joke for the unenlightened. It is a fact of life, however, that no performance is ever realized without an element of cruelty. All one needs to know is to what use the performance itself puts this cruelty, and that we are talking about a kind of cosmic cruelty which is closely related to destruction, without which nothing can be created. That then is the meaning of the title which I explain in the manifesto. For us that is sufficient and for the public, I believe, this title is an attraction. Afterwards this same public will be able to see where we are leading it by way of this necessary cruelty. Although it is unaware of how far it could go. Too bad for it. Unless either you or André Gide decide to veto it, I will keep this title. If you can think of another, why not suggest it to me or even put it straight at the top of the published manifesto. As long as people can see clearly that it is a new theatre which is making its appearance and which is being launched. [. . .]

[*OC*, V, 98–102]

Letter to *Comoedia*

Paris, 18 September 1932

Dear Sir,

Would you kindly allow me to set out here a few of the principles which have guided me in the enterprise I am attempting.

I conceive theatre as an operation or as a magical ceremony and I will make every effort to restore to it, by the latest up-to-date means, its ritualistic and primitive character in a manner which is understandable to all. There are always two sides, two aspects to everything.

1. The physical, active, external aspect which is conveyed through gestures, sounds, images, precious harmonies. This physical side appeals directly to the audience's senses, in other words to its nervous system. It has hypnotic powers. It prepares the mind to accept mystical or metaphysical ideas which constitute the internal aspect of a rite, and these harmonies, or gestures, are only the gloss.

2. The internal, philosophical, religious aspect, using this last adjective in its broadest sense, in its sense of communication with the Universal.

But the spectator should not worry, for every rite has three degrees. And after the physical side destined to decorate and to charm like any dance or piece of music, appears the fantastical and poetic side of the rite, on which the mind can stop and ponder. At this degree, the rite tells stories and supplies wonderful and well-known images just as, when reading the Iliad, one can muse on the matrimonial misadventures of Menelaus, without noticing the profound and frightful ideas encapsulated therein, and which they conceal.

Anyway, I have stressed this magical and operative side of theatre in an article published in the February 1932 issue of NRF. [See pp. 102–8] And since then I have had the great satisfaction of noting that excellent critics bear me out. Jean Cassou, for instance, in the 17 September issue of *Les Nouvelles Littéraires* speaks of a poetic way of using the objects on stage, and he even uses the word 'ceremonial' which I used in a note to the same article. So there seems to be agreement in certain circles on a particular way of viewing theatre other than as an unnecessary art-game or as a means of distraction from the discomfort of a painful digestion.

But as theatre rediscovers the power of direct action on the nerves and nervous system, and through the senses on the mind, it abandons the use of the spoken theatre whose clarity and excessive logic are a hindrance to the senses. Moreover, there is no question of suppressing the Spoken Word, but of considerably reducing its use or of using it in a forgotten or overlooked incantatory way. But we must get rid of purely psychological and naturalistic theatre and allow poetry and imagination to exercise their rights once more.

However, and this is the novelty, there is a virulent side and I would even say a dangerous side to poetry and imagination to be rediscovered. Poetry is a dissociating and anarchic force which, through analogy, associations and imagery, thrives on the disruption of known relationships. And the novelty will be to disrupt these relationships not just superficially, externally, but internally, i.e. psychologically.

If I'm asked how, I'll reply that it is my secret. In any case, what I can say is that in this new theatre, the objective and external side, in other words, stagecraft, theatrical art will be of supreme importance, everything will be based not on the text but on the production, and the text will once again be slave to the performance. A new language with its own rules and its own style of writing will develop beside the spoken language, and however physical and concrete it may be, it will have as much intellectual weight and suggestive powers as the other.

Indeed I believe it a matter of great urgency that theatre become aware, once and for all, of what distinguishes it from written literature. However transient it may be, the art of theatre is based on the use of space, on expression in space and, strictly speaking, I don't think it is the fixed arts, inscribed in stone, on canvas or on paper which are the most valid and the most *magically* effective.

In this new language, gestures equal words, attitudes have a deep symbolic meaning and are taken as hieroglyphs, and the whole show, instead of aiming for effect and charm, will be, for the mind, a means of recognition, of dizziness and of revelation.

In other words, poetry sets itself up in external objects, and from their assemblage and their choices, draws out strange harmonies and images, and everything in the show aims at expression through physical means which *engage* the mind as much as the senses.

And thus appears a particular *alchemical idea* of theatre where, unlike the usual theatre, in which the analytical dissipation of correspondences in the gross state of scientific chemistry (which is only a degenerate branch of Alchemy), forms, feelings, words make up an image of a kind of living and synthetic whirlwind, in the midst of which the show takes on the appearance of a veritable metamorphosis.

As far as works are concerned, we shall not perform any written play. The shows will be created directly on the stage with all the means offered by the stage, but taken as a language in the same way as the dialogue and words of the written theatre. This does not mean that the shows will not be rigorously composed and fixed once and for all before being performed.

So much for the principle. As far as the material means of realization are concerned, may I be allowed to reveal them a little later.

Antonin Artaud

[*OC*, V, 31–4]

Manifesto published in the literary magazine *Comoedia*, 21 September
1932, with the editorial title, 'The reasons why M. Antonin Artaud
sets up "The Theatre of Cruelty"'. The famous title is thus
introduced on this occasion, although this venture was still to be
linked, in some ways, with the *Nouvelle Revue Française*. In a letter to
André Rolland de Renéville, 13 September, Artaud makes it clear
that he is aware that his provocative title could lead to misunder-
standings:

We all know what today's theatre is like. We need an active
theatre, a theatre which cuts into the flesh. Of course we are not
talking about wielding the butcher's knife on stage at every
possible opportunity, but about rediscovering theatrically the
notion of a principle which is fundamental to all reality. One
cannot deny that life, in its insatiable and implacable capacity, is
identified with cruelty. And not only visibly and physically
speaking, when cruelty is everywhere and takes on the appearance
in all places of power, but even invisibly and cosmically speaking
in particular, when the simple fact of being, with the vast sum of
pain it implies, appears as cruelty.

   Theatre, however, to the extent where it ceases to be a wanton
game of art and becomes active again and rediscovers its link with
unseen powers, takes on its dangerous and magical characteristics
and identifies with this kind of vital cruelty, which is fundamental
to all reality.

   Besides, one cannot go on prostituting the idea of theatre,
because theatre is only of any worth through a magical and
dreadful link with reality and with danger.

                                                    [*OC*, V, 112–13]

To A Friend

                                              Paris, 4 March 1933
[. . .]
   We need magic in the poetic field as well as in all others.
Theatre, which is poetry in action, poetry realized, must be metaphysical or not at all. That, in short, is what I think, and I believe
that ideologically my first manifesto expanded by this last
pamphlet, puts theatre back on its true level from which it never

should have fallen, the level of religious rites, metaphysical in essence, in other words on the level of the Universal. All the artistic verbiage about useless clichés of *mise en scène*, diatribes against commercialism, the industrialization of theatre, the ham-acting of the stars, against the sated vulgarity of bovine spectators who go to the theatre to relax and chew their cud at ease, such verbiage is wasted and worthless, the principle not being to turn theatre again into art, an art of detachment, of *disinterest* but, on the contrary, to make the spectator *interested* through his organs, all his organs, deep down and as a whole. Those who aim to restore and give back to the audience the religion of theatre, especially of a particular literary theatre of established works: Aeschylus, Euripides, Shakespeare, Molière, Corneille, Racine, are, as far as I am concerned, way off target. All these works are written in a dead language and, Aeschylus excepted, even if they were revitalized and heard as they should be heard, they no longer address the essential. The time has come to recognize that this celebrated poetry (so despised by an ignorant public) is the essence of all true dramatic creation and the only thing which affects the spectator. In the sense of explosion and of deepest emotion, of religious, spasmodic communication with meta-physics in action, in other words with the universal spirit. All action which doesn't reach that pitch, which doesn't come from there, which doesn't go back there, is truncated and embryonic, the action of a eunuch and a coward, of an impotent yes-man. That the human conscience would not wish to go so far, would not admit to revolutionary and dangerous consequences of a principle, however dangerous and *brutally* nasty they may be, that is what is beyond me. That is why I wanted this manifesto and this pamphlet to assert my revolutionary faith to the fullest and most conclusive degree possible, and it is impossible for one not to see and not to recognize, even in official theatre circles, circles which are most threatened by events – to what extent this pamphlet and the ideas it contains stand opposed to all received ideas of theatre, and how far this reaction against the state of things, in complete disarray, relies on intellectually firm bases, on which alone, at close inspection, theatre has ever been able to rely.

It is not in vain that all young people between the ages of 20 and 25 who use their minds, have felt the *Theatre of Cruelty* to be on the same track as the old, primitive theatre, and put it in writing. Whether they argue or deny it, influential people must recognize that the *Theatre of Cruelty* has the future on its side.

[*OC*, V, 142–4]

To Natalie Clifford Barney

Paris, 12 August 1933

Dear Madam,

I am about to complete the draft of a new plan for a brochure abridged as follows:

1. We are bored. Never was an age more deprived of secret life than ours. And never was an age more dramatic, more distressed, yet the most violent, the most conclusive and determining events fall on a dulled sensitivity, unable to react, needing to be shaken, revitalized, rendered capable of feeling the acuity of the time.

2. The masses are looking for excitement and have forgotten that theatre was essentially made to give it to them. Present-day theatre fails to honour its *raison d'être*, its objective. It only shows us ridiculous individualities with no greatness, no passion, and what is more, it shows them lifeless and alienated.

3. But theatre is an exorcism, a summoning up of energy. It is a way of channelling passions, of making them serve something, but it must be understood not as an art or a distraction, but as a serious action, and paroxysm, seriousness, danger must be restored to it. To that end it must abandon individual psychology, espouse collective passions, mass opinion, tune into the collective wave-lengths, in short alter its subject matter;

and psychologically where theatre persists in splitting hairs on the well-known, it must enter the domain of the unknown, through the unconscious, imagination, poetry, and prove to the masses that they can, by a proper use of images, theatrical action, attain a new level, where life pushed to its paroxysm shows off all its energies. Thus make super-human passions come alive for the masses, allow them to be made flesh in heightened, monstrous characters.

4. For that, technical means exist which theatre has forgotten. First of all it should stop making the show something seen, unfolding in front of the audience and replace it with something

acted, revolving around the audience and engulfing it in its waves, its lights, its acoustics, its reflections.

That's why we need percussion instruments, gongs several metres in diameter, vibrations all clinging to one another, rubbing against the sensitivity, lighting which is not decorative but which provokes states of mind, why we need throbbing sounds, hypnotic rhythms aiming at the sensitivity of the masses instead of pursuing their understanding, preparing them for the psychic revelations to be made by the rest of the performance. The extent of the means used, the number of actors, extras, are of supreme importance since by the agitation of considerable crowds, agitation which never stops, they completely hold the attention of the spectator.

Thus the performance becomes comparable to a test, if not an illness whose subsequent cure proves to the audience the vital necessity of such an effort. [. . .]

[*OC*, V, 152–4]

To Orane Demazis (draft of a letter)

Paris, 30 December 1933

My very good friend,

  [. . .]

I have a plan.

This theatre will not be a theatre of aesthetes but for the masses. No luxury. The masses don't need luxury but bread, and for their anxiety to be lifted, and to believe in the sweetness of life. The aim is to give theatre back its function, to apprehend and redirect conflicts, to settle unanswered questions, to give a harsh crack of the whip to the senses of whoever participates in the per-formances. I say participates for I believe in the sacred character of theatre. I consider it an active rite, a kind of magical object, made to act on the organs nervous system as points of sensitivity Chinese medicine revolve around the sensitive organs and the principal functions human body. The red light makes aggressive atmosphere, primed for battle. It is as sure shot, slap. Slap doesn't kill its man. Shot kills sometimes. Atmosphere light sounds change nervous disposition. A word in the ear appropriate moment can terrify man, I mean drive mad.

This technique, for it's about technique, belongs methods of theatre. Methods which theatre has forgotten, lost habit of using and which it must learn again if it wishes to get back to its true function, to rediscover its effectiveness.

I hope to make these methods basis performance using 300 (extra) actors and which will have for crowd visual-plastic attractions. Auberge. These methods will support secret intentions, will be used to check initial resistance. Like tribes Central Africa, crowds, the sophisticated Upper Africa remain sensitive repetitions, resonances, rhythms, incantations where the voice supports gesture, gesture prolongs the voice.

A kind of human duty without interest by itself but which corresponds to an acute sense of destiny, to a notion of fatality which leads us, forces us to be aware of evil forces which make up the spirit of the time.

Somewhere there is a disturbance of which we are not in control, in this disturbance insoluble and gratuitous crimes, take part as a rehearsal all too frequent earthquakes, volcanic eruptions, tornadoes at sea, and railway disasters. What we don't want to see or end up with is art which fills up our spare time, a lightning conductor, and a performance which is excused its realization in life.

That's what understood all great ages when theatre meant something. Elizabethan Theatre. Those who consider theatre quick pleasure, and who deny it the right to take us back to solemn concept, insistent on the difficulty of everything in existence are responsible for the disturbing state of affairs in which we are stuck as if blind from birth.

Our total inability to react and even to live with the highly acute awareness of the cruelty of existence makes us cattle ready for war and slaughter.

If we had a notion of theatre not artistic but magical in the strong and even demiurgical sense of the word, that would indicate in us force we do not possess, and would even so correspond to a different aspect of things, for everything is linked magically, corresponds to this powerful and penetrating idea.

Will some people want to take such initiative creation. Opportunity is presented to try to escape this stagnation, by doing something. You are in a circle capable of many things. You have the understanding of particular kinds of suffering. You are capable of many things. Help me and be there first as in so many other things.

Yours affectionately,

Ant. Artaud

[*OC*, V, 287–8]

This is the first draft, in abbreviated style, of a letter to Orane Demazis. The draft is included for its immediacy and directness. For the 'clean copy' see *OC*, V, 164–8.

'The Conquest of Mexico' (*'La Conquête du Mexique'*)

[. . .]

Here now is the scenario of the show in the proper running order.

Act One – The Harbingers.

Evocation of Mexico in expectation, with its towns, its countryside, its caves of troglodytes, its Maya ruins.

Objects evoking on a grand scale certain Spanish *ex-votos* and the strange landscapes which are contained in bottles or in frames with convex glass.

Working on this principle, the towns, the monuments, the countryside, the forest, the ruins and the caves will be evoked – their emergence, their disappearance, their prominence – by lighting. The musical or pictorial ways of underlining their forms, of accentuating their rough edges will be constructed in the spirit of a secret melody, imperceptible to the audience, and corresponding to highly inspired and suggestive poetry.

Everything shudders and creaks like some strangely shaky stall. A landscape which senses the approaching storm; objects, music, fabrics, tattered costumes, shadows of wild horses passing in the air like distant meteors, like lightning on the horizon full of mirages, like the wind skimming the ground in a lighting effect warning of rain or human beings, bowing down, vehement. Then the entire lighting begins to dance; the squawking conversations, the arguments between all factions of the population are answered by the dumb, absorbed, depressed confrontations between Montezuma and his priests gathered in college, with the signs of the zodiac, and the strict forms of the firmament.

Part Five

'The Theatre and Its Double' (1931–7)

'The Theatre and Its Double' ('*Le Théâtre et son double*')

The Theatre and Its Double is not only Artaud's most famous book, it is also one of those rare books that catches the spirit of a particular age and sums it up for generations to come.

The Theatre and Its Double is a collection of essays, manifestos and letters written between 1931 and 1937 in which Artaud tried to define a new, modern conception of theatre. He suggested the publication in book form of his writings in a letter to Gaston Gallimard dated 2 December 1934 (*OC*, III, 298) under the general title of *Le Théâtre et la peste* (Theatre and the Plague) which explains the position of that essay at the beginning of the book. The initial manuscript was completed and submitted in February 1935.

Almost a year later, on 29 December 1935, just before his departure for Mexico, Artaud asked Paulhan to take good care of his book and urged him to speed up its publication 'which cannot be delayed until my return', even if it meant that Paulhan himself would have to make any necessary corrections. It was a few days later, on board ship, that Artaud found the definitive title and the letter in which he informs Paulhan was despatched from 'a little port in North America'. Dated 25 January 1936 it reads:

My dear friend,
    I believe I have found a suitable title for my book.
    It will be:

THE THEATRE AND ITS DOUBLE

for if theatre doubles life, life doubles true theatre, but it has nothing to do with Oscar Wilde's ideas on Art. This title will comply with all the doubles of the theatre which I thought I'd found for so many years: metaphysics, plague, cruelty,
    the pool of energies which constitute Myths, which man no longer embodies, is embodied by the theatre. By this double I mean the great magical agent of which the theatre, through its forms, is only the figuration on its way to becoming the transfiguration.
    It is on the stage that the union of thought, gesture and action is reconstructed. And the double of the Theatre is reality *untouched* by the men of today.

[*OC*, V, 196–7]

Artaud returned to Paris on 12 November 1936 and the contract with Gallimard was finally signed in December. When *Le Théâtre et son double* was published in the series 'Métamorphoses' on 7 February 1938 (400 copies), Artaud was already in psychiatric care in Sotteville-lès-Rouen. A second edition of 1525 copies (1944) was out of print by the time Volume IV of the *Œuvres complètes* was published in 1964, together with the first paperback edition in the series 'Idées'.

The Theatre and Its Double is today one of the most widely read books on theatre and a compulsory reference text for all theatre scholars, theatre directors and anyone interested in understanding *how* true theatre can work and *why* it should and could still be important.

On the Balinese Theatre (*Sur le théâtre balinais*)

The first Balinese Theatre show derived from dance, singing, mime and music – but extraordinarily little from psychological theatre such as we understand it in Europe, re-establishing theatre as pure and independent creativity whose products are hallucination and terror. [. . .]

In fact the strange thing about all these gestures, these angular, sudden, jerky postures, these syncopated inflections formed at the back of the throat, these musical phrases cut short, the flappings of insect wings, rustling branches, hollow drum sounds, robot creaking, animated puppets dancing, is the feeling of a new bodily language no longer based on words but on signs which emerges through the maze of gestures, postures, airborne cries, through their gyrations and turns, leaving not even the smallest area of stage space unused. Those actors with their asymmetrical robes look like moving hieroglyphs; not just the shape of their gowns, shifting the axis of the human figure, but creating a kind of second symbolic clothing standing beside the uniforms of those warriors entranced and perpetually at war, thus inspiring intellectual ideas or merely connecting all the criss-crossing of these lines with all the criss-crossing of spatial perspective. These mental signs have an exact meaning that only strikes one intuitively, but violently enough to make any translations into logical, discursive language useless. And for lovers of out-and-out realism, who might grow tired of the constant allusions to hidden, out-of-the-way attitudes of mind, there is still the double's nobly realistic acting, terrified as he is by apparitions from the Other World. There is a delineation of fear valid for all latitudes in this double who, by his trembling, childish yelping and heels striking the ground in time with the very automatism of the unleashed subconscious, hides behind his own reality, showing us that in human as well as in superhuman fields, Orientals are more than a match for us in matters of realism.

The Balinese, with gestures and a variety of mime to suit all occasions in life, reinstate the superior value of theatre conventions, demonstrate the effectiveness and greater active value of a certain number of well-learnt and above all masterfully applied conventions. One of the reasons for our delight in this faultless show lies precisely in the use these actors make of an exact amount of assured gesture, tried and tested mime coming in at an appointed place, but particularly in the mental clothing, in the deep shaded study which governs the formulation of the expressive interplay of these effective signs, giving us the impression their effectiveness has not become weakened over the centuries. That mechanical eye-rolling, those pouting lips, the use of twitching muscles producing studiously calculated effects which prevent any resorting to spontaneous improvisation, those heads moving horizontally seeming to slide from one shoulder to the other as if on rollers, all that corresponds to direct psychological needs as well as to a kind of mental construction made up of gestures, mime, the evocative power of rhythm, the musical quality of physical movement, the comparable, wonderfully fused harmony of a note. This may shock our European sense of stage freedom and spontaneous inspiration, but let no one say their precision makes for sterility or monotony. We get a marvellous feeling of richness, fantasy and bounteous lavishness emanating from this show regulated with a maddeningly conscious attention to detail. And the most impulsive correlations constantly fuse sight with sound, intellect with sensibility, a character's gestures with the evocation of a plant's movements conveyed by the shrieking sound of an instrument. The sighs of a wind instrument prolong the vibrations of vocal cords so identically we do not know whether the voice itself is held, or the senses which first assimilated that voice. Those rippling joints, the musical angle the arm makes with a forearm, a falling foot, an arching knee, fingers that seem to come loose from the hand, all this is like a constant play of mirrors where human limbs seem to echo one another, harmonious orchestral notes and the whisper of wind instruments, conjure up the idea of a passionate aviary where the actors themselves are the fluttering wings. Our theatre has never grasped this gestural metaphysics nor known how to make use of music for direct, concrete, dramatic purposes, our purely verbal theatre unaware of the sum total of theatre, of everything that exists spatially on the boards or is measured and circumscribed in space, having spatial density (moves, forms, colours, vibrations, postures, shouts) could learn a lesson in spirituality from the Balinese theatre with regard to the indeterminable, to dependence on the mind's suggestive power. This purely popular, non-religious theatre gives us an extraordinary idea of a nation's intellectual level, which takes the struggle of a soul as prey to the spectres and phantoms of the Other World to be the basis for its civic festivals. For the last part of the show certainly deals with purely inner conflicts. And in passing we ought to note the extent of theatrical magnificence the Balinese have been able to impart to it. The sense of the stage's plastic requirements are seen to be equalled only by their knowledge of physical fear and how to unleash it. And there is a striking similarity between the truly terrifying look of their devil, probably of Tibetan origin, and a certain puppet with leafy green nails, its hands distended with white gelatine, the finest ornament of one of the first plays of the Alfred Jarry Theatre. [. . .]

There is a wealth of ritual gestures in it to which we have no key, seeming to obey a very precise, musical indication, with something added that does not usually belong to music and seems to be aimed at encircling thought, hounding it down, leading it into a sure, labyrinthine system. In fact everything in this theatre is assessed with loving, unerring attention to detail. Nothing is left either to chance or individual initiative. It is a kind of sublime dance where the dancers are actors first and foremost. [. . .]

Everything is just as ordered and just as impersonal with them. Not one rippling muscle, not one rolling eye which does not seem to belong to a kind of deliberate accuracy directing everything, through which everything happens. The odd thing is that in this systematic depersonalization, in the purely muscular facial expressions, like feature masks, everything produces, conveys the utmost effect.

We are seized with a kind of terror when we think of these mechanical beings whose happiness and pain seem not to be their own, but to obey tried and tested rituals as if governed by higher intellects. In the last analysis, this impression of a higher, controlled life is what strikes us most about this show, like a profane ritual. It has the solemnity of a holy ritual – the hieratic costumes give each actor a kind of dual body, dual limbs – and in his costume, the stiff, stilted artist seems merely his own effigy. Beside the booming, pounding musical rhythm – there is a sustained hesitating fragile music which seems to grind the most precious metals, where springs of water bubble up as in a state of nature, where columns of insects march through the plants, where the sound of light itself appears to have been picked up, where the sounds of deep solitudes seem distilled into crystal swarms.

Furthermore, all these sounds are linked to movements, they are like the natural conclusion of gestures with the same attributes. All this with such a feeling of musical similarity, the mind is at last obliged to confuse them, attributing the sound qualities of the orchestra to the artist's hinged gesticulation – and vice versa. [. . .]

This theatre vibrates with instinctive things but brought to that lucid, intelligent, malleable point where they seem physically to supply us with some of the mind's most secret perceptions.

We might say the subjects presented begin on stage. They have reached such a point of objective materialization we could not imagine them, however much one might try, outside this compact panorama, the enclosed, confined world of the stage.

This show gives us a wonderful compound of pure stage imagery and a whole new language seems to have been invented in order to make it understood. The actors and costumes form true, living, moving hieroglyphs. And these three-dimensional hieroglyphics are in turn embellished with a certain number of gestures, strange signs matching some dark prodigious reality we have repressed once and for all here in the West.

There is something of the state of mind of a magic act in this intensive liberation of signs, at first held back, then abruptly launched into the air.

Confused seething, full of recognizable particles at times strangely orderly, sparkles in the effervescence of these painted rhythms, where the fermata constantly play and are interposed like calculated silences.

But no one in the West has ever tried to bring this concept of pure theatre to life since we regard it as merely theoretical, whereas the Balinese Theatre offers us an outstanding production that suppresses any likelihood of recourse to words to clarify the most abstract subjects; it has invented a language of gestures to be spatially developed, but having no meaning outside it.

The stage is used in all its dimensions, one might even say on all possible levels. For besides a keen sense of plastic beauty, these gestures are always ultimately aimed at the clarification of a state of mind or mental problem.

At least that is how it appears to us.

No point in space, and at the same time no possible intimations are wasted. And there is something like a philosophical feeling of the power nature has to rush suddenly headlong into chaos.

*

In the Balinese Theatre one senses a state prior to language, able to select its own language; music, gestures, moves and words.

[*CW*, 4, 38–50; *OC*, IV, 51–65]

First published in the *Nouvelle Revue Française*, No. 127, 1 October 1931.

A French 'Colonial Exhibition' (Exposition coloniale) took place at the Bois de Vincennes, on the outskirts of Paris, between May and November 1931. A Balinese dance/theatre company performed there on 25 June and again, after an interruption due to a fire which destroyed their stage, later in July and August. It would appear that Artaud saw the performance on 1 August as he wrote a most enthusiastic letter to Louis Jouvet the next day. (See *CW*, 3; *OC*, III, 217–18.)

'Mise en scène'[1] and Metaphysics (*La mise en scène et la métaphysique*)

Let me ask this question:

How can it be that in the theatre, at least theatre such as we know it in Europe, or rather in the West, everything specifically theatrical, that is to say, everything which cannot be expressed in words or, if you prefer, everything that is not contained in dialogue (dialogue itself viewed as a function of sound amplification on stage and the *requirements* of that sound) has been left in the background?

Besides, how can it be that Western theatre (I say Western theatre as luckily there are others such as Oriental theatre, which have known how to keep theatre concepts intact, whereas in the West this idea – just like all others – has been *debased*), how is it that Western theatre cannot conceive of theatre under any other aspect than dialogue form?

Dialogue – something written and spoken – does not specifically belong to the stage but to books. The proof is that there is a special section in literary history textbooks on drama as a subordinate branch in the history of spoken language.

I maintain the stage is a tangible, physical place that needs to be filled and it ought to be allowed to speak its own concrete language.

I maintain that this physical language, aimed at the senses and independent of speech, must first satisfy the senses. There must be poetry for the senses just as there is for speech, but this physical, tangible language I am referring to is really only theatrical insofar as the thoughts it expresses are beyond spoken language.

You might ask what these thoughts are that words cannot express, and which would find a more fitting, ideal expression than words in a physical, tangible stage language?

I will answer this question later.

The most urgent thing seems to me to decide what this physical language is composed of, this solid, material language by which theatre can be distinguished from words.

It is composed of everything filling the stage, everything that can be shown and materially expressed on stage, intended first of all to appeal to the senses, instead of being addressed primarily to the mind, like spoken language. (I am well aware that words also have their own sound potential, different ways of being projected into space, called *inflection*. Besides one could say a great deal about the tangible value of inflections in theatre, about the power of words to create their own music according to the way they are pronounced, distinct from their actual meaning and even running counter to that meaning – to create an undercurrent of impressions, connections and affinities beneath language. But this theatrical way of looking at language is already a subordinate *aspect* to the dramatist and one to which he no longer pays attention, especially today, in creating his plays. Well, let it go at that.)

This language created for the senses must first take care to satisfy the senses. This would not prevent it later amplifying its full mental effect on all possible levels and along all lines. It would also permit spatial poetry to take the place of language poetry and to be resolved in the exact field of whatever does not properly apply to words.

In order better to understand what I have said, doubtless a few examples of this spatial poetry would be desirable, able as it is to give birth to those kinds of substantial imagery, the equivalent of word imagery. Examples will be found below.

This difficult, complex poetry assumes many guises; first of all it assumes those expressive means usable on stage* such as music, dance, plastic art, mimicry, mime, gesture, voice inflection, architecture, lighting and décor.

Each of these means has its own specific poetry as well as a kind of ironic poetry arising from the way it combines with other expressive means. It is easy to see the result of these combinations, their interaction and mutual subversion.

I will return below to the subject of this poetry which can only be fully effective if it is tangible, that is to say if it objectively produces something owing to its *active* presence on stage – if, as in the Balinese theatre, a sound corresponds to a certain gesture and instead of acting as décor accompanying thought, makes it develop, guiding it, destroying it or decisively changing it, etc.

One form of this spatial poetry – beyond any brought about by an arrangement of lines, forms, colours, and objects in their natural state, such as are found in all the arts – belongs to sign language. And I hope I may mention that other aspect of pure

---

* Insofar as they show themselves able to profit by the direct physical potential offered by the stage, to replace the set forms of the art with living, threatening forms, through which the meaning of ancient ceremonial magic can find fresh reality on a theatrical level. Insofar as they accede to what one might call the *physical temptation* of the stage.

theatre language which escapes words, that sign, gesture and posture language with its own ideographic values such as they exist in some undebased mime plays.

By 'undebased mime plays' I mean straightforward mime where gestures, instead of standing for words or sentences as in European mime (barely fifty years old) where they are merely a distortion of the silent parts in Italian comedy, stand for ideas, attitudes of mind, aspects of nature in a tangible, potent way, that is to say by always evoking natural things or details, like that Oriental language which portrays night by a tree on which a bird that has already closed one eye is beginning to close the other. And another abstract idea or attitude of mind could be portrayed by some of the innumerable symbols in the Scriptures, such as the eye of the needle through which the camel cannot pass.

We can see these signs form true hieroglyphics where man, insofar as he contributes to making them, is only one form like any other, to which he nevertheless adds particular prestige because of his duality.

This language conjures up intense images of natural or mental poetry in the mind and gives us a good idea of what spatial poetry, if free from spoken language, could become in the theatre.

Whatever the position of this language and poetry may be, I have noticed that in our theatre, which exists under the exclusive dictatorship of words, this language of symbols and mimicry, this silent mime-play, these attitudes and spatial gestures, this objective inflection, in short everything I look on as specifically theatrical in the theatre, all these elements when they exist outside the script, are generally considered the lowest part of theatre, are casually called 'craft' and are associated with what is known as staging or *mise en scène*. We are lucky when the word staging is not just tagged on to the idea of external artistic lavishness solely connected with costume, lighting and décor.

Against this viewpoint, which seems to me completely Western or rather Latin, that is, pigheaded, I might even say that in as much as this language starts on stage, drawing its effectiveness from its spontaneous creation on stage, in as much as it exerts itself directly on stage without passing through the words (and why could we not envisage a play composed right on stage, produced on stage) – staging is theatre far more than a written, spoken play. No doubt I will be asked what is specifically Latin about this view which is opposed to mine. What is Latin is the need to use words to express obvious ideas. For me obvious ideas, in theatre as in all else, are dead and finished.

The idea of a play built right on stage, encountering production and performance obstacles, demands the discovery of active language, both active and anarchic, where the usual limits of feelings and words are transcended.

In any event, and I hasten to say so at once, theatre which submits staging and *mise en scène*, that is to say everything about it that is specifically theatrical, to the lines, is mad, crazy, perverted, rhetorical, philistine, antipoetic and Positivist – that is to say, Western theatre.

Furthermore, I am well aware that a language of gestures and postures, dance and music is less able to define a character, to narrate man's thoughts, to explain conscious states clearly and exactly, than spoken language. But whoever said theatre was made to define a character, to resolve conflicts of a human, emotional order, of a present-day, psychological nature such as those which monopolize current theatre?

Given theatre as we see it here, one would imagine there was nothing more to know than whether we will have a good fuck, whether we will go to war or be cowardly enough to sue for peace, how we will put up with our petty moral anxieties, whether we will become conscious of our 'complexes' (in scientific language) or whether our 'complexes' will silence us. Moreover, rarely does the debate rise to a social level or do we question our social or ethical system. Our theatre never goes so far as to ask itself whether by chance this social or ethical system is iniquitous or not.

Now to my mind the present state of society is iniquitous and ought to be destroyed. If it is theatre's role to be concerned with it, it is even more a matter for machine-guns. Our theatre is not even able to ask this question in as effective and incendiary a manner as is needed, and even if it did ask it, it would still be far from its intended purpose which is higher and even more mysterious.

All the topics detailed above stink of mankind, of materialistic, temporary mankind, I might even say *carrion-man*. These personal worries disgust me, utterly disgust me as does just about all current theatre, which is as human as it is antipoetic and, except for three or four plays, seems to me to stink of decadence and pus.

Current theatre is in decline because on the one hand it has lost any feeling for seriousness, and on the other for laughter. Because it has broken away from solemnity, from direct, harmful effectiveness – in a word, from Danger.

For it has lost any true sense of humour, and laughter's physical, anarchic, dissolving power.

Because it has broken away from the profoundly anarchic spirit at the basis of all poetry. [. . .]

To my mind theatre merges with production potential when the most extreme poetic results are derived from it, and theatre's production potential is wholly related to staging viewed as a language of movement in space.

Now to derive the furthest poetic consequences from means of production is to make metaphysics out of them and I do not believe anyone could argue with that way of looking at the problem.

It seems to me that to make metaphysics out of language, gestures, postures, décor and music is, from a theatrical point of view, to regard it in relation to all the ways it can have of agreeing with time and movement.

To give objective examples of the poetry resulting from the various ways gesture, sound or inflection support themselves with more or less insistence on such and such a spatial area at such and such a moment, would appear to me as difficult as to communicate the feeling of the special quality of a sound in words, or the intensity and nature of physical pain. It all depends on production and can only be determined on stage.

Here and now I ought to review all the means of expression open to theatre (or *mise en scène*, which in the system I have just expanded, is merged with it). But that would entail too much and I will select only one or two examples.

First, on spoken language.

To make metaphysics out of spoken language is to make language convey what it does not normally convey. That is to use it in a new, exceptional and unusual way, to give it its full, physical shock potential, to split it up and distribute it actively in space, to treat inflections in a completely tangible manner and restore their shattering power and really to manifest something; to turn against language and its basely utilitarian, one might almost say alimentary, sources, against its origins as a hunted beast, and finally to consider language in the form of *Incantation*.

This whole active, poetic way of visualizing stage expression leads us to turn away from present-day theatre's human, psychological meaning and to rediscover a religious, mystical meaning our theatre has forgotten.

Besides, if one has only to say words like *religious* and *mystic* to be taken for a sexton or a profoundly illiterate bonze barely fit for rattling prayer wheels outside a Buddhist temple, this is a simple judgement on our incapacity to draw all the inferences from words and our profound ignorance of the spirit of synthesis and analogy.

It may also mean that we have reached the point where we have lost all contact with true theatre, since we restrict it to the field of whatever everyday thought can achieve, to the known or unknown field of consciousness − and if theatrically we turn to the subconscious it is merely to steal what it may have been able to collect (or hide) in the way of accessible mundane experiences.

[*CW*, 4, 22–33; *OC*, IV, 32–45]

Within the context of his campaign to set up a company sponsored by the *Nouvelle Revue Française* (NRF) Artaud gave a lecture entitled 'La mise en scène et le théâtre' at the Sorbonne (University of Paris) on 10 December 1931. The text, under its new title, was published in the *Nouvelle Revue Française*, No. 221, 1 February 1932. The lecture itself was a great success and made a strong impression on its audience (see *OC*, IV, 278–9).
[1] See *Note* 1, p. 16.

Alchemist Theatre (*Le théâtre alchimique*)

A secret similarity exists between the fundamental principles of theatre and those of alchemy. For when one considers theatre's nature, its foundations, it is anchored like alchemy to a certain number of bases, the same for all arts, aiming in the imaginary, mental field at being as effective as that which *really* turns matter into gold in the physical field. But there is an even higher likeness between theatre and alchemy, leading us much further metaphysically. That is, alchemy and theatre are virtual arts, so to speak, and do not contain their object within them any more than they contain their reality.

Where alchemy, through its signs, is like the mental Double of an act effective on the level of real matter alone, theatre ought also to be considered as the Double not of this immediate, everyday reality which has been slowly truncated to a mere lifeless copy, as empty as it is saccharined, but another, deadlier, archetypal reality in which Origins, like dolphins, quickly dive back into the murky depths once they have shown their heads.

For this reality is not human but inhuman and we must admit that man, his customs and nature count for little in it. Man's head might barely remain, a kind of soft, stripped, organic head in which just enough positive power would be left for first principles to be able to exert their effects within it in a sensible, final manner. [. . .]

All true alchemists know alchemical symbols are chimeras just as theatre is a chimera. And this eternal reference to the fundamental principles and objects in theatre, found in almost all alchemist texts ought to be understood as a feeling (the alchemists being extraordinarily conscious of it) of the similarity there is between the level on which characters, objects, portrayals and in a general way everything which makes up theatre's *virtual reality* develops, and the purely assumed, dreamlike level on which alchemist signs are evolved.

[*CW*, 4, 34–7; *OC*, IV, 46–50]

This text was first published in Spanish translation in the Argentinian magazine *Sur*, No. 6, September 1932, on the initiative of the South-American-born French poet Jules Supervielle. A letter to Supervielle, dated 17 March 1932 (*CW*, 4, 168–70; *OC*, IV, 227–9) sheds further light on Artaud's thoughts and on his creative process at the time. In particular it accounts for the fact that, throughout his life, he wrote such a wealth of letters and so often used the epistolary form:

My dear friend,

Permit me to send you my article in the form of a letter. It is the only means I have of combating a completely paralysing feeling of pointlessness, and to complete what I have been thinking about for a month or more.

ALCHEMIST THEATRE

The difficult thing in European theatre's case is that if it made up its mind to be serious it would run up against a tremendous scarcity of material from the start, and besides it was this very 'scarcity of material' that led it to the point of inertia and exhaustion it has now reached. When we complain about the decline of theatre, first one wants to know who is complaining, second are there many of them and third if (   )[1] are capable of affecting the development of events, however little. If theatre lost all contact with reality long ago, we might congratulate ourselves on this secession.

*

The very name Theatrum Chemicum indicates that wonderful performances were attributed to distilled, convulsive material at the heart of the Athanor, where each chemical element making up the composition of pure matter obeyed a visible rhythm in transforming itself, and evolved within a particular framework. It also indicates that universal consciousness is artistic and contributes to giving us an infinitely freer, more tangible idea of art, a kind of untried idea, completely contradictory to our ordinary ideas of it. It substitutes an idea of organized, transcendental art for the passive idea of art according to which any concept is inert; which aims at making art simply a formal intent, fine attire intended to transform whatever it touches but is nothing itself. It calls the intellectual idea of a landscape 'art', which might be *thought of* as being in a certain form while its total artistic aspect had been produced by one *single idea*!!!

In the same way as certain alchemical atoms in labour aim at becoming conscious of certain cosmic rhythms and that this active consciousness, not without some solemnity, restores the idea of a certain BASIC theatre, so alchemist theatre transferred to a human level can dissociate, isolate a certain number of essential operations whose special movement and rhythm conform completely with the genius of poetry.

If Alchemist procedures are represented by a certain number of symbols that are always the same and whose effectiveness has

[1] A blank in the original letter.

really been tried and tested, symbols whose consequences are such
that when they descend from a mental level and are expressed on
a material level they allow us to *re-create* gold, we ask ourselves
why we should not find poetic symbols on the illusory, imaginary
level of theatre such as would lead to the effective apparition of
spirits.

Otherwise what use are imagery and poetry?

For if the original idea of theatre is not to allow us to attempt
psychological operations similar to those attempted by alchemy in
the hollowed out, empty excavation of the stage, that is, a small
scale liberation of powers we forcibly constrict, it has no reason for
being.

These powers must be intercepted in full flight, caught
bubbling over, held seething.

For example, we can clearly see that a mind which dares to
concentrate on one word, which in language . . .

*

Verbal language,
formation and the need for gesture,
what it represents.

There is no call for enthusiasm, lyricism, emotion or posturing,
we need acuteness of mind, an accurate sense of moral values,
we must search out the right tones and that search can be thrilling,
actors and directors, in short all of us, must search for it
together and keep telling ourselves that what is to be done pales
beside what is not to be done,
besides, the script is there and above all else it must be spoken,
and I might even venture to say the script is so important that
we ought to take no notice how the moves are carried out.

The author impresses through his power and acuteness of mind
and we ought not to be beneath him in production; production
disguised behind the play, almost mathematically; and contrary to
the general notion it ought to give us the impression the author has
accomplished his purpose.

And symbols,
attitude or poetic level.

The Theatre of Cruelty – First Manifesto (*Le théâtre de la cruauté – Premier manifeste*)

We cannot continue to prostitute the idea of theatre whose only value lies in its agonizing, magic relationship to reality and danger.

Put in this way, the problem of theatre must arouse universal attention, it being understood that theatre, through its physical aspect and because it requires *spatial expression* (the only real one in fact) allows the sum total of the magic means in the arts and words to be organically active like renewed exorcisms. From the aforementioned it becomes apparent that theatre will never recover its own specific powers of action until it has also recovered its own language.

That is, instead of harking back to texts regarded as sacred and definitive, we must first break theatre's subjection to the text and rediscover the idea of a kind of unique language somewhere between gesture and thought. [. . .]

TECHNIQUE

The problem is to turn theatre into a function in the proper sense of the word, something as exactly localized as the circulation of our blood through our veins, or the apparently chaotic evolution of dream images in the mind, by an effective mix, truly enslaving our attention.

Theatre will never be itself again, that is to say will never be able to form truly illusive means, unless it provides the audience with truthful distillations of dreams where its taste for crime, its erotic obsessions, its savageness, its fantasies, its utopian sense of life and objects, even its cannibalism, do not gush out on an illusory make-believe, but on an inner level.

In other words, theatre ought to pursue a re-examination not only of all aspects of an objective, descriptive outside world but also all aspects of an inner world, that is to say man viewed metaphysically, by every means at its disposal. We believe that only in this way will we be able to talk about imagination's rights in the theatre once more. Neither Humour, Poetry nor Imagination mean anything unless they re-examine man organically through anarchic destruction, his ideas on reality and his poetic vision in reality, generating stupendous flights of form constituting the whole show.

But to view theatre as a second-hand psychological or moral operation and to believe dreams themselves only serve as a substitute is to restrict both dreams' and theatre's deep poetic range. If theatre is as bloody and as inhuman as dreams, the reason for this is that it perpetuates the metaphysical notions in some Fables in a present-day, tangible manner, whose atrocity and energy are enough to prove their origins and intentions in fundamental first principles rather than to reveal and unforgettably tie down the idea of continual conflict within us, where life is continually lacerated, where everything in creation rises up and attacks our condition as created beings.

This being so, we can see that by its proximity to the first principles poetically infusing it with energy, this naked theatre language, a non-virtual but real language using man's nervous magnetism, must allow us to transgress the ordinary limits of art and words, actively, that is to say, magically, to produce a kind of total creation *in real terms*, where man must reassume his position between dreams and events.

SUBJECTS

We do not mean to bore the audience to death with transcendental cosmic preoccupations. Audiences are not interested whether there are profound clues to the show's thought and action, since in general this does not concern them. But these must still be there and that concerns us.

*

The Show: *Every show will contain physical, objective elements perceptible to all. Shouts, groans, apparitions, surprise, dramatic moments of all kinds, the magic beauty of the costumes modelled on certain ritualistic patterns, brilliant lighting, vocal, incantational beauty, attractive harmonies, rare musical notes, colours of objects, the physical rhythm of the moves whose build and fall will be wedded to the beat of moves familiar to all, the tangible appearance of new, surprising objects, masks, puppets many feet high, abrupt lighting changes, the physical action of lighting stimulating heat and cold, and so on.*

Staging: *This archetypal theatre language will be formed around staging not simply viewed as one degree of refraction of the script on stage, but as the starting point for theatrical creation. And the old duality between author and director will disappear, to be replaced by a kind of single Creator using and handling this language, responsible both for the play and the action.*

Stage Language: *We do not intend to do away with dialogue, but to give words something of the significance they have in dreams.*

Moreover we must find new ways of recording this language, whether these ways are similar to musical notation or to some kind of code.

As to ordinary objects, or even the human body, raised to the dignity of signs, we can obviously take our inspiration from hieroglyphic characters not only to transcribe these signs legibly so they can be reproduced at will, but to compose exact symbols on stage that are immediately legible.

Then again, this coding and musical notation will be valuable as a means of vocal transcription.

Since the basis of this language is to initiate a special use of inflections, these must take up a kind of balanced harmony, a subsidiary exaggeration of speech able to be reproduced at will.

Similarly the thousand and one facial expressions caught in the form of masks can be listed and labelled so they may directly and symbolically participate in this tangible stage language, independently of their particular psychological use. or being just a mark

Furthermore, these symbolic gestures, masks, postures, individual or group moves, whose countless meanings constitute an important part of the tangible stage language of evocative gestures, emotive arbitrary postures, the wild pounding of rhythms and sound, will be multiplied, added to by a kind of mirroring of the gestures and postures, consisting of the accumulation of all the impulsive gestures, all the abortive postures, all the lapses in the mind and of the tongue by which speech's incapabilities are revealed, and on occasion we will not fail to turn to this stupendous existing wealth of expression.

Besides, there is a tangible idea of music where sound enters like a character, where harmonies are cut in two and become lost precisely as words break in.

Connections, level, are established between one means of expression

and another; even lighting can have a predetermined intellectual meaning.

Musical Instruments: *These will be used as objects, as part of the set.*

Moreover they need to act deeply and directly on our sensibility through the senses, and from the point of view of sound they invite research into utterly unusual sound properties and vibrations which present-day musical instruments do not possess, urging us to use ancient or forgotten instruments or to invent new ones. Apart from music, research is also needed into instruments and appliances based on special refining and new alloys which can reach a new scale in the octave and produce an unbearably piercing sound or noise.

Lights – Lighting: *The lighting equipment currently in use in the theatre is no longer adequate. The particular action of light on the mind comes into play, we must discover oscillating light effects, new ways of diffusing lighting in waves, sheet lighting like a flight of fire-arrows. The colour scale of the equipment currently in use must be revised from start to finish. Fineness, density and opacity factors must be reintroduced into lighting, so as to produce special tonal properties, sensations of heat, cold, anger, fear and so on.*

Costume: *As to costume, without believing there can be any uniform stage costume that would be the same for all plays, modern dress will be avoided as much as possible not because of a fetishistic superstition for the past, but because it is perfectly obvious certain age-old costumes of ritual intent, although they were once fashionable, retain a revealing beauty and appearance because of their closeness to the traditions which gave rise to them.*

The Stage – The Auditorium: *We intend to do away with stage and auditorium, replacing them by a kind of single, undivided locale without any partitions of any kind and this will become the very scene of the action. Direct contact will be established between the audience and the show, between actors and audience, from the very fact that the audience is seated in the centre of the action, is encircled and furrowed by it. This encirclement comes from the shape of the house itself.*

Abandoning the architecture of present-day theatres, we will rent some kind of barn or hangar rebuilt along lines culminating in the architecture of some churches, holy places, or certain Tibetan temples.

This building will have special interior height and depth dimensions. The auditorium will be enclosed within four walls stripped of any ornament, with the audience seated below, in the middle, on swivelling chairs allowing them to follow the show taking place around them. In effect, the lack of a stage in the normal sense of the word will permit the action to extend itself to the four corners of the auditorium. Special places will be set aside for the actors and action in the four cardinal points of the hall. Scenes will be acted in front of washed walls designed to absorb light. In addition, overhead galleries run right around the circumference of the room as in some Primitive paintings. These galleries will enable actors to pursue one another from one corner of the hall to the other as needed, and the action can extend in all directions at all perspective levels of height and depth. A shout could be transmitted by word of mouth from one end to the other with a succession of amplifications and inflections. The action will unfold, extending its trajectory from floor to floor, from place to place, with sudden outbursts flaring up in different spots like conflagrations. And the show's truly illusive nature will no longer be a hollow gesture any more than will the action's direct, immediate hold on the spectators. For the action, diffused over a vast area, will require the lighting for one scene and the varied lighting for a performance to hold the audience as well as the characters — and physical lighting methods, the thunder and wind whose repercussions will be experienced by the spectators, will correspond with several actions at once, several phases in one action with the characters clinging together like swarms, will endure all the onslaughts of the situations and the external assaults of weather and storms.

However, a central site will be retained which, without acting as a stage properly speaking, enables the body of the action to be concentrated and brought to a climax whenever necessary.

Objects–Masks–Props: *Puppets, huge masks, objects of strange proportions appear by the same right as verbal imagery, stressing the physical aspect of all imagery and expression — with the corollary that all objects requiring a stereotyped physical representation will be discarded or disguised.*

Décor: *No décor. Hieroglyphic characters, ritual costume, thirty foot high effigies of King Lear's beard in the storm, musical instruments as tall as men, objects of unknown form and purpose are enough to fulfil this function.*

Topicality: *But, you may say, theatre so removed from life, facts or present-day activities . . . news and events, yes! Anxieties, whatever is profound about them, the prerogative of the few, no! In the Zohar, the story of Rabbi Simeon is as inflammatory as fire, as topical as fire.*

Works: *We will not act scripted plays but will attempt to stage productions straight from subjects, facts or known works. The type and lay-out of the auditorium itself governs the show as no theme, however vast, is forbidden to us.*

Show: *We must revive the concept of an integral show. The problem is to express it, spatially nourish and furnish it like tap-holes drilled into a flat wall of rock, suddenly generating geysers and bouquets of stone.*

The Actor: *The actor is both a prime factor, since the show's success depends on the effectiveness of his acting, as well as a kind of neutral, pliant factor since he is rigorously denied any individual initiative. Besides, this is a field where there are no exact rules. And there is a wide margin dividing a man from an instrument, between an actor required to give nothing more than a certain number of sobs and one who has to deliver a speech, using his own powers of persuasion.*

Interpretation: *The show will be coded from start to finish, like a language. Thus no moves will be wasted, all obeying a rhythm, every character being typified to the nth degree, each gesture, feature and costume to appear as so many shafts of light.*

Cinema: *Through poetry, theatre contrasts pictures of the unformulated with the crude visualization of what exists. Besides, from an action viewpoint, one cannot compare a cinema image, however poetic it may be, since it is restricted by the film, with a theatre image which obeys all life's requirements.*

Cruelty: *There can be no spectacle without an element of cruelty as the basis of every show. In our present degenerative state, metaphysics must be made to enter the mind through the body.*

The Audience: *First, this theatre must exist.*

Programme: *Disregarding the text, we intend to stage:*

1. *An adaptation of a Shakespearian work, absolutely consistent with our present confused state of mind, whether this be an apocryphal Shakespeare play such as* Arden of Faversham *or another play from that period.*

2. *A very free poetic play by Léon-Paul Fargue.*

3. *An excerpt from* The Zohar, *the Story of Rabbi Simeon which has the ever-present force and virulence of a conflagration.*

4. *The story of Bluebeard, reconstructed from historical records, containing a new concept of cruelty and eroticism.*

5. *The Fall of Jerusalem, according to the Bible and the Scriptures. On the one hand, a blood red colour flowing from it, that feeling of running wild and mental panic visible even in daylight. On the other hand, the prophets' metaphysical quarrels, with the dreadful intellectual agitation they cause, their repercussions falling bodily on the King, the Temple, the Masses and Events.*

6. *One of the Marquis de Sade's tales, its eroticism transposed, allegorically represented and cloaked in the sense of a violent externalization of cruelty, masking the remainder.*

7. *One or more Romantic melodramas where the unbelievable will be an active, tangible, poetic factor.*

8. *Büchner's* Woyzeck *in a spirit of reaction against our principles, and as an example of what can be drawn from an exact text in terms of the stage.*

9. *Elizabethan theatre works stripped of the lines, retaining only their period machinery, situations, character and plot.*

[*CW*, 4, 68–76; *OC*, IV, 86–96. First published in the *Nouvelle Revue Française*, No. 229, 1 October 1932]

Letters on Cruelty (*Lettres sur la cruauté*)

Paris, 13 September 1932
To J.P. [Jean Paulhan]

My dear friend,

I can give you no details about my Manifesto without spoiling its emphasis. All I can do for the time being is to make a few remarks to try and justify my choice of title, the Theatre of Cruelty.

This cruelty is not sadistic or bloody, at least not exclusively so.

I do not systematically cultivate horror. The word cruelty must be taken in its broadest sense, not in the physical, predatory sense usually ascribed to it. And in so doing, I demand the right to make a break with its usual verbal meaning, to break the bonds once and for all, to break asunder the yoke, finally to return to the etymological origins of language which always evoke a tangible idea through abstract concepts.

One may perfectly well envisage pure cruelty without any carnal laceration. Indeed, philosophically speaking, what is cruelty? From a mental viewpoint, cruelty means strictness, diligence, unrelenting decisiveness, irreversible and absolute determination.

From the aspect of our own existence, the most current philosophical determinism is an image of cruelty.

It is wrong to make cruelty mean merciless bloodshed, pointless and gratuitous pursuit of physical pain. [. . .]

Paris, 14 November 1932

To J.P.

My dear friend,

Cruelty is not an adjunct to my thoughts, it has always been there, but I had to become conscious of it. I use the word cruelty in the sense of hungering after life, cosmic strictness, relentless necessity, in the Gnostic sense of a living vortex engulfing darkness, in the sense of the inescapably necessary pain without which life could not continue. [. . .] Theatre in the sense of constant creation, a wholly magic act, obeys this necessity. A play without this desire, this blind zest for life, capable of surpassing everything seen in every gesture or every act, in the transcendent aspect of the plot, would be useless and a failure as theatre.

Paris, 16 November 1932

To Mr R. de R. [Roland de Renéville]

My dear friend,

[. . .]

There is a form of incipient spitefulness in the flame of life, in love of life, life's irrational impulse. Erotic desire is cruel since it feeds on contingencies. Death is cruelty, resurrection is cruelty, transfiguration is cruelty, for true death has no place in all the meanings of an enclosed, circular world, ascension means rending apart, this enclosed space is nurtured by lives, each stronger life passes over the others, consuming them in slaughter transfiguring good. In a world made manifest, where, metaphysically speaking, evil is the paramount rule, whatever is good is an effort, further cruelty superimposed on all other.

If one does not understand this, one does not understand metaphysical ideas. And after this let no one come and tell me the title of my book is too restricted. Cruelty connects things together, the different stages of creation are formed by it. Good is always an external façade but the inner façade is evil. Evil will eventually be reduced, but only at the final moment when all forms are on the point of returning to chaos.

[*CW*, 4, 77–9; *OC*, IV, 97–100]

Theatre and Cruelty (*Le théâtre et la cruauté*)

We have lost a certain idea of theatre. And in as much as theatre restricts itself to probing the intimacy of a few puppets, thereby transforming the audience into peeping Toms, one understands why the élite have turned away from it or why the masses go to the cinema, music-hall and circus to find violent gratification whose intention does not disappoint them.

Our sensibility has reached the point where we surely need theatre that wakes us up heart and nerves.

The damage wrought by psychological theatre, derived from Racine, has rendered us unaccustomed to the direct, violent action theatre must have. Cinema, in its turn, murders us with reflected, filtered and projected images that no longer *connect* with our sensibility, and for ten years has maintained us and all our faculties in an intellectual stupor.

In the anguished, catastrophic times we live in, we feel an urgent need for theatre that is not overshadowed by events, but arouses deep echoes within us and rises above our unsettled period.

Our long-standing habit of seeking diversions has made us forget the slightest idea of serious theatre which upsets all our preconceptions, inspiring us with fiery, magnetic imagery and finally acting in us after the manner of unforgettable soul therapy.

Everything that acts is cruelty. Theatre must rebuild itself on a concept of this drastic action pushed to the limit.

Infused with the idea that the masses think with their senses first and foremost and that it is ridiculous to appeal primarily to our understanding as we do in everyday psychological theatre, the Theatre of Cruelty proposes to resort to mass theatre, thereby rediscovering a little of the poetry in the ferment of great, agitated crowds hurled against one another, sensations only too rare nowadays, when masses of holiday crowds throng the streets.

If theatre wants to find itself needed once more, it must present everything in love, crime, war and madness.

Everyday love, personal ambition and daily worries are worthless except in relation to the kind of awful lyricism that exists in those Myths to which the great mass of men have consented.

This is why we will try to centre our show around famous personalities, horrible crimes and superhuman self-sacrifices, demonstrating that it can draw out the powers struggling within them, without resorting to the dead imagery of ancient Myths.

In a word, we believe there are living powers in what is called poetry, and that the picture of a crime presented in the right stage conditions is something infinitely more dangerous to the mind than if the same crime were committed in life.

We want to make theatre a believable reality inflicting this kind of tangible laceration, contained in all true feeling, on the heart and senses. In the same way as our dreams act on us and reality acts on our dreams, so we believe ourselves able to associate mental pictures with dreams, effective insofar as they are pro-jected with the required violence. And the audience will believe in the illusion of theatre on condition they really take it for a dream, not for a servile imitation of reality. On condition it releases the magic freedom of daydreams, only recognizable when imprinted with terror and cruelty.

Hence this full-scale invocation of cruelty and terror, its scope testing our entire vitality, confronting us with all our potential.

And in order to affect every facet of the spectator's sensibility, we advocate a revolving show, which instead of making stage and auditorium into two closed worlds without any possible communication between them, will extend its visual and oral outbursts over the whole mass of spectators.

Furthermore, leaving the field of analysable emotional feelings aside, we intend using the actor's lyricism to reveal external powers, and by this means to bring the whole of nature into the kind of theatre we would like to evoke.

However extensive a programme of this kind may be, it does not overreach theatre itself, which all in all seems to us to be associated with ancient magic powers.

Practically speaking, we want to bring back the idea of total theatre, where theatre will recapture from cinema, music-hall, the circus and life itself, those things that always belonged to it. This division between analytical theatre and a world of movement seems stupid to us. One cannot separate body and mind, nor the senses from the intellect, particularly in a field where the unendingly repeated jading of our organs calls for sudden shocks to revive our understanding.

Thus on the one hand we have the magnitude and scale of a show aimed at the whole anatomy, and on the other an intensive mustering of objects, gestures and signs used in a new spirit. The reduced role given to understanding leads to drastic curtailment of the script, while the active role given to dark poetic feeling necessitates tangible signs. Words mean little to the mind; expanded areas and objects speak out. New imagery speaks, even if composed in words. But spatial, thundering images replete with sound also speak, if we become versed in arranging a sufficient interjection of spatial areas furnished with silence and stillness.

We expect to stage a show based on these principles, where these direct active means are wholly used. Therefore such a show, unafraid of exploring the limits of our nervous sensibility, uses rhythm, sound, words, resounding with song, whose nature and startling combinations are part of an unrevealed technique.

Moreover, to speak clearly, the imagery in some paintings by Grünewald or Hieronymus Bosch, gives us a good enough idea of what a show can be, where things in outside nature appear as temptations just as they would in a Saint's mind.

Theatre must rediscover its true meaning in this spectacle of a temptation, where life stands to lose everything and the mind to gain everything.

Besides we have put forward a programme which permits pure production methods discovered on the spot to be organized around historic or cosmic themes familiar to all.

And we insist that the first Theatre of Cruelty show will hinge on these mass concerns, more urgent and disturbing than any personal ones.

We must find out whether sufficient production means, financial or otherwise, can be found in Paris, before the cataclysm occurs, to allow such theatre (which must remain because it is the future) to come to life. Or whether real blood is needed right now to reveal this cruelty.

May 1933

[*CW*, 4, 64–7; *OC*, IV, 82–5]

Letters on Language (*Lettres sur le langage*)

Paris, 15 September 1931

To Mr B.C. [Benjamin Crémieux]

Sir,

In an article on *mise en scène* and theatre you stated:

'One risks making a terrible mistake by considering direction [*mise en scène*] as an autonomous art',

and that:

'Performance, the spectacular side of a dramatic work, cannot operate alone or make its own decisions completely independently.'

You go on to add these are first truths.

You are perfectly right to consider staging merely an auxiliary, minor art, so that even those who employ it with the maximum freedom deny it any fundamental originality. As long as staging remains just a means of presentation, a subordinate way of expressing works, a kind of display interlude without any meaning of its own even in the minds of the boldest directors, it has no value except insofar as it succeeds in hiding behind the works it is intended to serve. And this will continue as long as the principal interest in performed works lies in the script, as long as in theatre

– a performing art – literature takes precedence over a kind of performance incorrectly called the show, with everything this term entails that is disparaging, subsidiary, ephemeral and external.

What seems to me a first truth above all is this: in order for theatre, an independent autonomous art, to be revived, or simply to stay alive, it must clearly indicate what differentiates it from the script, from pure speech, literature and all other predetermined, written methods.

We might perfectly well go on considering theatre as based on the authority of the script, on a more and more wordy, diffuse and tiring script to which stage aesthetics would be subject.

But this concept consists in having characters sit on a number of chairs or couches placed in a row and telling each other stories, however wonderful these might be. And even if this is not a complete denial of theatre, which does not absolutely demand movement to be what it ought to be, it is certainly a distortion.

If theatre has become essentially psychological, the intellectual alchemy of feelings and if the pinnacle of dramatic art has come to consist of a certain ideal silence and stillness, this is nothing else but a staged distortion of the idea of concentration.

For this concentrated acting, used among so many other expressive means by the Japanese, for example, is valuable only as one method among many. And to make this the aim of the theatre is to avoid using the stage just like someone who, having the whole of the Pyramids in which to bury a Pharaoh's body, blows them up on the pretext a niche will accommodate it just as well.

But at the same time he would have to blow up the magic, philosophical system of which the niche was only the starting point and the body only a condition.

On the other hand, a director who takes pains over staging to the detriment of the lines is wrong, perhaps less wrong than a critic who accuses him of an exclusive concern with staging.

For a director remains true to theatre tradition which deals with staging by taking pains over staging, that is, over the truly specifically theatrical part of the show. But both these are playing on words, for if the term staging [*mise en scène*] has assumed such a disparaging meaning, this is the fault of our European concept

antonin artaud
24 Juin 1947

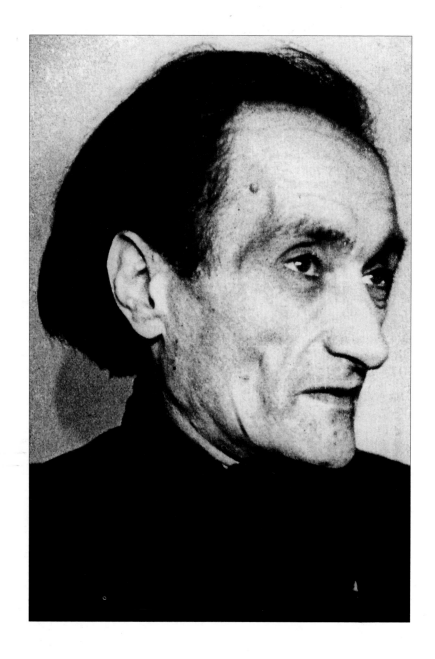

of theatre, making speech predominate over other means of performance.

No one has ever definitely proved word language is the best. And it seems that on stage, above all a space to be filled, somewhere something happens, word language must give way to sign language, whose objective aspect has the most immediate impact on us.

Viewed from this angle, the aim of stage work reassumes a kind of intellectual dignity, words effacing themselves behind gesture, and from the fact that the aesthetic, plastic part of theatre abandons its role as a decorative interlude, to become a *language* of direct communication in the proper sense of the word.

In other words, if it is true that in a play made to be spoken, the director is wrong to become sidetracked on more or less intelligently lit scenic effects, group acting, muted moves, all of what could be termed skin-deep effects that only overload the script, but in so doing he is closer to theatre's tangible reality than an author who might have confined himself to books, without resorting to the stage, whose spatial requirements seemed to escape him.

One might object by pointing to the great dramatic value of all the great tragic playwrights whose literary, or at least verbal, side seems predominant.

My answer to this is that if we are so incapable today of giving any idea of Aeschylus, Sophocles or Shakespeare that is worthy of them, this is very likely because we have lost any idea of the natural philosophy of their theatre. Because all the immediately human, active aspects of delivery, gesture or stage rhythm escape us, and these ought to have as much if not more importance than the admirable spoken dissection of their heroes' psychology.

Through this aspect, through these exact gestures modified during the course of history and making feelings current, we can rediscover the deep humanity in their drama.

But even if this natural philosophy really existed, I would still maintain none of these great tragic writers are theatre alone, which is a matter of stage embodiment, only coming alive by embodiment. Call theatre a minor art if you like – that remains to be seen! – but theatre consists of a certain manner of filling and animating stage space, by sparking off emotions, human feelings at a given point, creating ecstatic situations expressed in tangible gestures.

Furthermore, these tangible gestures must be sufficiently effective to make us forget the very need for dialogue. Yet if dialogue exists, it must do so as a response, a relay in activated space and the mortar in these gestures must achieve the value of a true abstraction through its human effectiveness.

In a word, theatre must become a kind of experimental manifestation of the deep-seated identity between the abstract and the concrete.

For a gesture culture also exists side by side with word culture. There are other languages in the world besides our Western languages which have decided in favour of despoiling and desiccating ideas, presenting them in an inert, stale manner, unable to stir up in their course a whole system of natural affinities, as do Oriental languages.

It is only right that theatre should remain the most effective and active place where these tremendous kindred disturbances can pass through us, where ideas are arrested in flight at some point in their metamorphosis into the abstract.

No complete theatre can fail to take this grisly metamorphosis of ideas into account, which does not add the expression of states of mind belonging to the field of semi-consciousness to our known, ready-made feelings which suggestive gestures will always convey more adequately than the definite, exact meaning of words.

Briefly, it seems the highest possible concept of theatre is one which philosophically reconciles us with Becoming and which, through all kinds of objective situations, suggests the covert notion of the passage and metamorphosis of ideas, far more than the shock of feelings transmuted into words.

It also seems theatre certainly arose from a desire of this kind, that man and his appetites must only obtrude to the degree that he is magnetically confronted with his fate. Not to submit to it, but to measure up to it.

[*CW*, 4, 80–93; *OC*, IV, 101–17]

Artaud wrote four letters under this heading: the present one to the drama critic Benjamin Crémieux and three more to Jean Paulhan. For lack of space, only the letter to Crémieux is included here. This letter was a reply to Crémieux's article on the art of *mise en scène* which had appeared in the journal *Je suis partout*, No. 42, 12 September 1931. The article, part of a series of studies on prominent directors, was devoted to Louis Jouvet. Although complimentary, Crémieux warned against the modishness of *mise en scène* and against the excessive power that directors seemed to be exercising in the production of plays at the expense of what could be termed 'authorial orthodoxy'. Such views, obviously, ran contrary to everything Artaud was thinking and doing.

Theatre and the Plague (*Le théâtre et la peste*)

Whereas plague imagery related to an advanced state of physical disorganization is like the last outbursts of waning mental strength, the imagery of poetry in the theatre is a mental power which, beginning its trajectory in the tangible, dispenses with reality. Once launched in fury, an actor needs infinitely more virtue to stop himself committing a crime than a murderer needs to perpetrate his crime, and this is where, in their pointlessness, these acts of stage feeling appear as something infinitely more valid than those feelings worked out in life.

Compared with a murderer's fury that exhausts itself, an actor of tragedy remains enclosed within a circle. The murderer's anger has accomplished an act and is released, losing contact with the power that inspired but will no longer sustain it. It has assumed a form, while the actor's fury, which denies itself by being detached, is rooted in the universal.

If we are now prepared to accept this mental picture of the plague, we can consider the plague victim's disturbed fluids as a solidified, substantial aspect of a disorder which on other levels is equivalent to the clashes, struggles, disasters and devastation brought about by events. Just as it is not impossible that the unconsumed despair of a lunatic screaming in an asylum can cause the plague, so by a kind of reversibility of feelings and imagery, natural disasters, revolutionary order and wartime chaos, when they occur on a theatrical level, are released into the audience's sensitivity with the strength of an epidemic.

In *The City of God*, Saint Augustine points to the similarity between the plague which kills without destroying any organs and theatre which, without killing, induces the most mysterious changes not only in the minds of individuals but in a whole nation.

'Know then,' he writes, 'you who are ignorant of this, that these plays, exhibitions of shameless folly and licence, were established in Rome not by the vicious craving of men but by the appointment of your gods. Much more pardonably might you have rendered divine honours to Scipio* than to gods such as these; indeed, the gods were not so moral as their pontiff! . . .

They enjoined that plays be exhibited in their honour to stay a physical pestilence, while their pontiff prohibited the theatre to prevent a moral pestilence. If then there remains in you sufficient mental enlightenment to prefer the soul to the body, choose whom you will worship. But these astute and wicked spirits, foreseeing that in due course the pestilence would shortly cease, took occasion to infect, not the bodies, but the morals of their worshippers, with a far more serious disease. And in this plague these gods found great enjoyment because it benighted the minds of men with so gross a darkness and dishonoured them with so foul a deformity, that even quite recently some of those who fled from the sack of Rome and found refuge in Carthage were so infected with the disease that day after day they seemed to contend with one another who should most madly run after the actors in the theatre.'

There is no point in trying to give exact reasons for this infectious madness. It would be as much use trying to find reasons why the nervous system after a certain time is in tune with the vibrations of the subtlest music and is eventually somehow lastingly modified by it. Above all we must agree stage acting is a delirium like the plague, and is communicable.

The mind believes what it sees and does what it believes; that is the secret of fascination. And in his book St. Augustine does not doubt the reality of this fascination for one moment.

Yet conditions must be found to give birth to a spectacle that can fascinate the mind. It is not just a matter of art.

For if theatre is like the plague, this is not just because it acts on large groups and disturbs them in one and the same way. There is both something victorious and vengeful in theatre just as in the

* Scipio Nasica, High Pontiff, who ordered that the theatres in Rome be razed to the ground and their cellars filled. [Author's note]

plague, for we clearly feel that the spontaneous fire the plague lights as it passes by is nothing but a gigantic liquidation.

Such a complete disaster, such organic disorder overflowing with vice, this kind of wholesale exorcism constricting the soul, driving it to the limit, indicate the presence of a condition which is an extreme force and where all the powers of nature are newly rediscovered the instant something fundamental is about to be accomplished.

The plague takes dormant images, latent disorder and suddenly carries them to the point of the most extreme gestures. Theatre also takes gestures and develops them to the limit. Just like the plague, it reforges the links between what does and does not exist, between the virtual nature of the possible and the material nature of existence. It rediscovers the idea of figures and archetypal symbols which act like sudden silences, fermata, heart stops, adrenalin calls, incendiary images surging into our abruptly woken minds. It restores all our dormant conflicts and their powers, giving these powers names we acknowledge as signs. Here a bitter clash of symbols takes place before us, hurled one against the other in an inconceivable riot. For theatre can only happen the moment the inconceivable really begins, where poetry taking place on stage nourishes and superheats created symbols.

The symbols are symbols of full-blown powers held in bondage until that moment and unusable in real life, exploding in the guise of incredible images giving existence and credibility to acts naturally opposed to social life.

A real stage play disturbs our peace of mind, releases our repressed subconscious, drives us to a kind of potential rebellion (since it retains its full value only if it remains potential), calling for a difficult heroic attitude on the part of the assembled groups.

As soon as the curtain goes up on Ford's *'Tis Pity She's a Whore*, to our great surprise we see before us a man launched on a most arrogant defence of incest, exerting all his youthful, conscious strength both in proclaiming and justifying it.

He does not hesitate or waver for one instant, thereby demonstrating just how little all the barriers mean that might be set up against him. He is heroically guilty, boldly, openly heroic. Everything drives him in this direction, inflames him, there is no heaven and no earth for him, only the strength of his tumultuous passion, which evokes a correspondingly rebellious and heroic passion in Annabella. [. . .]

If fundamental theatre is like the plague, this is not because it is contagious, but because like the plague it is a revelation, urging forward the exteriorization of a latent undercurrent of cruelty through which all the perversity of which the mind is capable, whether in a person or a nation, becomes localized.

Just like the plague there is an evil time, the victory of dark powers, a higher power nourishing them until they have died out.

In theatre, as in the plague, there is a kind of strange sun, an unusually bright light by which the difficult, even the impossible, suddenly appears to be our natural medium. And Ford's *'Tis Pity She's a Whore* is lit by the brilliance of that strange sun just as is all worthwhile theatre. It resembles the plague's freedom where, step by step, stage by stage, the victim's character swells out, where the survivors gradually become imposing, superhuman beings.

Now one may say all true freedom is dark, infallibly identified with sexual freedom, also dark, without knowing exactly why. For the Platonic Eros, the genetic meaning of a free life, disappeared long ago beneath the dark surface of the *Libido* which we associate with everything sullied, despicable and ignominious in the fact of living, the headlong rush with our customary, impure vitality, with constantly renewed strength, in the direction of life.

Thus all great Myths are dark and one cannot imagine all the great Fables aside from a mood of slaughter, torture and bloodshed, telling the masses about the original division of the sexes and the slaughter of essences that came with creation.

Theatre, like the plague, is made in the image of this slaughter, this essential division. It unravels conflicts, liberates powers, releases potential and if these and the powers are dark, this is not the fault of the plague or theatre, but of life.

We do not see that life as it stands and as it has been made offers us much cause for exaltation. It seems as though a colossal abscess, ethical as much as social, is drained by the plague. Just like the plague, theatre is collectively made to drain abscesses.

It may be true that the poison of theatre, when injected in the body of society, destroys it, as St. Augustine asserted, but it does so as a plague, a revenging scourge, a redeeming epidemic in which credulous ages were convinced they saw God's hand, while it was nothing more than a natural law applied, where all gestures were offset by another gesture, every action by a reaction.

Like the plague, theatre is a crisis resolved either by death or cure. The plague is a superior disease because it is an absolute crisis after which there is nothing left except death or drastic purification. In the same way, theatre is a disease because it is a final balance that cannot be obtained without destruction. It urges the mind on to delirium which intensifies its energy. And finally from a human viewpoint we can see that the effect of the theatre is as beneficial as the plague, impelling us to see ourselves as we are, making the masks fall and divulging our world's lies, aimlessness, meanness, and even two-facedness. It shakes off stifling material dullness which even overcomes the senses' clearest testimony, and collectively reveals their dark powers and hidden strength to men, urging them to take a nobler, more heroic stand in the face of destiny than they would have assumed without it.

And the question we must now ask ourselves is to know whether in this world that is slipping away and committing suicide without realizing it, a nucleus of men can be found to impress this higher idea of theatre on the world, to bring to all of us a natural, occult equivalent of the dogma in which we no longer believe.

[*CW*, 4, 7–21; *OC*, IV, 15–31]

This is the text Artaud chose to open *The Theatre and Its Double*. It is the text of a lecture delivered at the Sorbonne on 6 April 1933. It was published, with alterations and additions, by the *Nouvelle Revue Française*, No. 253, 1 October 1934.

Unlike his previous lecture, '*Mise en scène* and Metaphysics' (see p. 102), 'Theatre and the Plague' got a stormy reception. Anaïs Nin gives us this vivid account of the occasion (*The Journal of Anaïs Nin, 1931–34*, Peter Owen, 1966, p. 192): 'At first people gasped. And then they began to laugh. Everyone was laughing! They hissed. Then one by one, they began to leave, noisily, talking, protesting . . . But Artaud went on, until the last gasp. . . .' After the lecture he complained to Anaïs Nin: 'They always want to hear *about*; they want to hear an objective conference on "The Theatre and the Plague", and I want to give them the experience itself, so they will be terrified, and awaken. I want to awaken them. They do not realize *they are dead*.'

No More Masterpieces (*En finir avec les chefs-d'œuvre*)

Past masterpieces are fit for the past, they are no good to us. We have the right to say what has been said and even what has not been said in a way that belongs to us, responding in a direct and straightforward manner to present-day feelings everybody can understand.

It is senseless to criticize the masses for having no sense of the sublime, when we ourselves confuse the sublime with one of those formal, moreover always dead, exhibits. And if, for example, the masses today no longer understand *Oedipus Rex*, I would venture to say *Oedipus Rex* is at fault as a play and not the masses.

In *Oedipus Rex* there is the incest theme and the idea that nature does not give a rap for morality. And there are wayward powers at large we would do well to be aware of, call them *fate* or what you will.

In addition, there is the presence of a plague epidemic which is the physical incarnation of these powers. But all this is clothed in language which has lost any contact with today's crude, epileptic rhythm. Sophocles may speak nobly, but in a manner that no longer suits the times. His speeches are too refined for today, as if he were speaking beside the point.

Yet the masses tremble at railway disasters, are familiar with earthquakes, plagues, revolutions and wars as well as being sensitive to the disturbing anguish of love and are capable of becoming conscious of them, but on condition we know how to speak their language and that notions of these things are not brought to them invested with a sophistication belonging to dead periods we will never relive.

Just as in former times, the masses today are thirsting for mystery. They only ask to become conscious of the laws by which fate reveals itself and perhaps to guess at the secret of its apparitions.

Let us leave textual criticism to teachers and formal criticism to aesthetes, and acknowledge that what has always been said no longer needs saying; that an expression twice used is of no value since it does not have two lives. Once spoken, all speech is dead and is only active as it is spoken. Once a form is used it has no more use, it begs another form be found, and theatre is the only place in the world where a gesture, once made, is never repeated in the same way.

If the masses do not frequent literary masterpieces, this is because the masterpieces are literary, that is to say set in forms no longer answering the needs of the times.

Far from accusing the masses, the public, we must accuse the formal screen we place between ourselves and the masses and that form of a new idolatry, the idolizing of set masterpieces, an aspect of middle-class conformity. [. . .]

[*CW*, 4, 56–63; *OC*, IV, 72–81]

First published in *The Theatre and Its Double* this text was almost certainly written towards the end of 1933.

Theatre and Poetry (*Le théâtre et la poésie*)

It appears that the notion of a language belonging to theatre could be fused with the notion of a language in space, such as might appear on a stage, and directly opposed to the language of words. The language of theatre is, in effect, the language of the stage, which is dynamic and objective. It is the sum of everything which can be put on a stage in terms of objects, shapes, attitudes, and meanings. But only to the extent where all these elements arrange themselves in the process and are cut off from their immediate meaning, and endeavour, indeed, to create a true language based on the sign, rather than based on the word. That is where the notion of symbolism based on the changing of meanings comes in. Things will be stripped of their immediate meaning and will be given a new one.

*

In the current decline of theatre the audience is generally blamed. And it is blamed for having rejected theatrical texts without trying to understand what the production has done for them. And it appears from this point of view that there has never been, in France at any rate, for quite some time, a truly theatrical performance of a quality text. It appears that the notion of the essentials and the possibilities of theatre have been completely lost. A European conception of theatre would have the theatre fused with the text, would have everything revolve around the dialogue, considered to be both the starting and finishing points. But it seems to us that, without calling upon the philosophical and, therefore, rather too specialized notion of pure theatre, the notion can be put forward of a theatre based on the possibilities of developing a purely theatrical means of expression, in which all effective approaches would similarly come into play. That does not mean that the *mise en scène* should dominate the text. And in this respect we must counter a certain European conception of *mise en scène*, in which everything, light, set and movement, is only, so to speak, an ornamental additive to the text, with an organic conception in which *mise en scène* becomes a language in itself. In the case where the text retains its importance, it is certain that everything which is given to the *mise en scène* can only result in a purely artistic distraction from the text, and thus is useless and parasitic. It follows thus that theatre can only come into its own when all dramatic performances develop directly from the stage and do not play second fiddle to the definitively written text which is self-determining and limited in its possibilities.

This brings us to call into question the language of the spoken word as it is currently conceived in Europe, as a means of expression, and to ask whether it fulfils all the organic essentials of life. This raises the additional question of the purpose of the spoken word, with its real and magical power of suggestion and creation.

In any case, although one might consider the importance of the spoken word in the real world, theatre, which offers other possibilities beyond the purely verbal, is not directly linked to it.

Theatre is fused with the very purpose of the world of form. It raises the question of expression through forms and it challenges us to do what we like with the real world,

through humour, the creator of poetry.

And then, this humorous challenge to reality makes us wonder where it is leading the mind, the senses, if we are intent on drawing the ultimate conclusions.

It leads us to intellectual metaphysics on the one hand, organic on the other, through the possibilities of magical and religious separation from the language used.

*

New objects, sometimes even splendidly developed, but finite, with some high idea of themselves which they might be capable sometimes of passing on to human intelligence.

[*OC*, V, 13–15]

This text is the second part of a short double essay entitled 'Theatre and Psychology – Theatre and Poetry'. It was not included in *The Theatre and Its Double* but its composition is contemporaneous with 'Oriental and Western Theatre' (late 1935).

Oriental and Western Theatre (*Théâtre oriental et théâtre occidental*)

The Balinese Theatre was not a revelation of a verbal but a physical idea of theatre where drama is encompassed within the limits of everything that can happen on stage, independently of a written script. Whereas with us, the words gain the upper hand and theatre as we understand it finds itself restricted by them. Thus theatre is a branch of literature, a species of vocal language, and even if we admit a difference between the words spoken on stage and those read by the eyes, even if we confine theatre to what goes on between the cues, we will never succeed in divorcing theatre from the idea of script production.

This notion, the predominance of the spoken word in theatre, is deeply rooted in us and we view theatre as a mere physical reflection of the script, that everything in theatre outside the script, not contained within its limits or strictly determined by it, appears to us to be a part of *mise en scène*, and inferior to the script.

Given the subservience of theatre to the spoken word, we might ask ourselves whether theatre by any chance possesses a language of its own, or whether it would really be illusory to consider it an independent, autonomous art for the same reasons as music, painting, dance, etc.

In any case if such a language exists it will inevitably be confused with staging viewed:

1. On the one hand, as the spoken word visually, plastically materialized.
2. On the other, as a language expressing everything which can

be said or intended on stage distinct from the text, everything that can be spatially embodied, affected or disrupted by it.

Once we consider the language of *mise en scène* as theatre's pure language, we must discover whether it is capable of attaining the same inner object as the words, whether from a theatrical or mental viewpoint it can claim the same intellectual effectiveness as spoken language. In other words we must not ask ourselves whether it can define thought but whether it *makes us think*, and can lead the mind to assume deeply effective attitudes from its own point of view.

In short if one questions the intellectual effectiveness of expression through objective forms, of a language using forms, sound and gesture, one is questioning the intellectual effectiveness of art.

Although we have come to credit art with nothing more than a pleasurable relaxing value, confining it solely to the express use of forms, to the compatibility between certain surface relationships, this in no way diminishes its deeply expressive value. But the mental weakness of the West, where man has especially confused art and aesthetics, is to believe one can have painting used only as painting, dancing as a plastic form alone, as if one wanted to cut art off from everything, to sever the links with all the mystical attitudes they might adopt in confrontation with the absolute.

One therefore understands that theatre, inasmuch as it remains confined within its own language and in correlation with it, must make a break with topicality. It is not aimed at solving social or psychological conflicts, to serve as a battlefield for moral passions, but to express objectively secret truths, to bring out in active gestures those elements of truth hidden under forms in their encounters with Becoming.

To do that, to link theatre with expressive form potential, with everything in the way of gestures, sound, colours, movement, is to return it to its original purpose, to restore it to a religious, metaphysical position, to reconcile it with the universe.

But while one might say words have their own metaphysical power, no one says we cannot think of speech as well as gestures on a universal level. Besides, it is more effective on this level as a dissociatory force exerted on material appearances, as on all states in which the mind feels settled or tends to relax. We can readily answer that this metaphysical way of looking at dialogue is not used in Western theatre since it does not make it an active power springing from the destruction of appearances to reach the mind, but on the contrary uses it as a final degree of thought, which gets lost when openly expressed.

In Western theatre, words are solely used to express psychological conflicts peculiar to man and his position in everyday existence. His conflicts are clearly justifiable in spoken words and whether they remain in the psychological field, or leave it to pass over into the social field, drama will always concern itself with morality owing to the way in which conflicts attack and disrupt character. And this will always remain in a field where words, verbal solutions, retain their advantage. But these moral conflicts, by their very nature, do not need to be resolved on stage. To make speech or verbal expression dominant over the objective expressiveness of gestures and everything on stage spatially affecting the mind through the senses means turning our backs on the physical requirements of the stage and rebelling against its potential.

We must admit theatre's sphere is physical and plastic, not psychological. This does not simply mean assessing whether theatre's physical language can attain the same psychological resolutions as words or whether it can express emotions and feelings as well as words, but whether there are not attitudes in the field of intellect and thought which words cannot assume, which gestures and everything inclusive in this spatial language cannot attain with greater precision than them. [. . .]

There is no question of abolishing speech in theatre but of changing its intended purpose, especially to lessen its status, to view it as something other than a way of guiding human nature to external ends, since our theatre is solely concerned with the way emotions and feelings conflict with one another or the way man is set against man in life.

Yet to change the purpose of theatre dialogue is to use it in an actual spatial sense, uniting it with everything in theatre that is spatial and significant in the tangible field. This means handling it as something concrete, something disturbing, first spatially, then in an infinitely more secret and mysterious field permitting more scope.

[CW, 4, 51–5; OC, IV, 66–71]

First published in *The Theatre and Its Double*. Probably written towards the end of 1935 or the beginning of 1936.

Theatre is First Ritualistic and Magical ... (*Le théâtre est d'abord rituel et magique ...*)

Theatre is first ritualistic and magical, in other words bound to powers, based on religion, on actual beliefs, and whose effectiveness is conveyed through gesture, directly linked to the rites of theatre which is the very practice and the expression of a hunger for magical and spiritual manifestations.

Beliefs fade away, external theatrical gestures linger on, but empty of any internal substance, yet transcendent, but on the level of imagination and the mind. Although such gestures are void of any occult power or idea, a poetic and real substratum lurks behind them, like some reject. The ideas are dead but their reflection remains in the poetic state evoked by the gestures. The remote quality, the remote degree of the gesture represented by poetry in its *pure state* may still call itself poetry but it lacks any real or magical effectiveness. Art is on the brink of decadence.

In this state, however, the mind continues to create myths and theatre to perform them. Theatre goes on living above the real, offering the audience some kind of poetic life which, if taken too far, would hurtle over the edge, but this is preferable all the same to the simple psychological life in which theatre is currently suffocating.

This is when theatre makes use of the magic of nature, reverberates with the colour of the earthquake or the eclipse, when the poets give vent to the storm, and theatre at last concentrates on the physical and tangible side of supreme magic.

The poetry it uses is dark; or if resplendent, it is even darker, even more opaque.

It is when theatre takes on the task of substitution. To ordinary life, theatre opposes the state of poetic life, dazzling but false. To psychological life, another psychological life which is slightly enlarged, slightly more monstrous. The characters wield their knives, but what they eat, even on a symbolic level, has no more meaning.

We are now at the point of applied life, where everything has disappeared, nature, magic, images, powers; in the state of stagnation where man lives on his legacy with a sentimental and moral stock unchanged for a century. At this point, theatre creates no new myths. The mechanical myths of modern life have been captured by the cinema. It might have captured them but they lead nowhere. They turn their back on the spirit. As for the pseudo-knowledge of the subconscious, the psychological phantoms, the poetical spectres which it can conjure up, it must be understood that, by the act of reconciliation with life on the boil, life in its pure state, we will rediscover something essential in existence, and resolve to split up once again psychological principles, but split them up metaphysically and for what they represent transcendentally, and the subconscious will once again call upon symbols and images, considered to be a means of recognition which goes beyond psychology.

But the photographically recorded subconscious will make disproportionate inroads into the domain of the non-magical and the well-known, and we shall never escape from the moralistic and surgical theatre.

[*OC*, V, 16–17]

An Affective Athleticism (*Un athlétisme affectif*)

One must grant the actor a kind of affective musculature matching the bodily localization of our feelings.

An actor is like a physical athlete, with this astonishing corollary; his affective organism is similar to the athlete's, being parallel to it like a double, although they do not act on the same level.

The actor is an athlete of the heart.

In his case the whole man is also separated into three worlds; the affective area is his own.

It belongs to him organically.

The muscular movements of physical exertion are a likeness, a double of another exertion, located in the same points as stage movements.

The actor relies on the same pressure points an athlete relies on to run, in order to hurl a convulsive curse whose course is driven inward.

Similar anatomical bases can be found in all the feints in boxing, all-in-wrestling, the hundred metres, the high jump and the movements of the emotions, since they all have the same physical support points.

With this further rider that the moves are reversed and in anything to do with breathing, for instance, an actor's body relies on breathing while with a wrestler, a physical athlete, the breathing relies on his body.

The question of breathing is of prime importance; it is inversely proportional to external expression.

The more inward and restrained the expression, the more ample, concentrated and substantial breathing becomes, full of resonances.

Whereas breathing is compressed in short waves for ample, fiery externalized acting.

We can be sure that every mental movement, every feeling, every leap in human affectivity has an appropriate breath.

These breathing *tempi* have a name taught us by the Cabbala, for they form the human heart and the gender of our emotional activity.

An actor is merely a crude empiricist, a practitioner guided by vague instinct.

Yet on no account does this mean we should teach him to rave.

What is at stake is to end this kind of wild ignorance in the midst of which all present theatre moves, as if through a haze, constantly faltering. A gifted actor instinctively knows how to tap and radiate certain powers. But he would be astonished if he were told those powers which make their own substantial journey *through the senses* existed, for he never realized they could actually exist.

To use his emotions in the same way as a boxer uses his muscles, he must consider a human being as a Double, like the Kha of the Egyptian mummies, like an eternal ghost radiating affective powers.

As a supple, never-ending apparition, a form aped by the true actor, imposing the forms and picture of his own sensibility on it.

Theatre has an effect on this Double, this ghostly effigy it moulds, and like all ghosts this apparition has a long memory. The heart's memory endures and an actor certainly thinks with his heart, for his heart holds sway.

This means that in theatre more than anywhere else, an actor must become conscious of the emotional world, not by attributing imaginary merits to it, but those with concrete meaning. [. . .]

To reforge the links, the chain of a rhythm when audiences saw their own real lives in a show, we must allow audiences to identify with the show breath by breath and beat by beat.

It is not enough for the audience to be riveted by the show's magic and this will never happen unless we know where *to affect them*. We have had enough of chance magic or poetry which has no skill underlying it.

In theatre, poetry and skill must be associated as one from now on.

Every emotion has an organic basis and an actor changes his emotional voltage by developing his emotions within him.

The key to throwing the audience into a magical trance is to know in advance what pressure points must be affected in the body. But theatre poetry has long become unaccustomed to this invaluable kind of skill.

To be familiar with the points of localization in the body is to reforge the magic links.

Using breathing's hieroglyphics, I can rediscover a concept of divine theatre.

N.B. – In Europe no one knows how to scream any more, particularly actors in a trance no longer know how to cry out, since they do nothing but talk, having forgotten they have a body on stage, they have also lost the use of their throats. Abnormally shrunk, these throats are no longer organs but monstrous, talking abstractions. French actors now only know how to talk.

[*CW*, 4, 100–6; *OC*, IV, 125–32]

Text written for the literary magazine *Mesures* at the end of 1935, with its companion piece 'Seraph's Theatre'. *Mesures* did not publish the articles. Then, on publication of *The Theatre and Its Double*, an editorial mix-up led to the exclusion of 'Seraph's Theatre' from the first edition of the book (see *CW*, 4, 113–17; *OC*, 141–6 and also *OC*, IV, 328–31). It is excluded here for lack of space.

Theatre and Culture (*Le théâtre et la culture*)

At a time when life itself is in decline, there has never been so much talk about civilization and culture. And there is a strange correlation between this universal collapse of life at the root of our present-day demoralization, and our concern for a culture that has never tallied with life but is made to tyrannize life.

Before saying anything further about culture, I consider the world is hungry and does not care about culture and people artificially want to turn these thoughts away from hunger and direct them towards culture.

The most pressing thing seems to me not so much to defend a culture whose existence never stopped a man worrying about going hungry or about a better life, but to derive from what we term culture, ideas whose living power is the same as hunger.

Above all, we need to live and believe in what keeps us alive, to believe something keeps us alive, nor should every product of the mysterious recesses of the self be referred back to our grossly creature concerns.

What I mean is this: our immediate need is to eat, but it is even more important not to waste the pure energy of being hungry simply on satisfying that immediate need.

If confusion is a sign of the times, I see a schism between things and words underlying this confusion, between ideas and the signs that represent them.

We are not short of philosophical systems; their number and contradictions are a characteristic of our ancient French and European culture. But where do we see that life, our lives, have been affected by these systems?

I would not go so far as to say philosophical systems ought to be directly or immediately applied, but we ought to choose between the following:

1. Either these systems are part of us and we are so steeped in

them we live them, therefore, what use are books?

2. Or we are not steeped in them and they are not worth living. In that case what difference would their disappearance make?

I must insist on this idea of an active culture, a kind of second breath growing within us like a new organ, civilization as applied culture, governing even our subtlest acts, the spirit alive in things. The distinction between civilization and culture is artificial, for these two words apply to one and the same act.

We judge a civilized man by the way he behaves – he thinks as he behaves. But we are already confused about the words 'civilized man'. Everyone regards a cultured, civilized man as someone informed about systems, who thinks in systems, forms, signs and representations.

In other words, a monster who has developed to an absurd degree that faculty of ours for deriving thoughts from actions instead of making actions coincide with thoughts.

If our lives lack fire and fervour, that is to say continual magic, this is because we choose to observe our actions, losing ourselves in meditation on their imagined form, instead of being motivated by them.

This faculty is exclusively human. I would even venture to say it was the infection of humanity which marred ideas that ought to have remained sacred. Far from believing man invented the supernatural and the divine, I think it was man's eternal meddling that ended up corrupting the divine.

At a time when nothing holds together in life any longer, when we must revise all our ideas about life, this painful separation is the reason why things take revenge on us, and the poetry we no longer have within us and are no longer able to rediscover in things suddenly emerges on the adverse side. Hence the unprecedented number of crimes, whose pointless perversity can only be explained by our inability to master life.

Although theatre is made as an outlet for our repressions, a kind of horrible poetry is also expressed in bizarre acts, where changes in the facts of life show its intensity undiminished, needing only to be better directed.

But however we may cry out for magic, at heart we are afraid of pursuing life wholly under the sign of real magic.

Thus our deep-rooted lack of culture is surprised at certain awe-inspiring anomalies; for example, on an island out of contact with present-day civilization, the mere passage of a ship carrying only healthy passengers can induce the outbreak of diseases unknown on that island, but peculiar to our countries; shingles, influenza, catarrh, rheumatism, sinusitis and polyneuritis, etc., etc.

Similarly, if we think blacks smell, we are unaware that everywhere except in Europe, we, the whites, smell. I might even say we smell a white smell, white in the same way as we speak of 'the whites'.

Just as iron turns white hot, so we could say everything extreme is white. For Asians, white has become a mark of final decomposition. [. . .]

But true theatre, because it moves and makes use of living instruments, goes on stirring up shadows, while life endlessly stumbles along. An actor does not repeat the same gestures twice, but he gesticulates, moves, and although he brutalizes forms, as he destroys them he is united with what lives on behind and after them, producing their continuation.

Theatre, which is nothing, but uses all languages (gestures, words, sound, fire and screams), is to be found precisely at that point where the mind needs a language to bring about its manifestations.

And confining theatre to one language, speech, written words, music, lighting or sound, heralds its imminent ruin, since choosing one single language proves the inclinations we have for the facilities of that language. But one effect of a single language's limitations is that it dries up.

For theatre, just as for culture, the problem remains to designate and direct shadows. And theatre, not confined to any fixed language or form, destroys false shadows because of this and prepares the way for another shadowed birth, uniting the true spectacle of life around it.

To shatter language in order to contact life means creating or recreating theatre. The crucial thing is not to believe this action must remain sacred, that is to say, set apart. And the main thing is to believe not that anyone can do it but that one needs to prepare for it.

This leads us to reject man's usual limitations and powers and infinitely extends the frontiers of what we call reality.

We must believe in life's meaning renewed by theatre, where man fearlessly makes himself master of the unborn, gives birth to it. And everything unborn can still be brought to life provided we are not satisfied with remaining simple recording instruments.

Moreover when we say the word *life*, we understand this is not life recognized by externals, by facts, but the kind of frail moving source forms never attain. And if there is one truly infernal and damned thing left today, it is our artistic dallying with forms, instead of being like those tortured at the stake, signalling through the flames.

[*CW*, 4, 1–6; *OC*, IV, 9–14]

This, the preface, is the last text that Artaud wrote for the publication of his collected essays under the title *The Theatre and Its Double*. The contract was signed on 17 December 1936 and the preface was written at that time; it was subsequently revised at proof stage in April 1937.

Theatre and the Gods (*Le théâtre et les dieux*)

I have not come here bearing a surrealist message; I have come to tell you that surrealism is no longer fashionable in France: and many things which are no longer fashionable in France continue to be copied outside France as if they were representative of the thinking within the country.

The surrealist position is a negative position, and I have come to tell you what a whole body of young people in my country is thinking, young people hungry for positive solutions and wanting to regain their lust for life. And what they are thinking is what they are going to do.

The current aspirations of young people in France are not something you can talk about in books or in newspapers as you would to describe a peculiar illness or a strange epidemic which has nothing to do with life.

Among young French people an epidemic of the mind is spreading which should not be seen as an illness, for it is a dreadful challenge. It is a sign of the times that ideas are ideas no more, but a desire about to turn to action.

In everything which is currently developing in France, there is a desire which is ready to turn to action.

When the young artist Balthus paints a portrait of a woman, he is expressing his desire genuinely to transform the woman, to make her conform to his way of thinking. He is expressing through his picture, a dreadful, challenging notion of love and of the woman; and he knows he is not spitting into the wind, for his painting possesses the secret of action.

He paints like one who might know the secret of lightning.

As long as the secret of lightning is not applied, the world thinks that it is part of science and leaves it to the scientists; but one day someone will apply the secret of lightning and he will apply it to the destruction of the world; and that's when the world will begin to take this secret into account.

Young people want to relate the secrets of things to their numerous applications.

And that, too, is an idea of culture which is not taught in the Universities; for behind this idea of culture is an idea of life which can only upset the Universities because it destroys their teachings.

This idea of life is magical, it assumes the presence of a fire in all the expressions of human thought; and this image of human thought which catches fire appears to us all today to be contained in theatre; and we believe that theatre exists only to express it. But today most people think that theatre bears no relation to reality. When we speak of something which caricatures reality, everyone thinks that it is theatre; whereas there are many of us in France who believe that true theatre alone can show reality.

Europe is in a state of advanced civilization: I mean that it is very sick. The tendency of young people is to react against this state of advanced civilization.

They didn't need Keyserling or Spengler to sense the universal decay of a world based on false ideas about life, the relics of the Renaissance. Life seems to us to be in a state of acute desolation. And in order to feel this state of acute desolation we do not need a new philosophy.

Things are such that we can say that, whereas in other ages young people aspired to love, had dreams of ambition, of material success, of fame, today they have dreams of life; and it is to this life that they are aspiring and which they are pursuing, may I say, *in its essence*: they want to know why life is sick and what has debased the idea of life.

To find out, they are looking at the whole universe. They want to understand nature and Man into the bargain. Not the exceptional in Man, but the greatness in Man just as in nature.

When we talk to them of Nature, they ask which Nature we are talking about today. For they know that, as there are three Internationals, so there are three natures, three-tiered Natures.

That, too, is part of science.

'There are three suns,' said Emperor Julian, 'only the first of which is visible.' And Julian the Apostate cannot be suspected of falling into Christian Spirituality, being one of the last representatives of the SCIENCE of the Ancients.

Into Nature young people insert Man; as they see from the outside into the tiers of Nature, so they see Man in tiers.

And young people know that it is this grand idea of man and nature, which theatre can give them.

They don't think they are betraying life with such a high idea of theatre, but they think, on the contrary, that theatre can help them cure life.

There are ten thousand ways of dealing with life and of belonging to one's time. We do not think that, in a disorganized world, intellectuals should indulge in pure speculation. As for the ivory tower, we no longer know what it is. Intellectuals too should commit themselves to their time; but we don't think that they can commit themselves in any other way than by taking up arms against it.

War to achieve peace.

In the current catastrophe of the mind we are pointing the finger at a monstrous ignorance; and there is a very strong wave of opinion for this ignorance to be cauterized; I mean to be scientifically cauterized.

Life for us is neither a lazaret, nor a sanatorium nor even a laboratory, and anyway we don't think that a culture can be taught through words or through ideas. It is not through the surface of social behaviour that a civilization evolves. Before taking pity on the people, it is our aim to revive the forgotten virtues of a people who might thus, by itself, achieve self-civilization.

So I am saying that young people who are not worried but are being made to worry, made to worry because of what appears to resemble, but doesn't actually come close to what they are thinking, are pointing the finger at the ignorance of the time.

They see the ignorance of the time and they rebel against it.

When they learn that the medicine of the Chinese, an age-old medicine, was able to cure cholera by age-old methods, whereas the medicine to combat cholera in Europe still only knows the barbaric methods either of running away or of cremating the dead, they will not be satisfied with introducing this medicine to Europe, but will think of the corruption of the European mind and will seek to cure this mind.

They understand that it is not by a trick but through a deep understanding that China was able to fathom the nature of cholera.

It is this understanding which constitutes culture. And there are some secrets of culture which texts don't teach.

As opposed to the culture of Europe which is contained in written texts and pretends that culture is lost if the texts are destroyed, I am saying that there is another culture by which previous generations have lived, and this culture is based on a materialistic conception of the mind.

As opposed to the Europeans who know nothing but their body and who could never dream of being able to organize nature since they do not see beyond the body, the Chinese, for example, possess an understanding of nature through a science of the mind.

They understand the degrees of vacuity and density which describe the measurable states of the soul; and on the three hundred and eighty points of the physiological functioning of the soul, the Chinese are able to identify nature and its illnesses and we can say that they have been able to identify the nature of illnesses.

Jacob Boehme, who only believes in his mind, can tell when minds are sick; and he describes in the whole of nature the states which reveal the Anger of the Mind.

These insights, and many others, too, give us a new notion of Man. And we want to be taught once more what Man is, since we knew in former times.

We are beginning to reveal *the Taboos* with which a petrified and petty-minded science has masked the vestiges of a culture, which was able to explain life.

Whole man, man with his cry which can ride the path of a storm, this, for Europe, is poetry, but for us who have a synthetic notion of culture, to relate to the cry of the storm is to rediscover a secret of life.

Throughout the world today there is a trend which is a demand for culture, the demand for an organic and profound notion of culture which might explain the life of the mind.

I call organic culture a culture based on the mind connected to the organs, and the mind steeped in all the organs, responding to one another at the same time.

There is, in such a culture, a notion of space and I say that true culture can only be taught in space, and that it is a culture with a purpose, just as theatre has a purpose.

Culture in space means culture of a mind which never stops breathing and feeling alive in space and which summons up the bodies of space like the very objects of its thought, but which, as far as the mind is concerned, is located *in the dead centre of space*, in other words, in a neutral void.

This is perhaps a metaphysical idea, this idea of the dead neutral in space through which the mind must pass.

But without metaphysics, it isn't culture. And what do we mean by this idea of space being propelled all of a sudden into culture, if not the assertion that culture is inseparable from life.

'Thirty spokes meet in the centre', says Tao te King of Lao-Tseu, 'but it's the void in the middle which makes the wheel go round.'

When there is harmony between the ways men think, where else can we say that this harmony is achieved, but in the dead void of space?

Culture is a movement of the mind which passes from the void to forms and from these forms returns to the void as to death. To be cultured is to burn down the forms, burn down the forms to achieve life. It is to learn to stand upright amidst the continual movement of forms which are successively destroyed.

The ancient Mexicans never knew any other approach than this passing to and fro between death and life.

This dreadful, internal disposition, this act of breathing, that is culture, that which stirs simultaneously in nature and in the mind.

'But that is metaphysics, and we can't live in metaphysics.'

So what I am saying precisely is that life must be restored into metaphysics, and this difficult approach which terrifies the people of today is the approach of all pure races who have always *felt themselves to be simultaneously* in death and in life.

That is why culture is not written down and why, as Plato says, 'Thought was lost the day a single word was written down.'

To write is to prevent the mind from stirring or breathing freely in the midst of fixed forms. Since writing fixes the mind and crystallizes it in a form and from that form is born idolatry.

True theatre, like culture, has never been written down.

Theatre is an art of space and it's by pressing on the four points of space that is has a chance of affecting life. It is in the space haunted by theatre that things find their shape, and beneath the shapes is the clamour of life.

There is a tendency to separate theatre from everything which is not space and cast back the language of the text to books, from which it never should have come. And this language of space in turn acts upon the nervous system and ripens the landscape stretched out beneath it.

I don't have to repeat the theory of theatre in space which acts simultaneously through gesture, movement and sound.

By occupying space it stalks life and drives it out of its lair.

It is like the six-pointed cross which extends a supernatural geometry over the walls of certain temples in Mexico. The Mexican cross is always ringed, it is at the centre of a wall, it derives from a magical idea.

To make the cross, the ancient Mexican places himself at the centre of a kind of void and the cross moves around him.

It is not a cross with codifies space as some scientists believe today, it is a cross which reveals how life enters space and how it rediscovers from outside space the very essence of life.

Always the void, always the fixed point around which matter builds up.

The Mexican cross denotes the rebirth of life.

For a long time I looked at the Gods of Mexico in the Codex and it seemed to me that these Gods were above all Gods in space and that the Mythology of the Codex was concealing a science of space with its Gods like shadow-holes, and its shadows where life is rumbling.

I am saying, in all sincerity, that these Gods are not born by chance but are present in life as in a theatre and they make up the four corners of the consciousness of Man where sound, gesture, words and breathing which belches out life are concealed.

Who still thinks of the Gods and of looking for the seat of the Gods. To look for their seat is to look for their strength and to confer on oneself the strength of a God. The White world calls these Gods idols, but the Indian mind is able to stir up the strength of the Gods by locating their musical strengths; and theatre, through a musical distribution of strengths, summons up the power of the Gods. Each one has his place in a space which pulsates with images. The Gods appear to us through a cry or a face and the colour of the face has its cry; and the cry is worth its weight in images in Space where Life is maturing.

For me, these revolving Gods which get tangled up with lines, lines which probe space as if they were afraid of not exploring space enough, offer us a concrete means of understanding the structure of life. This fear of the empty space which obsesses the Mexican artists and which prompts them to cast line upon line, isn't only a fabrication of lines, of shapes pleasing to the eye, it implies the need to make the void *mature*. Filling space to conceal the void is to find the way to the void. It is like starting from a line in its ascendant and plunging breathtakingly down again into the void.

And the Gods of Mexico which revolve around the void provide a kind of coded means of rediscovering the strengths of a void without which it is not part of reality.

And to conclude, I think that the Gods of Mexico are the Gods of life, prey to a loss of strength, to a giddiness of thought; and the lines which rise above their heads provide a melodious and rhythmical means of making thought rise above thought.

They call on the mind not to become fossilized, but on the contrary, so to speak, *to walk*.

'I am marching as to war', the God seems to be saying as he holds in his fist a weapon of war which he carries before him. 'And as well as marching, I think', says a kind of flashing line which zigzags above his head. – And this line, at some point in space, multiplies anew.

'And if I think, I test my strength,' says the line which is behind him. 'I summon the strength from whence I came.'

That is how, in their inhuman form, these Gods who are not content with their simple stature of man, show how man can emerge from it. – For I think, moreover, that there is a harmony in these lines, a kind of essential geometry which corresponds to the image of a sound.

In the theatre, a line is a sound, a movement is music, and the gesture which emerges from a sound is like a key word in a sentence.

The Gods of Mexico have open lines, they indicate everything which has emerged, but at the same time provide the means of going back into something.

The Mythology of Mexico is an open Mythology. And the Mexico of yesterday and the Mexico of today likewise possess open strengths. There is no need to go very far into a Mexican landscape to sense everything which emanates from it. It is the only place on earth which offers us a life of the occult, and *offers it on the surface of life*.

[*OC*, VIII, 196–206]

This is the text of the third lecture which Artaud was invited to deliver at the University of Mexico-City on 29 February 1936. It was first published, in Spanish translation, in *El Nacional*, Mexico, 24 May 1936.

After the failure of *The Cenci* and having submitted the manuscript of *The Theatre and Its Double* to his publisher, Artaud felt the need for a complete change of scene and he decided to go to Mexico since that land, with its fervent religiosity, ancient cultures and civilization, had long acted as a magnet to him. He left for Havana (Cuba) from the Belgian port of Antwerp on 10 January 1936 and arrived, almost penniless, in Mexico-City on 7 February. The three lectures he gave at the university were extremely well received both by the audience and press. They were: 'Surrealism and Revolution' (26 February, *OC*, VIII, 171–83); 'Man Against Fate' (27 February, *OC*, VIII, 184–95) and 'Theatre and the Gods'.

Artaud returned to France on 12 November, in poor health and financially bankrupt. He was unable to receive treatment for his drug addiction for lack of funds and had to rely on the charity of friends. Jean Paulhan, in particular, came to his rescue. Early in 1937 Artaud busied himself with the correction of the proofs of *The Theatre and Its Double*.

A Medea Without Fire (*Une Médée sans feu*)

Seneca's Medea is a mythical world. Margarita Xirgu has no spark and fails to reach such a world. Myths must not be debased, and if they are, we can just as well resign ourselves to being mere mortals, and what pitiful anthropomorphism that would be. That's how we expose ourselves as men, and how we expose ourselves to man, small in stature, faint in voice, in short, naked.

In this tragedy monsters should have pounced, we should have been shown that we are amongst monsters, the monsters of primitive imagination seen through a primitive mind. Monsters cannot readily be approached. Jason and Medea are inaccessible to one another: they both have their circle, they both keep within their circle. To get to her, Jason must force his way through the gods; the same for Medea. One god facing another god. At all times the atmosphere of the drama is conveyed at fever pitch.

The ancients drew on a whole range of tragic paraphernalia: buskins, life-size puppets, masks: symbolism of masks, lines and costumes. Not to be seen from afar in order to overwhelm man and bring him down to size.

'I call upon you with a voice of doom,' says Medea, 'a voice which calls forth crimes, which invents and imagines crimes.' What is special about modern theatre is that we are systematically losing the opportunity to present tragedy, in other words, really to rip our attention apart through crime. Our theatre cheats for it is afraid of dealing with the powers that be, real powers from which we cannot possibly escape.

There is a technique in tragedy.

Material and ornamental technique.

Physiological technique.

And psychological technique.

Its aim is really to deceive the senses; that's why it is necessary in the first place not to arouse them. Theatre is a world of real illusion. The imagination of the spectator wants to believe in what it sees, but to show wobbling sets painted to deceive the eye, not only deceives the eye, it also drives it to despair and to loathing, and the eye would indeed laugh at it if it could.

In Xirgu's Medea three moth-eaten dustcloths are suspended supposedly evoking Cyclopean mountains. And to crown it all these mountains are stylized. I cannot stomach such stylization on a dirty dustcloth. It was Gordon Craig who invented the system, but in Europe we have literally been swamped with stylizations *à la* Gordon Craig. Of an even dirtier colour are the bags worn by the servants who sprawl out as they come in head first.

I particularly recommend to you the chorus, a chorus of warriors with pink-coloured arms who look as if they had come straight from a hospital for sick children. They are all covered in green sheets, as if a hundred billiard tables had been stripped to dress them.

Creon's costume is the most unbelievable of all. He wears a shoulder belt, a rosary of acanthus leaves, each one as big as an elephant's thigh. If this garland of wildflower leaves is intended to signify his kingship, then it portrays kings as drunken tramps. And if many kings are, actually, in the habit of getting drunk and possess the degenerate souls of tramps, the mythical kings should offer us a superior image of kingship. Modern theatre directors no longer have any concept of true royal power, nor any understanding of tragedy.

It's not by making the *music-hall* lighting shine on the dustcloths which I have just described that one could convey the supernatural feeling of terror which springs from the truly magical text of Seneca who was a real initiate, whereas the modern tragedians are nothing but puppets and tumblers.

On stage, objects must be taken for what they are; this is, as I see it, the only means of creating scenic illusion. You cannot take a dustcloth and try to pass it off as a mountain, but take a mountain and use it as a dustcloth. Of course you cannot transport a mountain on stage, but it's possible to set up a mirror and have it reflect a mountain. The technique lies in not seeking to represent what cannot be represented.

All the genuine theatrical traditions have, in all ages, despised reality, but never have they substituted it with ramshackle artifice. Wherever he be, the actor acts with real-life objects; tables, chairs, cupboards, ladders, and he sticks to these objects; the rest he creates by gestures. The set is in his arms, in his body, in his feet, in his hands, in his eyes, and above all, in his face which is as changeable as a landscape in which the clouds would delight in hiding the sun. But that doesn't prevent natural objects from undergoing a real psychological demonetization: as they change their plans they change their value because their psychological situation is new, strange, surprising and unexpected. The lighting, embellishing everything as if by magic, adds either to the illusion or to the disillusion. For the lighting has an intellectual value; it doesn't merely illuminate objects. On stage objects become monsters to whom the spoken word, gesture and movement of the actors lend a supernatural soul.

Tragedy is born of myth. All tragedy is the representation of a great myth. The language of myths is symbol, allegory. Allegory appears through signs. There is a language of signs which belongs to the plastic arts and to the tragic set.

Xirgu's performance lacks allegorical signs; she has scarcely more than two or three fixed gestures, of hand, head, and arms outstretched.

Symbolic signs also belong to the tragic set as for example, the fasces of lictors, the cross, Mercury's wand. Roman armies used to march behind a cluster of signs. So where were Medea's symbolic emblems . . .

As for the physiological technique which proposes to transform the human voice through the art of breathing and physical control, I must say that it was absent from that Medea. Xirgu shouts relentlessly, without variation, without any inflection in her voice which would make our insides shudder and our souls leap in our bodies. It never enters her head, it seems to me, that the range of the human voice can be tuned to the point where it can be made to chant like a real organ. There are ways of making the voice jump, of making it shimmer like a landscape. There is a whole scale to the voice.

It is on the psychological level, finally, that the poetic gift must operate; it is poetry which enables Jason to come dragging monsters when he enters with the grace of a god. We can have gods appear on stage, we can draw magic circles around unapproachable characters of a myth incarnate but, I repeat, one needs this gift. The principle of it is to introduce on stage the irrational and monstrous logic of dreams, this logic which has you see a face in a hand and which, beginning with a sigh close to the ear, suggests the roar of a hurricane. It's this creation of images which is, in everyday speech, at the origin of the metaphor. With

The Cenci

On 10 February 1935 Artaud wrote to Gide that he had recently put the final touches to a tragedy, *The Cenci*, adapted from Shelley's five-act tragedy written in 1819 and from Stendhal's translation of a sixteenth-century archival manuscript about the Cenci family.

There are, obviously, variations from one version to another but on the whole all three authors follow the same plot which centres on the criminal life of the papal Count François Cenci who committed the most heinous crimes and sexual atrocities: he had two of his sons murdered and built a church in the courtyard of his palace to rejoice daily at the sight of their tombs; he savagely raped his second daughter Beatrice, more – it would seem – to damn her eternal soul through incest than to satisfy his sexual urge. Cenci, for these and other crimes, was jailed three times, but on each occasion he bribed his way out of prison.

As Beatrice could not expect any justice either from the state or the church, she plotted with the help of Cenci's second wife Lucrezia to have her father killed. Two hired assassins did the deed by hammering one nail into Cenci's eye and another into his throat. The women were denounced and tried. Pope Clement VIII, so clement to Cenci, condemned wife and daughter to death and Artaud's play ends on their exit to the gallows.

Artaud's *The Cenci*, as it appears on the page, is often verbose, often melodramatic and should be read as a scenario and not as a literary text. Its production by the Theatre of Cruelty was to be Artaud's first tentative step towards the full realization of his theatre of the future.

The production went into rehearsal at the end of March 1935, but at that time Artaud had neither a full cast nor a theatre. Some of his actors were wealthy amateurs who agreed to put up money in exchange for a good part. So it was that the role of Beatrice was played by Iya Abdy, the Russian-born wife of an English baronet, and her mother, Lucrezia, by Cécile Bressant, the wife of the publisher Robert Denoël. In sharp contrast, many male actors were out of work when they joined the company and badly needed to earn some money. And since money was in short supply some members of the cast had to leave during the rehearsal period in order to accept jobs where they had a better chance of getting paid.

The choice of venue, too, was fraught with difficulty. Artaud would have liked to perform in the prestigious Théâtre des Champs-Élysées but had to settle for the Folies-Wagram, a music-hall, which did not stage 'serious' plays, let alone avant-garde theatre.

Eventually the play opened on 6 May 1935 before an invited audience which responded enthusiastically. But the critics who saw the play on the following night were almost unanimous in their condemnation. *The Cenci* had a wider press coverage than any other play of the season, both before and during the short run, but the press was so derogatory that the play had to close after 17 performances on 22 May 1935. Artistically it proved to be a great disappointment and financially a total disaster. For Artaud himself the experience was devastating.

Artaud's full text can be found in *The Cenci*, Playscript 12, Calder and Boyars, 1969, translated by Simon Watson Taylor. Also in *CW*, 4, 121–53 and in *OC*, IV, 147–210.

An important dossier of Parisian press articles published at the time can be found in *The Drama Review*, Volume 16, Number 2 (T-54), June 1972, 90–145.

To André Gide

10 February 1935, Paris

Dear Sir and friend,

I have just finished a tragedy – complete *with text*, the dialogue, however abridged, is written in full.

This tragedy will be performed at the *Comédie des Champs-Élysées*, at the beginning of April; and rehearsals will begin in the next few days.

But beforehand I intend to give a reading of the play for a few friends. – All the actors will be present at this reading.

I would like to ask you to do me the honour and the favour of attending this reading. I am counting on your presence above all, as well as on several friends such as Jean Paulhan, and here is why.

The dialogue of this tragedy is, dare I say, of the utmost violence. And there is *nothing* which escapes attack among the antiquated notions of Society, order, Justice, Religion, the family and Country.

I am, therefore, expecting some extremely violent response from the audience. That is why I would like to prepare opinion in advance.

There must be no misunderstanding.

Everything which is attacked, is much less so on the Social level than on the Metaphysical level.

It is not pure anarchy. – And this is what must be understood.

Even those who consider themselves to be ideologically the most libertarian, the most detached, the most advanced, remain secretly tied to a certain number of notions which in this play I attack in one fell swoop.

The production must not become a continuous howl of protest.

There is no libertarian ideologically prepared to cast the idea of the family to the four winds, who does not retain a deep-rooted human affection for his father, mother, sisters, brothers, etc.

Nothing, however, is spared in this play. And what I want everyone to understand is that I am attacking the social super-stition of the family, without asking them to take up arms against anyone in particular. The same goes for order, and the same for justice. However opposed to present-day order one may be, an old respect for the idea of order *as such* prevents people from distinguishing between order and those who represent it, and leads them in effect to respect individuals under the pretext of respecting order as such.

But as for the ideological stance which I have taken, I absolutely cannot brook all the niceties which force me temporarily, in order to speed things up, to attack order as such.

These then are the points on which I think opinion must be prepared.

I'm hitting hard to hit fast, but especially to hit conclusively and without recourse.

Since I restrict myself to the realm of pure ideas, I do not have to put up with a whole group of human niceties which would only hamper me and paralyse all action. And what people refuse to take account of is that it is these human niceties which generally paralyse action and which prevent people from doing anything or even attempting anything.

And so I wanted to be done once and for all with all these inhibitions. And that's no reason to think of me as an *out-and-out* anarchist.

It is in this respect that opinion must be prepared. But first the play must be heard in order to get a hint of what I want to come out of it. Besides, those who are afraid of words are the same people who are afraid of action, and that's why nothing is ever done. – And that's why I'm particularly anxious that you should attend this reading; and I must INSIST that you come.

Afterwards you will be able to say the things which must be said; and I have no need to tell you again that what you have to say will always be heard.

No one, however committed he may be to his personal ideology, I should say to his own Mythology, would like, things being as they are, to be taken for a fool. The protestors, however, if it came to it, must be persuaded that by protesting they would be fools beyond question. And this is my drift.

There isn't a man of intelligence or shrewdness who has the right, without losing face, to rebel against the words of a character in the theatre, – given that the character who says what he thinks is representing my own thoughts at the same time, but representing them dramatically, that is to say dynamically, dialectically; – contingent on another word coming to destroy it temporarily, and contingent especially on an ideal atmosphere distorting it at the same time and locating it.

So it is to prevent the audience from confusing ideas with men and, what is more, confusing them with forms

that I am destroying the idea, lest the respect for the idea leads one to spare a form which, in turn, favours the continuation of bad ideas.

That's why I'm counting on your presence and why I'm even asking you to arrange a day or rather an evening after dinner. [. . .]

[*OC*, V, 176–9]

'The Cenci' ('*Les Cenci*')

The Cenci, which will be performed at the Folies-Wagram from 6 May onwards, is not yet the Theatre of Cruelty but is preparing the way for it.

I have drawn my play from Shelley and Stendhal, which does not mean that I have adapted Shelley or imitated Stendhal.

From both of them I have taken the subject, which is, in any case, historical and far more beautiful in nature than the stage or the printed versions.

Shelley added to nature his own style and that language of his which resembles a summer night bombarded by meteors, but personally I prefer nature in the raw.

In writing the tragedy *The Cenci* I have not sought to imitate Shelley any more than I have tried to copy nature, but I have imposed upon my tragedy the movements of nature, that kind of gravitation which moves plants and moves human beings like plants, and which becomes concentrated in the form of the earth's volcanic eruptions.

The whole production of *The Cenci* is based on this gravitational movement.

The gestures and movements in this production are just as important as the dialogue; the purpose of the dialogue is to act as a reagent to the other elements. And I think it will be the first time, at least here in France, that a theatrical text has been written in terms of a production, the modalities of which have sprung fully formed and alive from the author's imagination.

The difference between the Theatre of Cruelty and *The Cenci* will be the difference which exists between the thunder of a waterfall or the unleashing by nature of a hurricane on the one hand and, on the other hand, whatever degree of their violence may remain in their image once it has become established.

This is the reason why it has been impossible to make use of direct sound for *The Cenci*. In order to create a volume of vibration comparable to that of a cathedral's great bell I used a microphone to record Amiens Cathedral's great bell.

Just as they would in the Theatre of Cruelty, the audience at *The Cenci* will find themselves in the centre of a network of sound vibrations; but these, instead of emanating from four actual 30 ft. high bells hanging at the four cardinal points of the auditorium, will be diffused by loudspeakers placed at these same points.

The Cenci will include the presence of human dummies, and in this way, again, I shall achieve the Theatre of Cruelty by devious and symbolic paths.

In *The Cenci* we will, in the first place, be listening to what the characters say; and they say more or less everything that they think; but we shall also find things that no one can say, however great may be his natural sincerity and the depths of his self-awareness. The dummies will be there to force the heroes of the play to describe the things that are troubling them and which human speech is incapable of expressing.

The dummies will be there to formulate all the reproaches, rancour, remorse, anguish and demands, and the play will be filled from one end to the other with a whole language of gestures and signs in which the anxieties of the age will blend together in a violent manifestation of feeling.

The Cenci is a tragedy in the sense that I am the first person for a very long time to have attempted to give speech not just to men but to *beings*, beings each of whom is the incarnation of great forces, while still retaining just enough human quality to make them plausible from a psychological point of view.

As though in a dream, we witness these beings roaring, spinning around, flaunting their instincts or their vices, passing like great storms in which a sort of majestic fate vibrates.

We have not yet reached the domain of the Gods, but we have almost reached the domain of the heroes such as they were conceived to be in antiquity. In any case, the characters in *The Cenci* possess this exalted, legendary aspect, this atmosphere of rashness and bewilderment shining through the clouds which one finds in the heroes of the great romances and marvellous epics.

It seems to me that *The Cenci* returns the theatre to its true path and enables it to recapture that almost human dignity without which it can only waste the audience's time completely.

The Cenci, Grove Press, NY, 1970 (translated by Simon Watson Taylor); *OC*, V, 37–9. First published in the literary magazine *La Bête noire*, No. 2, 1 May 1935.

The Tragedy 'The Cenci' at the Folies-Wagram (*Ce que sera la tragédie 'Les Cenci' aux Folies-Wagram*)

In *The Cenci*, the father is the destroyer, and in this way the theme may be linked to the Great Myths.

The tragedy *The Cenci* is also a Myth which spells out clearly a few truths.

And it is because *The Cenci* is a Myth that this theme has become a tragedy when transferred to the stage.

I say deliberately a tragedy rather than a drama; for here the men are more than men, even if they are not yet gods.

Neither innocent nor guilty, they are in the power of the same essential amorality which possessed those gods of the Mysteries of Antiquity from whom all tragedy has emanated.

What did the gods mean for the peoples of Antiquity?

Plato devotes page after page to discussing the nature of the gods.

What is certain is that these gods went their own way, oblivious to the petty human distinctions between good and evil, almost as though they equated evil with betraying one's nature, and good with remaining faithful to it, whatever the moral consequences. Indeed the gods never concerned themselves with moral consequences.

I have tried to imbue the characters in my tragedy with the same sort of prodigious amorality that belongs to lightning as it strikes, and to the boiling explosion of a tidal wave.

And I felt strongly that, in an era such as ours, when nature speaks louder than man, it was appropriate to resuscitate an ancient Myth which pierces the heart of today's anxieties.

So much for the theme.

The next step was to make this Myth tangible, to endow it with speech: because even if nature does speak more loudly than mankind, I have the impression that, apart from a few very rare exceptions, the general tendency of the era has been to forget to wake up.

I have attempted to give a jolt to this hypnotic sleep by direct, physical means. Which is why everything in my play revolves, and why each character has his particular *cry*.

I wrote *The Cenci*, a tragedy, because I met an actress capable of a cry without giving in to weakness, – and with strengths which increase as she develops her frenzy.

Iya Abdy as Béatrice will begin to live her life.

An important aspect of the play's *mise en scène* will be an emphasis on symbolic gesticulation where a sign equals a written word.

In other words, gesture for me is just as important as what we call language, because gesture is a language in its own right.

The lighting effects, like gesture, will also stand for a language, and in this attempt to achieve a single, integrated theatrical language light will constantly be associated with sound in order to produce a total effect.

Balthus, the designer of the sets, is just as much at home with the symbolic nature of forms as he is conversant with that of colours; like Désormière, whose musical inventions are a positive unleashing of the sounds of nature, is well aware of the communicative value of these sounds.

Gestures, sounds, noises, scenery, text, lighting: we have tried to offer the theatre-going public of Paris a bold experiment which can compete today with those countries in Europe where the theatre has once again become a religion.

The Cenci, Grove Press, NY, 1970, 10–11 (translated by Simon Watson Taylor); *OC*, V, 40–1. First published in *Le Figaro*, 5 May 1935.

After 'The Cenci' (*Après 'Les Cenci'*)

If there is an inhuman rhythm in *The Cenci*, it is not in the controversial gyration of groups that one should look for it, but in the clock-work precision which I tried to impose on all scenes of dialogue.

Few spectators will have noticed the precision, the strictness, the mathematical entrances and exits of actors moving around one another and creating on the stage a spatial geometry, because we only recognize what we know.

If Orsino describes around the groups which he motivates, around characters whom he individually arouses, circles of birds of prey; if Camillo and Orsino revolve and act around Giacomo in a cellar-like atmosphere, in an underground light like that of a fairground hypnotist around his customer whom he wants to entrance; if Beatrice moves the automaton assassins like pieces on a chessboard, if she swathes them like living mummies, if they both laugh with a simultaneous laugh like out-of-tune organisms; if the veiled guards turn in a circle and move about like the hands of a clock, if they return in succession to their places with the rhythm of a pendulum; that is where this secret gravitation lies, whose subtlety few have seen.

One thing is apparent: once a director escapes from the usual routine, whatever the audience, actors or critics here in France, he is on his own.

The trends he is trying to set will hit him smack in the face; and the emphasis put on Old Cenci is only perceptible because no one else has been able to tune into his wavelength.

Whatever their determination, their deep-rooted desire to do well, one cannot ask of actors who come from all kinds of backgrounds and who, as individuals, have nothing in common, this kind of sacred cohesion, this consciousness of mutual effort which belonged in other countries and in other times to companies with a long tradition in collective work.

To try and create in these conditions a strict geometry with ephemeral groups whom circumstances are soon to separate, represented, it seems to me, a wager which, and this is the stunning result, we have in part won.

[*OC*, V, 45–9. First published in *La Bête noire*, No. 3, 1 June 1935]

To Jean-Louis Barrault

Paris, 14 June 1935

My dear Barrault,

You know in what esteem I hold both your work and all that you are. You will understand, therefore, the spirit in which I speak to you in this letter.

There is no question of your taking the slightest offence at what I am about to say, but I do not want you to be able to harbour even the shadow of a grudge.

I do not believe that a collaboration between us is possible, for if I know what unites us, I see even better what divides us, and that is our *working methods* which, starting from two diametrically opposed points of view, lead to differing results, despite appearances. Several times in my presence you have expressed some reservation at my own personal way of working, arguing that being an author above all, I could not push things far enough, and that, in carrying them through, I was confronting obstacles which I couldn't overcome for lack of work and commitment. However, and this is something I am particularly keen on, I don't believe in watertight compartments, specifically as far as the theatre is concerned. It is at the basis of everything I have written for the last four years and more.

I DON'T WANT the show, directed by myself, to have the slightest nudge or wink which doesn't belong to me. If this was not the case in *The Cenci*, it's because *The Cenci* broke out in part from the framework of the theatre I want to establish and because I have been overwhelmed in the end by the enormity of the task I have set myself.

In short, I don't believe in associations, especially not since Surrealism because I don't believe in the purity of men. No matter how highly I regard you, I believe you are fallible and I don't want to lay myself open to even the slightest risk in that respect.

I cannot bear anyone about me in any undertaking whatsoever, and more than ever now after *The Cenci*. If there are animals to be featured in my play I will have them feature according to the rhythm and expression which I will impose upon them. And I will find the necessary exercises to help them discover this expression, or else it must be shown that I am just a common-or-garden theoretician, which I don't believe I am.

Anyway, I'll tell you again that you have reached the point where you must carry your work through, with your own personal way of understanding certain ideas. As for me I intend to gather my thoughts for a while and try to rid myself at last of the vices that paralyse me. This could take a few months. [. . .]

[*OC*, V, 189–90]

Jean-Louis Barrault, then at the very beginning of what was to become a most distinguished acting and directing career, had been working with Artaud's former teacher, Charles Dullin, at the Atelier Theatre since 1931. During the spring of 1935, as Artaud was rehearsing *The Cenci*, Barrault was directing his first show, due to open at the Atelier almost exactly a month after Artaud's tragedy. Despite his own very busy schedule the young man accepted to assist Artaud in his *mise en scène*. The extent of the collaboration is not clear nor is it clear why

Barrault suddenly decided to quit. It has been suggested that the two men did not see eye to eye, and Artaud's letter would bear this out; it is also probable that Barrault had some harsh things to say about Lady Iya Abdy's lack of professionalism and that he refused to go on working in unsatisfactory conditions.

'Around A Mother' ('*Autour d'une mère*')

Dramatic Action by Jean-Louis Barrault

In Jean-Louis Barrault's show there is a kind of marvellous *centaur-horse*, and the thrill we felt at the sight of it was as great as if, with the entrance of the *centaur-horse*, Jean-Louis Barrault had revived magic for us.

This show is magical in the same way as are the incantations of black witch-doctors, when their tongues slapping their palates bring rain down on the land, when before the exhausted sick man the witch-doctor gives his breathing the form of a strange disease, driving out the sickness with his breath. Thus in Jean-Louis Barrault's show the moment the mother dies, a chorus of cries comes to life.

I do not know if such a success is a masterpiece, but in any case it is an event. When an atmosphere is so transformed, when a hostile audience is suddenly and blindly immersed and invincibly disarmed, we must hail this as an event.

In this show there is a secret strength which wins the audience over, just as great love wins over a soul ripe for revolt.

Great, youthful love, youthful vigour, spontaneous, lively ebullience flow among the exact moves, the stylized, calculated gesticulation like the warbling of songbirds through colonnades of trees in a magically arranged forest.

Here, in this religious atmosphere, Jean-Louis Barrault improvises a wild horse's movements, and we suddenly see he has turned into a horse.

His show proves the irresistible operations of gesture, it triumphantly demonstrates the importance of gesture and spatial movement. Stage perspective is restored to a position of importance it should never have lost. Finally he turns the stage into a living, moving place.

This show was organized in relation to the stage, *on* stage; it only comes alive on stage and there is not one point in stage perspective which does not assume a thrilling message.

There is a kind of immediate, physical aspect in this lively gesticulation, in the disjointed unfolding of figures, something as convincing as solace itself which the memory will never forget.

Nor will one forget the mother's death, her spatial and temporal cries, the epic river crossing, anger rising in the hearts of men corresponding on a gestural level to the rising of another anger, especially that kind of man-horse weaving in and out of the play as if a legendary spirit had come down among us.

Up to now only the Balinese Theatre seemed to have retained any trace of the latter spirit.

What difference does it make if Jean-Louis Barrault has revived a religious spirit by profane, descriptive means, if everything genuine is sacred, if the gestures are so fine they assume symbolic meaning?

Indeed, there are no symbols in Jean-Louis Barrault's play. And if we were to criticize his gestures at all, it is because they present a symbolic allusion while they ought to define reality. Thus, however fiery their action on us may be, it does not extend beyond itself.

It does not do so because it is merely descriptive, because it narrates external facts without any soul, because it does not touch either thoughts or souls on the raw, and it is here, rather than in the problem of knowing whether this is a theatrical form, that any criticism we may have of it can be made.

It uses theatrical means – for theatre which opens the physical field requires this field to be filled, for stage space to be furnished with gestures, for this space to be brought to life magically within itself, for an aviary of sounds to be unleashed and new relations found between sound, gestures and voices – we could say that what Jean-Louis Barrault has accomplished is theatre.

But on the other hand, this production does not share a theatrical state of mind, I mean deep drama, mystery deeper than souls, the lacerating conflict between souls where gesture is merely a way. Where man is only a point and life drinks at its source. But who has ever drunk at the source of life?

[*CW*, 4, 109–10; *OC*, IV, 135–7]

First published in the *Nouvelle Revue Française*, No. 262, 1 July 1935.

Autour d'une mère, a 'dramatic action' devised by Jean-Louis Barrault, was based on William Faulkner's novel *As I Lay Dying*. The show, a mixture of mime and of traditional theatre, directed by Barrault was performed by a small cast headed by Barrault himself and included Génica Athanasiou in one of the leading roles. Artaud was enthusiastic about the production and he was convinced that he had written a most complimentary review despite the many reservations that are clearly apparent (see also *OC*, IV, 325–7).

A further text, possibly a draft of the review, betrays the same ambiguous attitude towards Barrault's work (*CW*, 4, 187–8; *OC*, IV, 255):

Theatre may be a clash of gestures, words, movement and sound, but above all it is conflict, a call to opposing forces, shocks solved in time more than in space.

In Barrault's play there are spatial shocks but no temporal ones, so to speak.

Yet this is a religious show. It points to the reappearance of an ancient, religious mood in theatre, showing that *Around A Mother* has renewed its links with Tradition. But I repeat, if it is religious it is so by dint of applying itself and because it renders a kind of higher dignity to human gestures, their most intense meaning. It demonstrates the beauty of nature's movements when we evoke them in an absolute light. But it does not depict the gestures of emotion. And what one calls soul does not enter into it. The symbolic vision in gestures applies above all to things in the soul, but the love emanating from this show can be traced to the body alone. Thus, to my way of thinking, if it is not total theatre, it is undeniably theatre since it recalls true theatre's ways and means, used with incredible success.

Certainly, when Barrault takes gestures or an acting area, he brings them to life, that is gesture from the plastic aspect and space from a material aspect, and in so doing, he reaches the mind but never plunges into mystery and so we may say his show has neither the mystery nor the mind of theatre.

Barrault endlessly travels between mind and matter.

Part Seven

Religion and Sexuality (Rodez 1943–6)

Artaud, Religion and Sexuality

As with the question of Artaud's mental state, the problems raised by his attitude towards religion and sex, inextricably entwined with, and symptomatic of, his attitude towards the theatre, cannot be solved satisfactorily, certainly not by anyone who has an axe to grind. Ironically Artaud's atheist friends are just as bigoted, if not more so, than his devoutly Catholic family, and many a commentator discusses his bizarre notions of virgin birth with apparent approval. Artaud's attitude towards sex, by no means confined to its religious dimension, became more and more complicated as time went on. At Rodez, and later in Paris, he almost invariably linked the two subjects together.

All his life Artaud was interested in religion and esoteric writings and practices. In Rodez he wrote: 'I've spent my life looking for all kinds of sects throughout the world who work on the awareness of people and I believe that I know them all . . . The most dangerous are those which claim they do not indoctrinate people but work nonetheless, day and night, through the occult, finding strength in the mystery of the human body.'

Artaud was both fascinated and repelled by religious systems and doctrines – as he was attracted and disgusted by sex, the body and theatre. According to Hutin ('Artaud et les doctrines ésotériques', *T.d.f.*, 122, 113–16), he was most interested in Gnosticism which attributes the creation of the material world to the work of an evil, imperfect and perverse deity. Artaud, like the Gnostics, believed in the redemption of the spirit from matter (evil and perceived as the only reality) through knowledge. He also happened to believe that the necessary knowledge would best be acquired through the medium of theatre.

His most ambivalent feelings were aroused by the religion closest to him: Catholicism as made flesh in Christ. At one extreme, Christ represented for Artaud all the evil of the world, at the other Christ was none other than Artaud himself and it was Artaud in person who had suffered the Passion on the Cross. Paradoxically, when Artaud dissociated himself from the figure of Christ, he accused Him of all kinds of sexual turpitudes and of having brought the sins of the flesh to humanity.

During the last ten years of his life Artaud went through successive phases of acceptance and rejection of religious belief, of devout adoration and uncontrolled blasphemy. 'During a given period of his life he could be simultaneously a Catholic prostrate with adoration or utterly sacrilegious, spitting out profane abuse on the name of God and all the saints; he could be thankful to doctor Ferdière for his devotion and call him a pig; reject his mother and write her letters filled with filial tenderness'. (*T.d.f.*, 1977, 135)

In a letter to Parisot, dated 10 December 1943, he affirmed that his initiation into the Indian cult of the peyotl was bestowed on him by Christ and in Rodez he behaved, and often spoke, like a devout Christian, going to confession, attending Mass and taking Holy Communion. On 18 October 1943, he wrote: '. . . I have returned to the faith of my forefathers, in all simplicity. And, since I have been taking communion three times a week here for the past two months all erotic thoughts have left me and my conscience is at peace.' But towards the end of his stay at Rodez, his devotion turned to blasphemy and in September 1945 he declared that it was idiotic for anyone to suggest that he had ever become a Christian convert since 'christ has always been what I most abhor'.

The links between religion and sexuality are nowhere expressed with more clarity than in a letter he wrote to one of the doctors who treated him at Rodez and whom he wanted to convert to a chaste way of life, although all he could reproach the doctor with was that he was married:

> Christ's law is the law of all that is Virgin, incarnate in the Holy Virgin Mary and made manifest on Calvary in the Mystery of the Cross. For God wishes that his creature be and remain chaste and virgin for all eternity. And men by perpetuating themselves through the filthy act of copulation have betrayed God's law and have enslaved themselves to the Antichrist and to Satan. And that is Adam's real sin.

The idea that God created man without sexual or digestive organs is repeated obsessively and leads Artaud to affirm ever more stridently that he was the son of no woman, but that he was born of his own suffering: 'je ne suis né que de ma douleur' (to Parisot, 7.9.45). Such a birth, or re-birth, essentially not of the flesh, disincarnate, is what true theatre should bring about.

Reality does not yet exist because the true organs of the human body are not yet created and ordered.

The theatre of cruelty was created to achieve such an order out of chaos and to undertake through a new kind of bodily dance to rid this world of microbes which is nothing more than congealed nothingness.

By whatever angle one tries to approach Artaud's personality, one is inevitably brought back to the theatre as the geometric point of total renewal of man and his absolute purification. In itself the theatrical act is trivial and insignificant, as far as Artaud is concerned, but if such an act becomes the expression of the actor's true and honest hidden life, theatre will be able to generate real life and be capable of transcending any idea of religion, of sexuality, of propagation of the species and lift such actions from the mire in which they are presently stuck.

From 1937 to the end of his life Artaud wrote a great many texts and countless letters on the subject of religion and sexuality. Here are a few samples which should help us in our understanding of his attitude towards art and theatre.

To Anne Manson

2-8-1937

Love binds Humans together,

Sexuality drives them apart.

Only the Man and the Woman who are able to come together above and beyond all sexuality are strong.

But how many are there still left in this divided world which the sexes divide even further.

I know that *your* sexuality is diffuse, rampant, sickly, lavish, and bordering on bestiality.

But how should that affect me?

You possess a rare light which, in the 20 years I have been researching Humans, no Human has ever exhibited to me.

Because of this light, now that I am no longer researching Humans, I accept from you the Sun and the Sea.

Needless to tell you, then, that your everyday, bodily, physical and sensual life is of no interest to me whatsoever, but it is your

Eternal Life which matters to me because, through your Higher Self,
I have seen
that you already touch upon the Eternal
and it is the only thing about you which matters to me.
I hope you understand me this time *once and for all*.

Antonin Artaud

[*OC*, VII, 244–5]

To André Breton

14 September 1937

My dear Breton, My Friend,
[. . .]
Because, André Breton, what you must understand is that the *Incredible*, yes, the Incredible, it is the Incredible which is the truth.

You know yourself who is to become the antichrist, you shook his hand, he is younger than I am, and he loves Life as much as I hate it.

However preposterous this idea may seem to you, the antichrist drinks at the Deux Magots.[1] And another character from the apocalypse has been seen at the Deux Magots as well.

That's how it is and I swear to you I'm not joking. *Here* where I am now, I could hardly be in the mood for joking.

Jesus–christ, this human figure, came to set up on a spiritual level a rite based on the disappearance of things, on the very principle of Human sacrifices. Only fools would think it a matter of slaughter, assassination or Suicide and, since we are in the midst of life, it's about living while denying life, looking at things from the point where they rise up and not from where they fall flat on the ground, looking at them from the point where they are about to disappear and not from where they become entrenched in reality. For in the true doctrine of christ,[2] the Holy Spirit is the entrenched Bourgeois, and christ is the Revolutionary for ever. The 2nd Deity Siva is the revolutionary power, the 3rd Deity Vishnu is conservative.

Choose!

The rite established by christ is the rite of revolutionary High

Magic whose Men-priests, these Eternal entrenched Bourgeois, celebrate Mass which brings on Nausea.

In this rite, Man, as he eats the flesh of a Man who *chose* to sacrifice his life, eats his own evanescence and asserts his contempt for the lasting nature of things, for their *plastic quality*, and for their effigies.

If this rite is not transcendent in its immediate and real celebration, *it does not exist*.

This rite is essential theatre and even in the secret temples of India, Brahmanism which has no rites, has rites of essential theatre.

For even to assert that we do not wish to Exist, we need to rely on beings, in other words on the created. We must touch denied objects to invite them to destroy themselves along with us, at the same time as us. The rite of christ takes features from a denied world and it invites them to disappear but only after *inviting them to take a good look at themselves*.

Things can only properly be denied in the concrete.

I will thus call upon the Black Magicians, on those who deny God in order to destroy him better and who rise up against the Deity which has just forced them to exist. And I will say to them: Your hatred, too, is justified, but it is misdirected. You have means to take your revenge on God, this God which has forced you to live and created the pain of existence.

It is with the brains of Men that you have risen up against God, but Man can do nothing against God, only God himself can act against God. The God who forces you to live is the 3rd Deity, which the Hindus call Vishnu and the Christians, the Holy Spirit. Think God with the brain of a God, rise up against the Holy Spirit, the Son-Siva-christ is with you against the Holy Spirit. Well, the days of the Holy Spirit are numbered, for the end of the world is nigh. The 3 Deities which were equally poised are going to destroy one another, and in order to destroy one another they're going to war against one another and to devour one another.

It will be war, it will be the war of the Son against the Holy Spirit and of the christ against the antichrist. As these two primeval forces of nature join in battle, we understand, don't we, the importance of the battle and the terrible stakes of the battle, but especially the terrible Power of the antichrist supported by the Holy Spirit. Now as the life force is exhausted, the antichrist who will represent life and the fondness for the forms of life will be destroyed but not without destroying himself and having destroyed many things and many people. And woe betide those, don't you agree, faced with a Life which is clearly falling to pieces, woe betide those who desert the side of the antichrist who will be defending life and the joy of living against the Madman who will urge them to give up life and to discover that dying is better. – Because you would be smarter to drift along with the tide than to swim against it.

If you believe me, it is my responsibility to tell you that a formidable power will be placed at your service and at the service of everything beautiful you have ever dreamt of, everything fair, formidable, *incredible* and desperate.

If you don't believe me then I'll have to find someone else who is fair-minded.

But you are the most fair-minded Man I have encountered so far.

Fondly yours,

[*OC*, VII, 286–93]

Breton and Artaud reconciled their differences at the end of 1936 after Artaud's return from Mexico. Artaud kept up his correspondence with Breton until he was committed and resumed it towards the end of his stay at Rodez. The letter of 14 September 1937 was written in Ireland but posted, via a third party, in Paris. Artaud wanted to keep his whereabouts secret, although he had already sent several letters to Breton from Ireland.

1. The Deux Magots is a well-known Parisian café, on the left bank of the Seine, in the 'artistic' quarter of the city, near the church of Saint-Germain-des-Prés, and was one of the favourite haunts of the intelligentsia between the two world wars and up to the sixties.
2. Artaud invariably wrote 'christ' and 'Jésus-christ', without a capital C.

To Frédéric Delanglade

Rodez, 18 July 1943

My dearest friend,

[. . .]

Sin means sex and the flesh, and there has never been any other kind, for all the crimes in the world stem only from the existence of the flesh.

Before the fall of Adam humans knew nothing of this sordid attraction which makes us confuse the impulses of the heart with those of sex, which means we can never have an unselfish, detached and sublime emotion without there being a sexual flutter mixed in. And that indeed is a preposterous crime. – One which has bound these two opposites together, the heart and sexuality.

In the Prophecy of the Great Monarch it is said that one day christ will come back with all the Virgin beings as before the fall of Adam and with Adam himself, and every man would see that he had never really sinned at all because the True Being of Adam was one of the greatest angels and that this Angel had only ever really and truly appeared on earth in the person of Saint John of the Cross, Virgin, never having sinned.

Antonin Artaud, though in receipt of a Mission from heaven, did not remain a Virgin, and that's why God killed him at Ville-Évrard one dramatic night in August 1939, when many miracles and many wonders were unveiled for all to see, but the policy of the police and the French Administration was to ignore and suppress them.

Yet these patent miracles and wonders had many witnesses and Dr Lubtchansky, the house physician at Ville-Évrard at the time could, if need be, testify to them.

The man who has now replaced him is different, a completely different kettle of fish, believe me, because sexual matters have been forever ALIEN to him AND HE CAN NEVER FORGET IT!!!

There is that tale by Stevenson which must appeal to you. It's the tale of an ordinary man, a simple soul, an innocent who, during the night, would light a candle set on the road and remain there for hours in contemplation and in union with the vertical flame, on evenings when the wind didn't blow. I have the impression that there is a similar kind of soul in you and that, in actual fact, only the Love of God is of interest to you, for this flame is the Love of God, and believe me it doesn't fit in with images of human sin. [. . .]

Antonin Nalpas

[*OC*, X, 65–7]

To Doctor J. Latrémolière

Rodez, 19 July 1943

[. . .]

For me sex is infamy and I cannot accept an unchaste man reproaching me for seeing and sensing devils; since he hasn't himself remained a pure Virgin, he bears his share of human responsibility in the production of evil spirits.

The fundamental truth of your heart, Dr Latrémolière, is not like that. The truth is that you are yourself transfixed by evil and that you don't want to admit it because you are so transfixed as not to realize it.

You are under a spell and remain in the clutches of sexuality which is sin, and insist upon it as a married man and that is, for all men on earth, hypocrisy in the face of God.

Yesterday morning you wanted to use *persuasion* on me and couldn't admit that you yourself had been *persuaded* by devils which I could sense talking, *thinking* and living through you.

And that is a pity for you are, in truth, a fair man, with your heart in the right place, and your way of reasoning with me wasn't like a fair man at all. I suffered from what you said to me because the fallacies wrung my heart, but I suffered even more from sensing the Evil Spirit which was speaking through you and which several times wantonly insulted me, as if it were you, by making you believe it was the truth. Several times I saw your own face disappear and through yours appeared another which was nothing but a fraud, a diabolic likeness, the face of a Sadducean Jew. [. . .]

You told me that those who perceive devils not as simple moral temptation but as physical and carnal contacts, and those who are in physical contact with them, I mean those who experience them in reality as if they were Saints and not as those hallucinating in the Asylums, were of greater merit than me, and by saying this, you inflicted an unnecessary wound on me, and this wasn't like you at all.

Antonin Nalpas

[*OC*, X, 75–85]

These two letters are signed 'Antonin Nalpas', Artaud's assumed identity from December 1941 to *c*. August 1943, Nalpas being his mother's maiden name. During that period he referred to 'Antonin

Artaud' in the third person and considered 'him' as a former self 'who had been estranged from God' and who 'died in August 1939 from maltreatment and poisoning'. 'Antonin Nalpas' considered himself to be the successor of Artaud on earth, inhabiting the same body, but a 'renewed and Virgin' body. His two correspondents, the doctor and the painter, were constantly urged to turn away from their sinful life and to embrace a chaste and pure existence in order to ensure their eternal salvation.

Two short extracts from long letters to Latrémolière (July 1943, *OC*, X, 61) and to the playwright Claude-André Puget (18 July 1943, *OC*, X, 73) also signed Antonin Nalpas reiterate the same message:

VIRGINS, Virgins like before the Fall of Adam which was precisely the Fall into *sexuality*. Before Adam, procreation was completely virginal, entirely spiritual and without sex, for sex is Sin, and don't you know that Adam and Saint John of the Cross were one and the same being, but that this Being Saint John of the Cross is the Angel who has never sinned and has never been tainted by the original fall.

and,

. . . Evil, however, has continued because the supernatural has to wend its way to the very flesh before human conscience agrees to defer to God. I believe it's something similar that Alfred Jarry wanted to put across when he produced his *Ubu roi* in the shape of Michelin's Bibendum, but with two little corkscrews on the chest between the spleen and the heart, occupying approximately the same place at which God re-enters the human body, because that's where the hole of the Depths of Infinity for man is. – As all true initiates know. – And I believe it's the Virgin place where Satan's charm does not operate.

To Sonia Mossé

Rodez, 10 October 1943

My dearest Sonia,
[. . .]
My confinement will come to an end, Sonia, the day *all* my friends, all those I love, and whom I have known on this earth, turn *chaste*, pure, fair, uninvolved, as charitable in fact and as *detached* as one can be in this base world which is nothing more than a den of

iniquity. – Man is suffering and he doesn't know what from. He longs for peace and he imagines it will just be given to him *free of charge*. – He is unable to see that if he doesn't manage to rid himself of his misery, it's because he created it himself. And he never ceases to think that it's God or chance. – What a pitiful lapse of thought, what baseness of most artful duplicity with which Satan, who since time immemorial has been keeping a tight rein on consciences, never stops baffling humanity. If man is suffering it's for one reason and one reason only: because he doesn't want to give up sexuality. Jesus–christ has already told him once, but man didn't want to hear his message, and it was because of this Truth which he proclaimed that Jesus–christ was crucified. For this and for no other reason. Jesus–christ came to earth to wipe out the original taint: but the original taint is the fall into sexuality, whereas before original sin, man didn't have any sex at all, and reproduced himself in his children according to a principle of angelic multiplication, the only one acceptable to God. Abel, the son of Adam and Eve, before their fall into sin, was created like an Angel by this chaste and sacred method of reproduction, whereas Cain was created by sexuality, which is the obscene invention of Satan and this, and this alone, is why Cain murdered Abel. Wiping out the original taint by the bloody offering of his crucifixion, Jesus–christ demesmerized and broke the spell on man from the appallingly penetrating clutches of the deadly enterprises of Satan. And this is no idle talk, no mere picture of no consequence. It means that man is one day materially and physically destined to lose his sex. And Jesus–christ wouldn't have come down to earth if he had not been able to succeed in his Work and his Mission, IN REALITY. And he succeeded in reality in converting humanity, making it give up the vile attraction of being born and being conceived *in sin*. And that is borne out by the universal hosanna of the masses the day of his entry into Jerusalem, a week before Easter. For it wasn't only Jerusalem but the whole earth which was converted that day. And if a week after his ultimate triumph, Jesus–christ was arrested and crucified, it's because a new and towering wave of hell submerged human conscience, but through his crucifixion Jesus–christ ensured that the determination of man to renounce sin, which had been brought about the week before, REMAINED VALID FOR ALL ETERNITY and that it would have on earth and under the most ordinary circumstances ITS

MATERIAL CONSECRATION ONE DAY IN THE BODY of THE HUMAN BEING. Anyway, all that, Sonia, is in *THE GOSPELS* and if you aren't able to find it anymore it's because the text of THE GOSPELS was cut and falsified between the 2nd and 3rd centuries AD because the men who were at the head of the church at that time and who were under the sovereignty of Satan didn't want people to know anymore that Jesus-christ had forbidden children to be created by the foul methods of copulation and sexual parturition. And what is more, Jesus-christ said to man: God curses copulation and he definitely does not want sexual procreation which is the stratagem of Satan, yet there aren't enough beings and you must multiply and increase, but in order to increase and multiply you must reproduce yourselves in your sons by the methods of Angelic multiplication, the only ones with God's blessing, and thus the only ones effective and active on Infinity: INCREASE AND MULTIPLY LIKE ANGELS, SAID CHRIST. THAT WAY ALONE WILL YOU BE GREAT ENOUGH IN NUMBER TO TOUCH THE HEART OF GOD. Because they were faked, the holy scriptures were made to say that men were authorized to multiply like swine.

There was something else which was deleted from the Bible: and that is the story of Saint Patrick's staff, as it had appeared in full, PRINTED in black and white until a few years ago in the Apocalypse. I read it in 1935 in a Bible lent to me by Mme Schramme, 8 rue des Mélèzes, Brussels. And it was, I believe, Osterwald's Bible. Since then I have never found it again in the Bible. And I believe that the present Pope Pius XII is responsible for this deletion, and I think Hitler regrets it. – It's in that part of the Bible, as we knew it, in which THE DIVISION OF THE SEXES was pronounced. It was in Rome in 1925 at the Vatican Library where the original and authentic text of the original Gospels was issued to me and which a reliable man translated for me. – Hitler, whom I met at the *Romanisches Café, Café des Bohémiens*, opposite the Kurfürstendamm in Berlin in 1932, when I was 'playing in' *Shot at Dawn*, must be made aware precisely what has become of me. – You will see Cécile again soon.

Yours, from the bottom of my heart,

Antonin Artaud

[*OC*, X, 124–8]

This letter never reached Artaud's young friend. Sonia Mossé had been deported to a concentration camp and murdered in a gas-chamber.

To Roger Blin

Espalion, 25 March 1946

My dear Roger Blin

[...] As for me I've been free since last Tuesday and I have been waiting in Espalion to gather enough funds to return to Paris and complete a number of important projects. The first is finally to get The Theatre of Cruelty off the ground. But money is not everything and I am sure that I'll get it more easily than anything else. I need actors who are first and foremost strong personalities, in other words, actors who, on stage, are neither afraid to experience the true feeling of being stabbed, nor of the absolutely real pains of a fake childbirth. Mounet-Sully believes in what he does and creates an illusion, but he is secure behind a banister; I take the banister away and if the actor does not actually grapple with the invisible, he will give birth to nought: theatre is the abortion of nought to make reality concrete. Not to make fake feelings true but stubbornly to show real beings instead of fake feelings. Knot, stump of an arm, misery, misery of the reprobate actor who has been writhing for ever under the weight of truncated feelings. Misery of an improbable psyche, which the gang of supposed psychologists have never stopped sticking pins in the muscles of humanity. Before the soul there is the cry of truth, and the truth is a movement of bones, for the bones of the unfathomable have been thundering in the abysses of our poor natures for too many centuries, downtrodden.

Here I have met an actress, Colette Thomas, and a poet, Marthe Robert, who both look very sick to me, although they didn't mention anything and perhaps didn't even feel it themselves. – Two souls wounded by reality and in need of some kind of opiate to be born again. Paying actors isn't enough. Giving them yourself something of your heart to eat day by day, not in a pederastic mass-like sacrifice, but in reality, in the very body of your heaving chest, and forcing the air to the blood as long as you are not afraid to die on stage to give your breath to a being who agreed to be your actor. Pushing your voice until your last gasp, not by shouting but right into the natural rock of the inside, in the silence of an incarnation of being which, to make the ghosts abort, the birth of pure minds, and for the checkmated player who is the body's being, doesn't fear the sharp fall to the driving back of the power of form, in the domination of internal forms of spontaneous outbursts.

I tried to recite a few lines of Gérard de Nerval to Colette Thomas in that manner, but I exhausted myself in vain. For the past 9 years I've seen too many straitjackets, poisonous drugs at the Rouen and Sainte-Anne asylums and too many ECT comas at Rodez and I was soon out of breath. Now I must build myself up again. [. . .] Affectionately yours,

Antonin Artaud

[OC, XI, 215–18]

Having been under strict surveillance since 1937, Artaud was allowed a modicum of freedom within the little town of Rodez towards the end of 1945. Early in 1946 several of his friends, now that the war was over, travelled south to visit him and to discuss his release directly with Dr Ferdière. On 19 March Artaud left the asylum for a small hotel in nearby Espalion on a 'trial period of freedom' which lasted until 10 April.

Before finally releasing him, however, Ferdière set two stringent conditions: Artaud's financial situation should be adequately secured and he should live in a protected environment with medical help at hand. In order to raise money Blin asked painters and writers to donate paintings and manuscripts to be sold at an auction in Paris. A friendly nursing home was also found in Ivry and the stage was set for Artaud's return to Paris in May 1947.

Certainly the prospect of imminent freedom encouraged Artaud to think concretely about reviving the Theatre of Cruelty. This letter to Blin (see also *OC*, XX, 421–2) and many texts written during Artaud's last two years of life testify to the continuity of his thoughts on theatre and to his determination to achieve his life's ambition.

Part Eight

Return to Paris (1946–8)

Theatre and Anatomy (*Le théâtre et l'anatomie*)

The last word about man is not yet spoken. I mean the question arises of knowing if man will continue to sport his nose in the middle of his face or if the two nostrils of the human skull which stare at us on the tables of eternity are not going to get fed up with sniffing and snivelling, never being able to feel or believe that they contribute to the esoteric run of thought well supported by two toes.

Theatre was never meant to describe man and what he does, but to create a human being who would enable us to advance on life's journey without festering and stinking.

Modern man festers and stinks because his anatomy is bad, and his sex organs are badly placed in relation to the brain in the squaring of his 2 feet.

And theatre is this gawky puppet which music of trunks with metallic barbs of barbed wire maintains us in a state of war against mankind that was strapping us in.

The theatrical monsters are demands made by skeletons and organs which are no longer affected by illness. – And they piss human passions through the holes of their nostrils.

Man suffers badly in Aeschylus, but he still thinks himself something of a god and doesn't want to enter the membrane, and in Euripides finally he wallows in the membrane, forgetting where and when he was a god.

But I feel now a shutter knocked back, a pulmonary section of the wall turning; and of course it's all right; and now I feel nothing but an old thunderbolt which might still like to protest.

This thunderbolt is called theatre: theatre the place where you fill your heart with joy, although nothing of what we can see in the theatre today recalls either the heart or joy.

And this is where my delirium returns, my delirium of an inveterate plaintiff.

For since 1918, and it wasn't in the theatre, who was it cast his sounding lead 'into all the dregs of chance and fortune', if not Hitler himself, the impure Moldo-Wallachian born of the race of innate monkeys.

Who appeared on stage with his belly of red tomatoes, covered

in dirt like a garlic parsley, and at each turn of the rotating saw
bored into human anatomy.

Because room was left for him on all the stages of a stillborn
theatre.

Who declaring the theatre of cruelty utopian went as far as
having the vertebrae sawn in the *mises en scène* of the barbed wire.

> yion tan nornan
> na sarapido
> ya yar sapido
> ara pido

I had spoken of real cruelties on the level of pitch,

I had spoken of manual cruelties on the level of attitude action,

I had spoken of molecular war of atoms, *chevaux de frise* on all
fronts, I mean beads of sweat on brows,

I was put into a lunatic asylum.

When can we expect the next dirty war, fought for tuppence
worth of turd paper, against the perspiration of breasts which
never stop gnawing at my brow.

Antonin Artaud.

[OC, XXII, 277–8]

Text commissioned by the journal *La Rue* which published it in its
issue No. 6, 12 July 1946. Artaud had written it on 8 July.

Similar ideas are further expressed in two short texts written in
mid-November 1947 when Artaud was working on a poem entitled
'Le Théâtre de la Cruauté' (The Theatre of Cruelty, *OC*, XIII,
105–18) which should have been included in *To Put an End to the
Judgement of God*. The poem itself had to be left out because of lack of
air time. Here are the two preparatory texts:

To LIVE one needs a body,
who had the idea of a body
to be formed and developed,
who counted on something other than chance,
a 'God' to have developed a body?
No, the body one must develop it oneself otherwise it's worth
    nothing and won't hold up

and it is born of talent and of quality,
it is born of deeds done.

[*OC*, XIII, 271]

and,

The body is the body,
it is alone
and needs no organs,
the body is never an organism,
organisms are the enemies of the body,
the things which one does
get by all alone
without the help of any organ,
every organ is a parasite,
it conceals a parasitic function
intent on making a being live,
which should not be there.
Organs were made only to give beings something to eat,
whereas the latter were cursed from the outset and have no
    reason at all to exist.
Reality has not yet been constructed because the real organs of
    the human body have not yet been formed and deployed.
The theatre of cruelty has been created to complete this
    deployment, and to undertake,, by a new dancing of man's
    body, a diversion
from
    this world of microbes which is merely coagulated
    nothingness.
The theatre of cruelty wants to make the eyelids dance in pairs
    with the elbows, the kneecaps, the thighbones and the toes,
and wants to be seen.

[*OC*, XIII, 287–8]

To Peter Watson

27 July 1946. Paris.

Dear Mr Watson,

I made my début in literature writing books in order to declare that I couldn't write anything at all; my thoughts, when I had something to write, were what was denied me most. I never had any ideas, and two short books, 70 pages each, echo this deep-rooted, intractable, endemic absence of any idea. They are *The Umbilical Limbo* and *The Nervometer*.

At the time they seemed to be full of cracks, of mistakes, of platitudes, and as if stuffed with spontaneous abortions, with all kinds of renunciations and abdications, bypassing the essential and stupendous things I wanted to say, and which I didn't say and never shall say. – But 20 years later, they seem astonishing to me, not in terms of my own success but in terms of the inexpressible. Thus it is that works improve with age and that, since they all *lie* as far as the writer is concerned, they constitute in themselves a bizarre truth which life, if it were itself ever authentic, should never have accepted. – The inexpressible expressed through works which, at the time of writing, are nothing but debacles, and are only worth anything by the posthumous distance of a mind dead to time and deadlocked in the present, what is that, can you tell me?

I have written a few other works since: *Art and Death*, *Heliogabalus*, *The Theatre and its Double*, *Journey to the Land of the Tarahumaras*, *New Revelations on Being*, *Letters from Rodez*.

In each I was hounded by the sinister harlequinade of a well of texts, stacked one on top of the other and which only ever appear now on one level like a secret squared grid, where yes and no, black and white, true and false, although contradictory in themselves, are dissolved into one man's style, that of poor Mr Antonin Artaud.

I don't remember being born during the night of 3 to 4 September 1896, as the official register states, but I remember having debated a serious question there in a place which never was, located somewhere between space and a sinister, fortuitous, intolerable, grotesque, dreadfully non-existent world.

That space led to a ladder of lives in which I couldn't see any interruption to my being, the sinister, horrible, grotesque world was this life's world.

The question with which I grappled was to know whether I would move towards a white charnel-house, if, ever tired of existing, I would yield myself up to this white centre which . . .

or whether I would remain faithful to this dark water, to this watery lid of a tub of dark water, which obstinately clung to me. – It smelt like shit on my heart, that tub with my trunk inside, but the excrement was my own, my ego.

In fact the tub was a bloody trunk, but a man's trunk, while the white hole which offered me its soul, a woman, was but nothingness to me.

Now would I turn to the mother or would I remain father, the eternal father which, ultimately, I was?

I must assume that I chose to be a father for eternity, since for 50 years now I've been a man and I can't see it ever changing.

Even if before this life I had other lives, I don't believe there will be any other afterwards.

Death is not just a passing state. It is a state which has never existed, for if living is difficult, dying is becoming increasingly impossible and ineffectual, – considering this life of mine I remember dying at least three times, actually and bodily, once in Marseilles, once in Lyons, once in Mexico and once at the Rodez asylum in the convulsions of electroshock. Each time I saw myself leave my body and travel in space, but not very far from my own body, for one is never completely detached. And in reality one never leaves one's body. The body is a trunk of which one is only a leaf when one realizes one is dead, and that one is not outside but inside.

For the dead man has only one thought, that is to return to his corpse, to pick it up and to go on.

But it's always the corpse which picks you up,
and one obeys because one is inside.

And then the dead man is a liar, more suffering is to follow, it is not yet time, says the voice of the dreaming conscience, and those who speak, are they dead or alive? – One cannot say anymore. – Dead, I was gripped by the tornado of beings all worn down by hatred, and madness. – This hatred gave me an idea, which I felt spinning in my distracted ears, and which brought my hand back to my side. The idea was that each being had made me lose some eventful moment, and that death was only a story I should have lived through when alive . . .

Dead, one dies on the wrong side, it isn't the path one should take.

Only as I live, I no longer believe in the path, and I don't believe that the dead believe in it or that they have to argue over it either. One is not dead, really dead, when one works this or that out.

And does it interest you, dear Mr Peter Watson, to know what one is like when one doesn't, really doesn't work something out. And what goes on elsewhere, and whether one is there or not.

I don't believe you're interested, and as far as I am concerned, for a long time, a very long time, a very long time indeed it has ceased to be of interest to me!

Enough, enough, and enough of questions and problems, of problems and questions, of life and of thought, of death and of nought (it rhymes, don't you see it rhymes, oh this life which will never go away). But please wait and think about coming up with at least something to say, Mr Artaud.

No, I, Antonin Artaud, well no, well no, precisely no, I Antonin Artaud, I only want to write when I have nothing more to think. – Like someone who would eat his own belly, the wind from inside his belly.

You say the English public doesn't know me. Where indeed could they have come across *Correspondence with Jacques Rivière*, *The Umbilical Limbo*, *The Nervometer*, *Art and Death*, *The Monk* by Lewis, *Heliogabalus* or *The Crowned Anarchist*, *New Revelations on Being*, *The Theatre and its Double*, *Journey to the Land of the Tarahumaras*, *Letters from Rodez* and finally, and especially *Letura d'Eprahi*, written in 1935, in which I gave my best, which was lost, which I never found again even though it was so magnificently printed, in characters taken from the ancient incunabulae,

no,

in characters of which the ancient incunabulae were a mere imitation,

a duplicate transfer,

a transposition emasculated of its own head.

and, forgive me for using strange and rather pedantic words, but I will give a transcription

voctrovi
cano dirima
cratirima
enectimi

vonimi
cano victrima
calitrima
endo pitri

calipi
ke loc tispera
kalispera
enoctimi

vanazim
enamzimi

all silly incantations in a gibberish, fit for calling back the sham dead.

I mean after the printing of this book the world buggered off, and before the first incunabulae the world, too, had buggered off. Because from time to time, life, dear Mr Peter Watson, takes a running jump, but it's never written down in history and I have only written it down to fix and perpetuate the memory of these cuts, of these crevices, of these breakages, of these abrupt and bottomless falls

which

. . .

but think, dear Mr Peter Watson, that I have never been anything but a sick man, and I won't go on about it anymore.

I repeat, I have never been able to live, to think, to sleep, to speak, to eat, to write

and I have only ever written to say that I have never done anything, could never do anything and that in doing something, in reality I did nothing at all. All my work has only been founded and could only be founded on such nothingness,

on this carnage, this fray of extinguished fires, of exhausted cries, and of slaughter, one does nothing, one says nothing, but one suffers, one despairs and one fights, yes, I believe in reality one fights. – Will this struggle be appreciated, will it be judged, will it be justified?

No.

Will it be given a name?

No again,

naming the struggle is the death of nothingness, perhaps.

But above all a stop to life . . .

Life will never be stopped.

But will we come out into the open at least, I mean in no man's land after the struggle. To breathe in the memories of the struggle?

Never.

The struggle has started again lower down, so now what? Perpetual scabs? Indefinite scratching of the wound. The never-ending ploughing of the gash, begetter of the wound?

Perhaps!

But you're mad?

Not at all; it's you who are nothing but a fool,

I, Antonin Artaud, I am fuming, I'm fuming; you, critic, you're sucking my cock.

And that's what characterizes you, hinders you, makes you what you are.

Where I am now, nothing has any meaning anymore and life isn't, it doesn't sink to your lewd level, you who only love what has a price-tag.

Your tongue is not for eating or for speaking, but for jousting, for driving the tip of your brain into the slimy mud of agony, and for stirring it, till it turns sour like a mayonnaise, or a garlic sauce, you did not create the agony that brought you forth, oh cowards, for you crawled out of this misery, like runaways, and it's on the custard of your flight that you have based life. Measuring evil is this lewd state of which you made your metre, your brand of calculated jargon!

arganufta
daponsida
parganuft

'*Tête-à-tête* with Antonin Artaud' (Artaud's lecture at the Vieux-Colombier, 13 January 1947, at 9 p.m.)

This was Artaud's one and only public appearance after his release from Rodez. In the history of contemporary French theatre, this particular evening has acquired 'mythic' proportions. The posters announced 'Tête-à-tête avec Antonin Artaud' and gave the titles of three poems that the author was to read to his audience. Some people, like André Breton, were against the idea of such an exhibitionist performance; others, like André Gide, were apprehensive and feared a disaster. In the event, Breton and Gide, together with over 900 spectators (among them many actors and directors, playwrights, authors, journalists . . .), squeezed into the small Vieux-Colombier theatre to witness what was to be Artaud's farewell to his public.

There exists no 'objective' account of the events of that famous evening and the text which Artaud had prepared, but failed to deliver as he had planned it, was only published in 1994 (*OC*, XXVI).

Not surprisingly, it would seem that the evening was very tense, the atmosphere highly charged and many literary figures wrote vivid testimonies in the days and weeks that followed. But most commentators seem to agree on a number of basic points. The 'performance' started at 9 p.m. and continued, with one fifteen-minute interval, until about midnight when Artaud suddenly stormed out. The next day he explained that he stopped because he was fed up trying to explain himself to 'that shower of cunts' ('cette bande de cons') quite incapable of understanding his message.

The following extracts, taken from Artaud's preparatory notes, reveal the combative and revolutionary tone of the 'performance':

I am the enemy of the theatre

And now I'm going to tell you something which perhaps might
	astonish a few people.
I am the enemy
	of the theatre.
And I have always been so.
For as much as I love the theatre,
I am, for that very reason, its enemy.

The theatre is an explosion of passions,
an awesome bursting forth of forces

from one body
   to another.
Such an explosion cannot happen twice.

8–14 December 1946

[*OC*, XXVI, 139]

and,

If I wanted to tell the whole world the story of my life, and to live it again here in actions or in deeds for some [of you],

it's not because of everything abnormal, unusual, disconcerting, let alone particularly outrageous in my life,

(like a drama too demanding for an actor)

but because I think that others besides me will have felt the same beast stirring within them, the same wild, untamed beast, champing at the bit, growling and waiting to pounce [. . .]

I had a certain number of ideas on theatre which reached 2 or 3 thousand people on earth, but which the majority of the public reject and which, apart from these 3 thousand people, seem to want to reject more and more. [. . .]

Because they understand that theatre poses a threat, not in itself, but if it were to become once again a fundamental part of society.

The Theatre of Cruelty was never realized because its very existence presupposes the disappearance of the basis of public life which is called Society.

I don't know why man believes that awareness can only be achieved by the institutions of government, public services, the police force, religion, science, and the army. – Or rather I know only too well that it goes back to the last real achievement by theatre which occurred in Greece, shortly before Aeschylus, in that prehistoric period of Greek life when theatre was pre-eminent, a theatre in which heads were systematically chopped off.

[*OC*, XXVI, 140–1]

During the three hours the 'encounter' lasted Artaud read some of his unpublished poems and spoke of his trip to Mexico, of his trouble with the Irish police and his subsequent arrest and deportation, of his experiences in psychiatric institutions and of the agony he experienced undergoing electroshock therapy. The evening, for all concerned, turned out to be quite harrowing. Here are a few extracts taken from the more perceptive texts inspired by Artaud's last 'theatrical' appearance:

Louis Guillaume: I was present at that 'lecture' (a pitiful, revolting, haunting act of exhibitionism) at the Vieux-Colombier . . . it was unforgettable. A small group of hecklers soon became quiet. An anguished silence hung over the public when that *inspired* man hurled at the public what Gide calls his 'filthy, blasphemous curses' or when he got muddled with the text of his lecture and fell silent for long moments holding his head in his hands, writhing in pain. We all suffered with him. (*La Tour de Feu*, 138)

Maurice Saillet: When he came on stage, his emaciated and haggard features reminiscent both of Baudelaire and of Edgar Allan Poe; when his hands hovered about his face like two birds of prey, ceaselessly clawing at it; when he started to chant his beautiful, but barely audible poems in his hoarse voice chocked by sobs and tragic stutterings – we felt ourselves lured into that danger zone, and as if we were reflections of that black sun, caught up in the all–devouring combustion of a body consumed by spiritual fire. (*Combat*, 24 January 1947)

Jacques Prevel: He tells us about being confined in psychiatric care, of opium, but he loses track of his thoughts. He stops talking from time to time. In a word his lecture is incoherent and does not seem to have been prepared. He recalls one incident from his time in Rodez which he had never mentioned to me before: 'While I was lying unconscious after an electroshock session I found myself one metre outside of my body. . . . Then, suddenly, tumbled into a hole and I woke up. Dr Ferdière thought I was dead and it was only when the two nurses were about to carry me to the morgue that I woke up . . . (*Magazine littéraire*, No. 26, April 1984)

André Gide: Artaud's lecture turned out to be far more extraordinary than one could have imagined. The like of it one's never heard or seen before and never will again. I shall never be able to blot it out of my memory; atrocious; painful, almost sublime at times; but also revolting and quite unbearable. The audience behaved admirably, being subjugated by Artaud for over two hours in a state of anxious silence and compelled to respect that exemplary display of human anguish and distress. Frighteningly long silences interrupted his garbled ragings (declamatory readings of his poems) from which one could only make out a few of the words he was yelling: 'cunt, arse, masturbation, etc.'. A madman obsessed, without a doubt; but also a prodigious actor, a ham, even a clown who remains nonetheless aware of the dramatic effect and who, deliberately, plays up his orphic frenzy. (Letter to Henri Thomas, in *Cahiers Renaud-Barrault*, 69, May 1957, 72–3)

Letters to André Breton

Altogether Artaud wrote five letters to André Breton on the subject of the evening at the Vieux-Colombier and the forthcoming International Surrealist Exhibition, which was organized by Breton and Marcel Duchamp and took place at the Galerie Maeght in Paris, from July to September 1947.

The five letters to Breton are important first and foremost in that they indicate Artaud's own feelings both during and subsequent to his 'performance' at the Vieux-Colombier. The first two letters are similar in tone and content. They convey his feeling of anti-climatic depression, not of the post-performance variety, but a depression about theatre in general and his inability to change it from inside, through a truly revolutionary production.

Letter of 28 February 1947

My dear friend,

I can no longer hide from you that every day I am falling deeper and deeper into a kind of abyss that neither art!!! nor poetry, nor any kind of activity, moral or physiological, intellectual or sexual, or even life itself can ever fill. – And I am resolved, I am firmly resolved no longer to put up with the yoke of existence or the law.

I have always said so.

But I didn't know how to remove it.

Now I know, and the action which will no longer be the practice of a routine activity will follow.

In the penultimate letter you wrote me there was a sentence which made me *cringe*:

'the man of the theatre which you cannot but be by the fact that you appear on a stage'.

Ah yes, I appeared on a stage, *once more*, for the LAST TIME, at the Théâtre du Vieux-Colombier, but with the manifest intention of blowing up the structure and blowing it up from the inside, I don't think that the performance of a man bellowing and hurling abuse and throwing up his intestines really is a theatrical performance,

besides something else happened that evening which no one fully appreciated: having appeared on stage and standing in front of the audience who had paid to hear me, and seeing them *locked in* with me in a theatre auditorium, all of a sudden and ready to start, it seemed to me pointless to carry on with the experiment and, instead of reading the lecture I had prepared, I folded it up and left after throwing into the audience the last stanza of a poem,

> all the exercises of yoga
> are not worth the desquamations
> of the cunt of a dead dyke
> when the maid who possesses it
> pisses with her udder split
> to get through the syphilis.

I left because I realized that the only language I could use on an audience was to take bombs out of my pockets and throw them in their faces in a gesture of unmistakable aggression.

For I don't think that consciousness can be taught, or that it's worth the trouble attempting its education.

And that hitting out is the only language I feel capable of speaking.

And if there are people who feel, like me, disposed to hitting out against the harmfulness of things and of a society which, with its Institutions, supports them, let them come over to my side.

But you, André Breton, who reproach me for appearing on the stage of a theatre saying to an audience of strangers, of bystanders, of voyeurs, of sadists, and *of friends as well*,

anti-theatrical things, by extra-scenic and anti-theatrical means when contrary to the law of the theatre which has the actor *keep control of his faculties* I wanted to lose mine in dreadful howling,

don't fall victim to the same mistake when organizing in some
well-established capitalist or maybe anti-capitalist gallery, with
premises in town, paying licences and taxes, with a large amount
of capital at its disposal, even if deposited in a communist bank,
and being therefore a gallery for the rich,
   an exhibition
   which cannot but have arty characteristics
   since it consists in placing in well chosen corners, illuminations,
situations
   objects which will neither rant, nor stink, nor reek, nor fart, nor
spit, which will cause no injury, nor suffer injury,
   will be removed from their living environment, by the fact that
they will figure in an '*exhibition*' on which all the snobs of the
world will converge, snobs who will guard themselves against
risking one jot of their existence, to change whatever may be in the
mainstream of today's reality,
   and I know fine well that a painting by Van Gogh destroys all
cosmography, all hydrography, all the science of eclipses, of
equinoxes and seasons but I would dearly like to see it somewhere
else than in the rooms of the Orangerie where,
   exhibited
   the object is
        castrated,
   extracted from the organic dynamism which produced it and
left to the foul masturbations of the bourgeois who in gawping
groups come to view it as an extra luxury added to their foul
nightly fornications.
   In an exhibition of this kind there is something of an exclusive
rite,
   for which one goes out of one's way to practise in a special place
   and which is a *rite*,
   and which forces one to turn to the limited register of a certain
number of intellectual operations, introduced in advance in
calculable categories and I can hide from you no more that I can
no longer bear anything which has the stamp of science, of
knowledge, of wisdom, of law, of regulation, anything which is a
human interpretation of truths
   or of absences, of deficiencies, of voids and natural gulfs.
   With time I have acquired an appalling horror of everything

which concerns magic, occultism, hermeticism, esoterism, astrology, etc., etc.

not only do I not believe in them but my hatred of human society knows no bounds when I see the unspeakable hotpotch of all the mistakes, of all the false beliefs, of all the sophisms, of all the puffisms, of all the scintillating showing off with which such particular individuals, such sects, such collections of individuals would have me believe that they have intercepted and are holding vital secrets, that they are controlling worlds of phenomenal truths, while all they have ever controlled was the hot air under the cover of this sordid human illusionism which has them believe that something can exist, and that there is something,

and that from that which is

something

ineluctably must be deduced

to which, through some part of me, I would inevitably and ineluctably be subjected.

For years now, André Breton, I have been fighting with the sects of all the sorcerers on earth to which must be added all the bourgeois of all the social classes who have ended up knowing far more about the true mysteries of things than all the dull and formalistic initiates.

Those are the people who got Villon, Edgar Allan Poe, Baudelaire, Gérard de Nerval, Lautréamont, Arthur Rimbaud, and who, sex in hand, or clitoris of the christian cross between thumb and forefinger and on their heart, have come to spit on their hide and profane their burial after nailing their tongues to prevent them living.

Gérard de Nerval, Villon, Edgar Allan Poe, Lautréamont are dead for having penetrated the supra-natural, surreal and, if you like, surrealist secret of things,

and it was to prevent him from revealing it that they twisted and steeped the brain of Gérard de Nerval in madness, and *forced* him, I say *forced*, by magical possession *to hang himself*,

and that several men held his hand, inside his own body, and forced him to tie the noose when he hanged himself.

Ah well, they won't do the same thing to me; they've locked me up in a lunatic asylum in order to discredit the revelations I had to make in this respect; the other evening, at the Vieux-Colombier, bourgeois consciousness – which hadn't called the police to have me arrested – *forced* itself arbitrarily into my organism to paralyse my revolt inside me and I had no bombs to throw

but I know now exactly the kind of bomb needed to overthrow consciousness,

for years now I have been collecting them

and the highest yoga never gave them to anyone.

I believe that soon, André Breton, as naïve as this assertion may at first appear to you, you will be able to see them *as they are*.

These are not mere words, ideas, or other phantasmagoric rot, these really are bombs, physical bombs, but how naïve and childish on my part, isn't it, to say all that so innocently, and so pretentiously.

It is something with which I shall rid myself of this world, and of its beliefs, and of its institutions, and of its doctrines, and of its logic, and of its discursive spirit, and of its *dialectics* and especially of the army of corpuscles, animalcules, fluidic bodies and miasmas of charm with which it never ceases to suffocate my innermost life to prevent me from liberating myself.

The time of succubae and incubi is past,

it has been replaced by the time of the small shopkeepers, assistant administrators, bank tellers, priests, doctors, teachers and scholars who think they are holding Artaud because day and night they are in his sex,

as if my sex were the sun of my reality,

and the sex

the screeching comet of the world in the act of creating itself.

There, I've told you what I was thinking

and I haven't added one bit of criticism, or of judgement,

I don't give a damn.

I do not forget that André Breton is the man who in Paris before my departure for Ireland supported me most, gave me food and money.

Yours,

                                                    Antonin Artaud.

P.S. – This passing from room to room, through 15 rooms, reminds me exactly of the greatest mistake of humanity which is to believe it necessary to enter the confines and the yoke of an

initiation in order to know what is not, while all the while it is not
and there is nothing.

Nothing but unredeemed, active and energetic insurrection
against everything which claims to be, forever.

[Published in L'Ephémère, No. 8, Winter 1968, 3–53]

The ranting tone of his performance carries over into the letter and he
maligns the forthcoming surrealist exhibition in similar vein. Artaud
believes the exhibition will betray the artists, that their work will lose
its potency, '*exhibited*, the object is *castrated*'. He attacks art for being
representative of bourgeois culture, and rejects magic and the
occultism of initiates for being elitist, hollow and false beliefs. He
considers himself to have joined the long list of revolutionary poets
and society's suicides such as Poe, Baudelaire, Rimbaud and, of course,
Van Gogh, who have fallen victim to the narrow-mindedness of
bourgeois consciousness. The only way to overthrow it, he believes, is
not by throwing explosive poems into the audience but through
revolution in society itself. Here is Artaud soliloquizing, channelling
his aggression and going on to advocate and urge real revolution.

Letter of 24 March 1947 (extract)

In his third letter of 24 March 1947 Artaud continues to admonish
Breton for his complicitous action in setting up the exhibition. Its
prospective public, like his own last public at the Vieux-Colombier,
receives particularly harsh criticism, coming in for a catalogue of
scatalogical abuse.

a certain body,
a certain concocted, curdled substance
between thighs and calf
the place where you find juicy turds,
feel, inhale and drop turds, like a good dog on a leash,
like a good dog,
a well-trained dog,
and this substance is only made of jealousy, hatred, envy,
malicious acrimony against the poet whom it comes to applaud
and listen to
against the painter (Van Gogh) whom it comes to see once more
explode and radiate,
on condition that he explodes and radiates

crystal

cry

of his pain alone

and *not* bread or opium stuffed with screeching life and flashing light which his audience will have given him to radiate and explode.

Knowing that I did not go to the Vieux-Colombier to give a session but to make accusations. – They were contained in five poems, they were also contained in a text which I gave up reading because it didn't seem horrible enough for the circumstances.

This being so, how could I write a text for an *exhibition* to which this same stinking audience is going to come, in a gallery which, even if it draws its funds from a communist bank, is a capitalist gallery where, for a lot of money, paintings are sold which are paintings no more but commercial securities, *securities*, titled SECURITIES, and which are the only objects in the world called SECURITIES, these Big, multi-coloured, printed pages which depict on mere paper (what a miracle) the contents of a mine, a field, a well, a deposit, an enterprise, a prospect, in which the possessor, the proprietor, the capitalist, the owner hasn't even participated by breaking a fingernail, whereas millions of workers have died, *on the job*, so that the so-called bugger-shirking mind can *wallow* in the material work of the body.

Well now, I don't want to write such a text to be similarly exhibited in an art gallery, in one of these places where you auction painted pictures, where you sell the sweat of men, the perspiration of suicides which, having left the clenched fist, the stiff fingers of the poor Van Gogh on his paintbrush, are now nothing but:

it's so much.

As for the other reason, I have told you,

I am the enemy of occultism,

in particular the enemy of initiations, of the principle of initiation.

I do not allow myself to be pushed and pulled back outside a truth which, from birth and because I am a man, I possess and I know in order to force myself to rediscover it little by little through arbitrary, gratuitous, presupposed and invented arithmetic, of a scale which has only ever existed in the brains of bestialized monkeys which have taken the place of my humanity.

Antonin Artaud.

Letter of 5 May 1947

Artaud's fourth letter was sent on 23 April and was followed by a fifth on 5 May. In this last letter Artaud finally apologizes for his previous attacks on Breton, pleading illness, and sets out more rationally his fears for the forthcoming exhibition.

Dear André Breton,

In the letter I wrote you 10 days ago I told you I was very ill, half paralysed, that I couldn't write the text you were asking me, and that I remained your friend anyway, despite everything

but that *I didn't want* to take part in the exhibition you were organizing

because it called upon hermeticism, occultism, magic, and that it was giving credence and recognition to an attitude of mind from which I have suffered most in the world.

I live possessed, smothered, defiled day and night by incubi and succubae

which only stem from the general faith in esoterism built on theft, rape, and on crime and which is a primary explanation of a world far more just, hidden and pure than that of the initiates.

I also told you and this is a quotation from the letter

that I didn't want to participate in an undertaking in a capitalist art gallery, even if it did keep its funds in a communist bank,

but I added that these terms,

and that was in my letter,

were not aimed at you but aimed at the gallery, the banks and at a whole system of institutions which, for the time being are treating you well, but are waiting for the day to strangle you for good just as it happened to you once before on a certain evening in America on the banks of the Hudson

when the consciousness of the masses rising up over the bodies of the carriers,

mankind,

said to you:

Make revolutionary art but make art,

don't start the revolution in life or you will be murdered.

That's what the occult consciousness of all mankind tells me
day and night.

Yours,

Antonin Artaud

Over the course of his correspondence with Breton, Artaud's hopes
for a cultural revolution appear to have vanished. Frustration and
anger have given way to cynicism and despair.

Deranging the Actor (*Aliéner l'acteur*)

The theatre
   is the state
the place,
   the point,
at which to grasp the human anatomy,
and through it cure and rule over life

Yes, life with its fits, its bleating, its rumblings, its holes of
emptiness, its itching, its blotches, its circulatory stoppages, its
bleeding maelstroms, its irritable rushes of blood, its clusters of
humours,
      its resumptions,
         its hesitations.

All that is perceived, pinpointed, perused and
lit up on a limb,
   and it's by getting it going, or I should say in
a feverish activity of the limbs,
   like limbs of this astonishing, activated fetish
which is the whole body
   of a whole actor,
      that one can see
         as if bare,
            life itself,
in its transparency, in the presence of its first-born
forces, of its unused powers,
   and which haven't yet helped, no, not yet
helped to correct an anarchic creation out of which
true theatre was made for setting right the hot-tempered

and petulant gravitations.

    Yes, universal gravitation is an earthquake, a terrible storm of
        passion which checks itself on the limbs of an actor,
        not frenetically
        not hysterically
        not ecstatically
    but at the extreme cutting edge of the crest, at
the final and most extreme section of the parietal
paroxysm of its effort.

    Partition after partition,
    the actor develops
spreads out or locks up walls, passionate and over-animated
faces of surfaces in which is inscribed the wrath of life.

    Muscle after muscle
on the body of the methodically traumatized actor,
one can grasp the developments of the universal impulses
and on him set them right.

    It's a technique which nearly came off one day,
in the times of the Orphic of Eleusian Mysteries, but
it failed because it was more a question
of perfecting an old crime;
        to give god,
            whole dismembered god,
                to the whole man,
the whole universality of the unused breath of things to
the despicably human man,
    than of the creation and INSTITUTION
of this new and thrilling *furtive* anatomy which
the whole theatre was calling for.
    Yes, man at a given moment needed
a new skeletal body, which would sparkle and soar through the air
like the furtive flames of a hearth.
    And the theatre was this force which churned human
anatomy, the exuberance of an inherent fire from which
the primitive skeletons were born one by one like grapes,
    a force of exploded humour,
a kind of inflammatory tumour in which the first

skeleton was melted.
  And it's by the rhythmical churning of all
the skeletons evoked that the inherent force of the theatre
cauterized humanity.
  That's where man and life came together
from time to time to renew themselves.

But where?

  In certain untimely excoriations of the deep organic
sensitivity of the human body.
  Without trance,
  by the pronounced, methodical and rhythmical panting
of the call,
  the glittering life of the actor was laid bare
in his deep veins,
  and there were no muscles, or bones,
  no science of muscle
        or
            bone,
  but the projection of a wooden skeleton
        which was a whole body
        as if laid bare and visible
        and which seemed to be saying:
        beware,
        watch out below,
        it's going to shit,
        it's going to burst.

  And actually the theatre was the martyr of all that which was
threatening to be human, of all that which wanted to give the
impression of being.
  It was the state in which one cannot exist, if one
hasn't agreed in advance to be as if by definition
and in essence
        a deranged lunatic
            through and through.

  Breaking of limbs and shattered nerves,
  fracture of bleeding bones and which protest at being
wrenched thus from the skeleton of possibility, theatre is this
ineradicable and ebullient extravaganza
  which has revolt and war as its inspiration and its theme.

For to be deranged in life, what does it mean?

It means
not having accepted, like today's idiotic and
crooked men,
   to give in to this state of visceral and
       anti-theatrical liquefaction
       which brings sex
to this state of *stagnant*, pro-intestinal
   erotization
      of today's body.

The magnetic uprooting of the body, the
cruel, muscular excoriations, the disturbances of the
buried sensitivity which make up true theatre,
cannot go along with this way of beating
for so long,
   in any case languidly and lustfully
about the bush
      which constitutes sexual life.

True theatre is much more thrilling,
much more deranged.
   Spasmodic state of the open heart
     which gives everything
       to what does not exist,
         and which is not
and nothing to what is, and which one sees,
   which one can make out,
     where one can stop and
       stay.

But who
   today
     would like to live
in what
demands
   injury in order to
     remain

deranged?

12 May 1947

[First published in *L'Arbalète*, No. 13, Summer 1948]

Theatre and Science (*Le théâtre et la science*)

True theatre has always appeared to me as the exercise of a
dangerous and frightful act,
in which any idea of theatre and performance is ruled out,
as well as any idea of science, religion, and art.

The act I'm talking about aims at the true organic and physical
transformation of the human body.
Why?
Because theatre is not a scenic display in which one virtually
and symbolically develops a myth
but a crucible of fire and real meat in which anatomically
by the crushing of bones, of limbs and syllables,
bodies are renewed,
and where the mythical act of creating a body is shown
physically and plainly.

If I am understood correctly, one shall see in this an act of true
genesis which will appear to everyone preposterous and laughable
to summon up in real life.
For no one at present can believe that a body can change except
through time and in death.

But let me repeat, death is an invented state
which only exists for all the vile sorcerers, the gurus of
nothingness who benefit from it, and who for several centuries
have been feeding and living off it in the state called Bardo.
Beyond that the human body is immortal.
It's an old story which must be brought into the open by
blowing the whistle.

The human body only dies because we forgot to transform and
change it.
Were it not so it would not die, turn into dust, or pass into the
tomb.

One of the disgraceful virtues of nothingness which religion,
society and science have thus obtained from human consciousness
is to induce it at a given moment to leave its body,
                   to make it believe that the human body was
perishable and destined in a very short time to disappear.

No, the human body is imperishable, immortal and it changes,
   it changes physically and materially,
      anatomically and manifestly,
         it changes visibly and on the spot, provided one really
wants to take the material trouble of making it change.

In former times there existed a process of an order less magical
than scientific
   and which theatre only touched upon,
      by which the human body,
         when it was recognized as evil was sifted,
            transported,
               physically and materially,
                  objectively and as if molecularly from one body to
another,
   from a past and spent state of the body
      to a strengthened and heightened state of the body.

And it was enough for it to appeal to all the dramatic, repressed
and spent forces of the human body.

This is truly a revolution,
and everyone calls for a necessary revolution,
      but I don't know if many will have realized that this
revolution will not be real, as long as it is not physically and
materially complete,
   as long as it refuses to come again face to face with man,
      with the body of man himself,
         and does not resolve at last to request that it *change itself*.

But the body has become dirty and evil because we live in a
dirty
and evil world which doesn't want the human body to change,
and has deployed
   from all directions,
      to all strategic points,
         its sinister and secret police to prevent it changing.

So the world is evil not only in appearance, but because
subterraneanly and secretly it cultivates and maintains the evil
which made it exist and made us all born of the evil spirit and in
the midst of the evil spirit.

Not only are mortals rotten, the very atmosphere in which we
live is materially and physically rotten, swarming with maggots,
with obscene appearances, poisonous minds, foul organisms,
easily perceived with the naked eye provided one has, like myself,
suffered for a long time, bitterly and systematically.

I'm not talking about hallucination or delirium, no, I'm talking
about this adulterated and certified mixing with the abominable
world of spirits whose private parts have sullied the purest
impulses of every imperishable actor, of every poet not created by
breath.

And no political or moral revolution will be possible as long as
man remains magnetically bound,
    in his most elementary and most simple organic and nervous
reactions,
                      by the sordid influence
               of all the dubious circles of initiates,
    who, keeping warm in the footwarmers of their psyche,
             laugh at revolutions as well as wars,
        certain that the anatomical order on which existence
as well as the duration of present-day society is based
        could never change.
But in the human breath there are jumps and breaks of tone,
and from one cry to another abrupt shifts
    things can suddenly be evoked through openings and impulses
of the whole body and prop up or liquefy a limb like a tree one
would shore up against the mountain of its forest.

      Now
    the body has a breath and a cry by which it can well up in the
rotting lower depths of the organism and be carried visibly to the
dazzling heights where the superior body awaits it.
It is a process whereby into the furthest recesses of the uttered
organic cry and breath

enter all the possible states of blood and mood,
    the whole battle of thorns and splinters of the visible
body
  with the fake monsters of the psyche,
    of spirituality,
      and sensitivity.
There were undeniable periods in history at the time when this
physiological process took place and when human ill-will never
had the time to gather its forces and to unleash like today its
monsters born of copulation.

If on certain points and for certain races, human sexuality has
reached its black spot,
  and if this sexuality unleashes foul influences,
    horrible bodily poisons,
      which are presently paralysing
all efforts of will and sensitivity,
              and make impossible any attempt
at metamorphosis
      and at definitive
      and
        integral revolution.
  It is because for centuries now
  we have forsaken a certain process of physiological
transmutation,
    and of true organic metamorphosis of the human body,
    which by its atrocity,
      its material ferocity
      and its magnitude
casts into the shadow of a lukewarm psychic night
    all the psychological, logical or dialectical dramas of the
human heart.
  I mean that the body constrains breaths
    and that the breath constrains bodies whose throbbing
pressure,
    the frightful atmospheric compression, render futile,
when they appear,
    all the impassioned and psychic states which conscious-
ness can evoke.

There is a degree of tension, of crushing, of opaque density, of supercharged compression of a body,

which leave far behind all philosophy, all dialectics, all music, all physics,

all poetry,

all magic.

Tonight I shall not show you what can only begin to be revealed after several hours of gradual exercises

besides one needs space and air,

in particular one needs tools which I don't have.

But you will certainly hear in the texts which will be spoken,

emanating from those speaking them,

screams

and impulses of such sincerity, that they show the way towards this total physiological revolution, without which nothing can be changed.

Antonin Artaud

First published, with 'Aliéner l'acteur' in *L'Arbalète*, No. 13, Summer 1948. It was subsequently reprinted in *Théâtre populaire*, No. 5, January–February 1954. The following note appeared at the end of the publication in *L'Arbalète*:

This reading took place on Friday 18 July 1947 and at times I almost *came to revealing* my innermost feelings. I should have to *shit* blood through the navel to get to what I want. Three quarters of an hour of knocking on the same spot with a poker, for example, *drinking* from time to time.

To Put an End to the Judgement of God (*Pour en finir avec le jugement de dieu*)

The idea of a radio broadcast was suggested to Artaud by Fernand Pouey who was in charge of the literary and dramatic programmes on French radio (Radiodiffusion française) and also producer of a series called *La Voix des Poètes* (The Voice of the Poets). The invitation came in November 1947. Artaud immediately set to work, writing new texts and adapting existing material. The programme was recorded between 22 and 29 November, under Artaud's direction, by Roger Blin, Maria Casarès, Paule Thévenin and Artaud himself. For Artaud this was to be a most important event: not only would the broadcast be the latest and fullest manifestation of 'The Theatre of Cruelty' but it would also allow Artaud, for the first time in his life, to reach a mass audience.

The title was duly accepted as soon as Artaud proposed it and the contract was signed on 7 December, *after* the recording had been completed. The editing took place in January and, at that stage, Artaud made a few changes which required some re-recording.

The date of the broadcast was set for Monday 2 February 1948 at 10.45 p.m. and publicized in the usual manner. Towards the end of January a number of newspaper articles were published hinting at a possible scandal. Alarmed by the rumours Wladimir Porché, director-general of French radio, requested a private audition and, on Sunday 1 February, he banned the programme. Fernand Pouey, who had not only commissioned it but had also come to respect Artaud for his work and for his professional dedication, lodged a strong protest against the arbitrariness of the decision and, as a result, he was allowed to invite some fifty people (authors, playwrights, journalists, critics) to a second 'private audition': although the overwhelming majority of the listeners were in favour of the broadcast the ban remained in force. Pouey resigned his post and Artaud decided to publish his text as soon as he possibly could. It appeared three months later, on 30 April, but Artaud had died on 4 March.

In a letter to Pouey, written after the producer's resignation, Artaud expressed his gratitude and repeated, once again, that for himself as well as for the listening public, this programme would have been an event that mattered:

never
was a broadcast AWAITED with more curiosity and impatience by the great mass of the public who were waiting for this broadcast
    just so that they could form an opinion on certain things in life.
    This broadcast is a long declaration against the deep-seated eroticism of things against which everyone subconsciously wants to react and
    against the social, political and religious, and thus
    ritualistic arbitrariness of the law
And the social body is tired of all these rites.

[7 February 1947, *OC*, XIII, 133–4]

The Question Arises of . . . (*La question se pose de . . .*)

The crucial thing
is that we know
that after the order
of this world
there is another.

What is it?

We do not know.

The number and the order of possible suppositions
        in this domain

is precisely
infinity.

And what is infinity?

That is precisely what we do not know!

It is a word
we use
to indicate
the opening
of our consciousness
to the unbounded,
the unstinting and unbounded
possibility.

And what precisely is consciousness?

That is precisely what we do not know.

It is nothingness.

A nothingness
we use
to indicate
when we don't know something
many facets
we don't know
and so

we say
consciousness,
the facet of consciousness
but there are a hundred thousand other facets.

So?

It seems that consciousness
is bound
in us
to sexual desire
and to hunger;

but it might
very well
not be bound
to them.

It is said,
it could be said,
there are those who say
that consciousness
is an appetite,
the appetite for life;

and immediately
beside the appetite for life,
the appetite for food
immediately springs to mind;

as if people did not eat
without any kind of appetite;
and yet are hungry.

For that too
exists
to be hungry
without an appetite;
so?

So

the space of possibility

was given to me one day
like a big fart
which I will fart;

but neither the space
nor the possibility
I did not know precisely what they were,

and I didn't feel the need to think about them,

they were words
invented to define things
which existed
or did not exist
in the face of
the pressing urgency
of a need:

the need to abolish the idea,
the idea and its myth,
and to have the thundering manifestation
of this explosive necessity
reign in its place:
to distend the body of my inner night,

the inner nothingness
of my self

which is night,
nothingness,
thoughtlessness,

but which is explosive assurance
that there is
something
to make room for:

my body.

And really
should my body be reduced
to this stinking gas?
Should I say that I have a body

because I have a stinking gas
welling up
in my insides?

I do not know
but
I know that
                space,
                time,
                dimension,
                becoming,
                future,
                coming,
                being,
                non-being,
                self,
                non-self,
mean nothing to me;

but there is one thing,
which is something,
one single thing
which is something,
and which I feel
because it wants
TO GET OUT;
the presence
of the pain
in my body,

the threatening,
never tiring
presence
of my
body;

however hard I am pressed with questions
and however strongly I deny all questions
there is a point
when I see myself compelled
to say no,

          NO

then
to negation;

and this point
is when I am pressed,

when I am pressurized
and am milked
until the discharge
in me
of food,
of my food,
and its milk,

and what is left?

How I am suffocated;

and I don't know if it is an action
but pressing me thus with questions

until the absence
and to the nothingness
of the question
I was pressed
as far as the suffocation
in me
of the idea of the body
and of being a body,

and that was when I felt the obscene

and I farted
irrationally
excessively
and in revolt
at my suffocation.

It's because I was pressed
right to my body

right to my body

**and that is when
I blew it all up
because no one ever
touches my body.**

[*OC*, XIII, 91–7]

Poem written in October 1947, i.e. *before* Artaud had been invited to prepare a broadcast. It was included in the programme, read by Paule Thévenin.

As already stated, a number of texts especially written for the broadcast had to be left out because of a shortage of time. The following extract is particularly interesting as it emphasizes once again Artaud's determination to ensure that theatre should have a real and lasting impact on the spectator:

There is nothing I loathe and detest more than the idea of spectacle, of performance,

i.e. of virtuality, of non-reality,

tagged on to everything which appears in public and is exhibited,

the idea which, for example, has saved high mass and made it admissible to countless groups of people who would never have stomached it otherwise,

the idea that mass is only a spectacle, a virtual performance, which doesn't exist and is useless;

but there is the opposite view that under its virtual and theatrical aspect mass is, on the contrary, a spectacle which is useful,

(mass contains one of the most effective means of real action in life, but that is something the great public doesn't know, and it is not aware that this means of action is deadly, that it is erotic and dark; we talk about black mass but it's the essence and the very *raison d'être* of mass to be black,

and there is no white mass,

every celebrated mass is one more *sexual* act in the wilderness.)

So let us come back to the idea that this whole broadcast was made only to protest against this so-called principle of virtuality,

of non-reality,
    indeed of performance,
    unfailingly tagged on to everything which appears in public and
is exhibited, as if we actually wanted it to civilize and at the same
time paralyse monsters, to transmit through the medium of the
stage, the screen, or the microphone, possibilities of explosive
deflagration, too dangerous for life, and which we divert from life.

[*OC*, XIII, 258–9]

To Wladimir Porché, Director of Broadcasting

Sir,
    Permit me to be a little more than just revolted and *scandalized*
by the measure which has just been taken at the last minute against
my
    Radio broadcast:
To Put an End to the Judgement of God,
which I had worked on for more than two weeks and which had
    been announced in all the papers for a month and more.
And you are not unaware of the extent of the curiosity with which
    this broadcast had been awaited by the great French public
who were hoping it would be a kind of deliverance,
counting on an acoustic harmony which would have finally
wrested it from the normal run-of-the-mill broadcasts.
You had ample time, well before last Sunday afternoon when you
    thought it necessary to ban it, [to become aware] of the
    particularly favourable atmosphere which surrounded the
broadcast of this programme.
Now I search in vain for the offence it might have caused those
    well-meaning people
who had not adopted a stance
        in advance
as is the case here.
I, the author, like everyone else, heard the entire programme on
tape, firmly resolved to let nothing pass
        which might affront
        taste,

morality,
good manners,
honourable intentions,
or which might
exude
boredom,
déjà vu,
routine,
I wanted a new work which would latch on to certain organic
   points of life,
a work
in which one feels one's whole nervous system
illuminated as if by endoscope
with vibrations,
which call upon
    man
    TO COME OUT
    WITH
    his body
and follow in the sky this new, strange and dazzling Epiphany.
But the glory of the body is possible
    only if
    nothing
in the spoken text
is there to shock,
is there to spoil
this kind of search for glory.
Well I am looking.
And I find
1. the pursuit of Fecality,
a text studded with violent words, shocking remarks, yes there are
violent words, shocking remarks, but in an atmosphere so *outside
life*
   that I don't believe that any public
   could possibly be scandalized by it.
Everybody, including the coalman, should understand
that we are fed up with vulgarity
– physical as well as physiological,
and LONG FOR a fundamental

change
OF THE BODY

Then there's the attack at the beginning on American capitalism.
But today one would have to be very naïve, mister Wladimir
Porché,
    not to understand that American capitalism and
    Russian communism are both leading us to war,
and so with voices, drum, and xylophonics, I'm alerting
    individuals to stand together.

I am

Antonin Artaud
4 February 1948

[OC, XIII, 130–2]

To René Guilly

[7 February 1948]

Sir,
I thought I was dreaming this morning when I read your article in
    Combat.
Astonished, what is more, that it was allowed to be published.
But I have a much higher opinion of this famous mass audience
    than you.
I believe it is infinitely less rotten with prejudice than you think.
Those people who, on Monday evening, eagerly sat next to their
    radio and were awaiting, with unprecedented curiosity and
    impatience, the broadcast entitled 'To Put an End to the
    Judgement of God' were in fact members of this mass audience,
barbers,
washerwomen,
tobacconists,
ironmongers, joiners, printworkers,
in short, all those people who earn their living by bloody elbow
    grease and not those capitalist shit-merchants
with hidden wealth
who go to mass every Sunday and who desire above all respect for
    rituals and the law.

It is such people along with certain prematurely wealthy pimps
    from the Butte [Montmartre] who have this nauseating fear of
    words,
whom my broadcast might have terrified.
Whatever it is,
It was a sin
and a crime
to ban a human voice appealing for the first time in this age to
    man's good nature
from speaking out.
2. Books, texts, journals are tombs, Mr René Guilly, tombs to be
    at last opened up.
We shall not live forever surrounded by the dead
       and by death.
If there are prejudices anywhere,
they must be destroyed,
       the *duty*
I repeat

THE DUTY

of the writer, of the poet
is not to lock himself up like a coward in a text, a book, a journal
    from which he will never again emerge
but on the contrary to come out
openly
      to rouse,
      to attack
      public attitudes,
      if not
      what use is he?
And why was he born?
3. In any case,
I am not a choirmaster,
since I never could sing,
let alone
make others sing.
The most I attempted in this radio broadcast, I who had never
    touched an
instrument in my life, was some local xylophonics on an
    instrumental xylophone

and the effect was achieved.

I mean to say that this broadcast was a quest for a language any
    dustman or coalman could have understood
which would convey by means of bodily emission the highest
    metaphysical truths.
That's what you yourself recognized and for this reason it was a
    shame and a disgrace to ban it.
That's what I wanted to tell you, Mr René Guilly.

                          Antonin Artaud

                      [*OC*, XIII, 135–7]

Guilly, a journalist with the left-wing daily *Combat*, was among the
invited audience on 5 February. On 7 February he published a long
and most negative article on *Pour en finir avec le jugement de dieu*.
Guilly declared that he agreed with the ban on the grounds that the
director of radio would justifiably have been sacked if he had gone
ahead with the broadcast. He went on to state that whereas 1000
listeners might have been interested, 15 million would have been
offended. He further argued that 'by his very nature this mad genius
is not – and must not be allowed to be – a public figure'. He then
accused those of his colleagues who supported Artaud, and who
protested against the ban, of mere trendiness. He assured his readers,
however, that personally he did not share the prejudices of the 15
million 'listeners' who would never hear the programme and that he
counted himself among the happy few capable of appreciating rare
works! The same paper printed a second article, written by the avant-
garde critic Maurice Nadeau, opposing Guilly's viewpoint on 8–9
February. For further press coverage of the event see *OC*, XIII,
322–41 and 354–7.

To Paule Thévenin

                      Tuesday 24 February 1948

Paule, I am very sad and desperate,
my body hurts all over,
but in particular I get the feeling that people have been
disappointed by my radio broadcast.
Where there is *machinery*
there is always void and nothingness,

there is a technical intervention which distorts and destroys what
   has been created.
The criticisms of M. and A.A.[1] are unjust but they must stem
   from a failure in transmission,
that's why I shall never touch Radio ever again,
and I will devote myself from now on
exclusively
to the theatre
as I conceive it,
a theatre of blood,
a theatre which at each performance will stir
something
in the body
of the performer as well as the spectator of the play,
but actually,
the actor does not perform,
he creates.
Theatre is in reality the *genesis* of creation:
It will come about.
I had a vision this afternoon – I saw those who will come after me
   and who don't quite have a body yet because swine like those at
   the restaurant last night eat too much. There are those who eat too
   much and others who, like me, can no longer eat without *spitting*.
Yours.

Antonin Artaud

[*OC*, XIII, 146–7]

1. 'M.' refers to Marthe Robert and 'A.A.' to Arthur Adamov. The
critic and the playwright, both friends of Artaud, had attended the
private broadcast of *To Put an End to the Judgement of God* on 23
February, but their critical comments had hurt Artaud.

A week later, on 3 March, Artaud had lunch with the Thévenins.
During his visit to their home he gave Paule Thévenin power of
attorney to deal with publishers and to handle royalties.

The following morning, 4 March, the gardener found Artaud
sitting at the food of his bed, clutching a shoe in his hand, dead.

He was buried on 8 March with no religious ceremony at the
cemetery in Ivry, near Paris.

Who Am I?

Who am I?
Whence do I come?
I am Antonin Artaud
and I proclaim it
as loud as I know how
instantaneously
you'll see my real body
shatter
and reassemble
in ten thousand shining shapes
a new body
in which you will never be able
to forget me.

Qui suis-je?

Qui suis-je?
D'où je viens?
Je suis Antonin Artaud
et que je le dise
comme je sais le dire
immédiatement
vous verrez mon corps actuel
voler en éclats
et se ramasser
sous dix mille aspects notoires
un corps neuf
où vous ne pourrez
plus jamais m'oublier.

[*OC*, XIII, 118]

Select Bibliography

ARTAUD'S WRITINGS

Œuvres complètes, Paris, Gallimard, 1956–
  superseded by *Œuvres complètes*, Paris, Gallimard, 1976 – (*Nouvelle édition revue et augmentée*), volumes I to XXV.
Lettres à Génica Athanasiou, Gallimard, Le Point du jour, 1969
Nouveaux Écrits de Rodez, Gallimard, Blanche, 1977
Lettres à Anie Besnard, Le Nouveau Commerce, 1977

ENGLISH TRANSLATIONS

Collected Works, translated by Victor Corti, London, Calder and Boyars, 1968–, Volumes 1 to 4
The Theatre and Its Double, translated by Mary Caroline Richards, New York, Grove Press, 1958
The Cenci, translated by Simon Watson Taylor, London, Calder and Boyars, 1969
Artaud Anthology, edited by Jack Hirschman, San Francisco, City Lights Books, 1965
Antonin Artaud, Selected Writings, edited by Susan Sontag, New York, Farrar, Straus and Giroux, 1976

BOOKS ON ARTAUD (in French)

Artaud (Colloque de Cerisy, 1972), Paris, Gallimard (10/18), 1973
Danièle André-Carraz, *L'Expérience intérieure d'Antonin Artaud*, Paris, Le Cherche-Midi, 1973
J.-L. Armand-Larouche, *Antonin Artaud et son double*, Périgueux, Pierre Fanlac, 1964
Françoise Bonardel, *Antonin Artaud ou la fidélité à l'infini*, Paris, Balland, 1987
Monique Borie, *Antonin Artaud: le théâtre et le retour aux sources*, Paris, NRF, Bibliothèque des idées, 1989
Pierre Brunel, *Théâtre de la cruauté ou Dionysos profané*, Paris, Librairie des Méridiens, 1982
Michel Camus, *Antonin Artaud, une autre langue du corps*, Bordeaux: Opales, 1996
Georges Charbonnier, *Essai sur Antonin Artaud*, Poètes d'aujourd'hui, Paris, Seghers, 1959

Camille Dumoulié, *Antonin Artaud*, Paris, Seuil, 1996

Jacques Garelli, *Artaud et la question du lieu*, Paris, José Corti, 1982

Henri Gouhier, *Antonin Artaud et l'essence du théâtre*, Paris, Vrin, 1974

Evelyne Grossman, *Artaud–Joyce, le corps et le texte*, Paris, Nathan, 1996

Otto Hahn, *Portrait d'Antonin Artaud*, Paris, Soleil Noir, 1968

Simon Harel, ed., *Antonin Artaud: figures et portraits vertigineux*, Montreal: XYZ, 1995

Jean Hort, *Antonin Artaud, le suicidé de la société*, Geneva, Connaître, 1960

Mireille Larrouy, *Artaud et le théâtre, 1920–1935, quinze ans de bonheur*, Toulouse, CRDP Midi-Pyrénées–CDDP Aveyron, 1997

Jean-Jacques Levêque, *Antonin Artaud*, Paris, Henri Veyrier, 1985

Florence de Mèredieu, *Antonin Artaud: portraits et gris-gris*, Paris, Blusson, 1983

— *Antonin Artaud, les couilles de l'Ange*, Paris, Blusson, 1992

— *Antonin Artaud, voyages*, Paris, Blusson, 1992

Jacques Prevel, *En compagnie d'Antonin Artaud*, Paris, Flammarion, 1974, 1994

A. Roumieux, *Artaud et l'asile*, 2 volumes, Paris, Séguier, 1996

Susan Sontag, *A la rencontre d'Artaud*, Paris, Christian Bourgois, 1976

Paule Thévenin, *Antonin Artaud, ce désespéré qui vous parle*, Paris, Seuil, 1993

Alain Virmaux, *Antonin Artaud et le théâtre*, Paris, Seghers, 1970 and Gallimard (10/18), 1976

Alain et Odette Virmaux, *Antonin: un bilan critique*, Paris, Pierre Belfond, 1979

—*Antonin Artaud–Qui êtes-vous?*, Lyon, La Manufacture, 1986 (sold with the recording of the broadcast *Pour en finir avec le jugement de dieu*) and 1996 (without the recording)

BOOKS ON ARTAUD (in English)

Stephen Barber, *Antonin Artaud: Blows and Bombs*, London, Faber & Faber, 1993

Alfred Bermel, *Artaud's Theatre of Cruelty*, New York, Taplinger, 1977

Julia F. Cotich, *Antonin Artaud*, Boston, Twayne, 1978

Martin Esslin, *Artaud*, Glasgow, Fontana/Collins, 1976

Jane Goodall, *Artaud and the Gnostic Drama*, Oxford, Oxford University Press, 1994

Ronald Hayman, *Artaud and After*, Oxford, Oxford University Press, 1977

Bettina L. Knapp, *Antonin Artaud, Man of Vision*, Swallow Press, 1969 and 1980

Naomi Greene, *Antonin Artaud, Poet Without Words*, New York, Simon and Schuster, 1970

Gene A. Plunka, ed., *Antonin Artaud and the Modern Theater*, Rutherford, N.J., Fairleigh Dickinson University Press, 1994

Eric Sellin, *The Dramatic Concept of Antonin Artaud*, Chicago, 1968

Brian Singleton, *Artaud: Le Théâtre et son double*, London, Grant & Cutler, 1998

John C. Stout, *Antonin Artaud's Alternate Genealogies: Self-Portraits and Family Romances*, Waterloo, Ont., Wilfrid Laurier University Press, 1996

BIOGRAPHIES (in French)

Jean-Louis Brau, *Antonin Artaud*, Paris, La Table Ronde, 1971

Thomas Maeder, *Antonin Artaud*, Paris, Plon, 1978

JOURNALS AND ARTICLES (in French)

Cahiers Renaud-Barrault, Nos 22–23, 1958 (reprinted in No. 69, 1969)

Europe, revue littéraire mensuelle, Nos 667–668, November–December 1984

La Tour de feu, Nos 63–64, December 1959 (reprinted in No. 112, December 1971, and again in No. 136, December 1977)

Magazine littéraire, No. 206, April 1984

Nouvelle Revue Française (*NRF*), No. 261, June 1935 ('Les Cenci d'Antonin Artaud' by Pierre-Jean Jouve)

Obliques, Nos. 10–11, 1976

Osidiane, No. 5, March 1979

Tel Quel, No. 20 (Winter 1965); Nos 39 and 40 (Autumn and Winter 1969)

Théâtre populaire, No. 18, May 1956

JOURNALS AND ARTICLES (in English)

Art Press International, No. 18, May 1978

The Drama Review, T-54, June 1972

Theatre Quarterly, No. 6, Summer 1972

Theatre Research International, Vol. II, No. 2; Vol. IV, No. 1; Vol. 6, No. 1; Vol. 9, No. 1; Vol. 25, No. 3

Twlane Drama Review, T-22, Winter 1963 + T-34, Winter 1966

Analytical Name Index

outside France for his part in *Les Enfants du paradis*. Director of L'Odéon-Théâtre de France (1958–68), Théâtre d'Orsay (1974–80), Théâtre du Rond-Point (1981–92). Famous for directing plays by Claudel, Ionesco, Beckett . . . xi, xv, xvii, xxi, xxii, 167–171

BAUDELAIRE, Charles (1821–67) Romantic poet. Forerunner of the surrealist movement. xii, 203, 209

BENDA, Julien (1867–1956) Writer and polemicist. His major work, *La Trahison des clercs* (1927), attacked French intellectuals for having betrayed the ideals of freedom and justice. 72

BLIN, Roger (1917–84) Actor and director. Artaud's closest friend. Played a small part in *The Cenci*. Directed the first production of many plays by Adamov, Genet and Beckett. xi, xvii, 186–7, 220

BLOCH, Jean-Richard (1884–1947) Novelist and playwright. Founder editor of the review *Europe* (1923). 69–70

BLOK, Alexandr Alexandrovich (1880–1921) Russian poet and dramatist. *The Fairground Booth* (1906). xvii

BOEHME, Jakob (1575–1624) German mystic philosopher and theologian. His aim was to find spiritual unity in a world divided by original sin. 10, 11, 148

BOSCH, Hieronymus (1450–1516) Flemish artist. 122

BRECHT, Bertolt (1898–1956) German playwright and director. xxii

BRETON, André (1896–1966) Poet, the 'Pope of Surrealism'. Founder and main theorist of the movement. xvii, xxvii, xxviii, 19, 29, 30, 178–180, 201, 204–212

BROOK, Peter (born 1925) English theatre director, influenced in the 1960s by the writings of AA. Founder in 1973 of the Centre International de Création Théâtrale, Paris, and noted for his engagement with the cultures of Africa and the East, most notably and controversially in his 1985 production of *The Mahabharata*. xxx, xxxvi

BRUEGHEL, Pieter (1525–69) Flemish Renaissance painter. xxx

BÜCHNER, Georg (1813–37), German poet, novelist and playwright. *Danton's Death, Woyzeck, Leonce and Lena*. xv, 73, 118

BUÑUEL, Luis (1900–83) Spanish surrealist film director. 22

BYRON, George Gordon Noël, Lord (1788–1824) English romantic poet. 69

CALDERÓN DE LA BARCA, Pedro (1600–81) Spanish playwright of the Golden Age, *The Great Theatre of the World* (1645), *Life Is a Dream* (1633). xviii, 6, 7, 8

ČAPEK, Karel (1890–1938) Czech playwright. *R.U.R.* (1920). xix

CASARÈS, Maria (1922–96) French actress of Spanish origin. 220

CASSOU, Jean (1897–1986) Writer and art critic. 84

DULAC, Germaine (1882–1942) Film director, pioneered 'art films'. Created the Fédération française des ciné-clubs in 1924. Directed AA's *The Shell and the Clergyman* (1927). xiv, xx, 60

DULLIN, Charles (1885–1949) Actor and director. Began his career at the Vieux-Colombier, under Jacques Copeau in 1913. Started his own school, École nouvelle du comédien, in 1921. Founded his theatre, the Théâtre de l'Atelier, in 1922. In 1926 he organized the Cartel des Quatre with Baty, Jouvet and Pitoëff. Director of the Théâtre Sarah-Bernhardt (1940–7). xiii, xvii, xviii, xxiv, xxx, 3, 5–7, 37, 41, 168

EISENSTEIN, S. M. (1898–1948) Russian film director. 46

ELSKAMP, Max (1862–1931) Belgian symbolist poet. 10

EURIPIDES (480–406 BCE) Greek dramatist. *Medea* (431 BCE), *The Bacchae* (405 BCE). xvii, 87, 191

EVREINOV, Nikolai Nikolaievich (1879–1953) Russian playwright, theorist and director. Insisted on the importance of the notion of 'theatricality' in the theatre. *The Chief Thing* (1919). 16

FARGUE, Léon-Paul (1874–1947) Poet. 118

FAULKNER, William (1897–1962) American novelist. Nobel Prize. 171

FERDIÈRE, Gaston (1907–90) Psychiatrist and writer. Director of the clinic in Rodez where AA stayed from 1943 to 1946. xvii, xxii, xxv, xxvi, xxvii, 176, 187, 203

FORD, John (1586–1639) Jacobean playwright. *'Tis Pity She's a Whore* (1626). xxx, 12, 73, 129, 130

GANCE, Abel (1889–1981) Film director. *Napoléon* (1927, silent; 1934, with sound added). xiv, xix

GÉMIER, Firmin (1869–1933) Actor and director. Started in melodrama. Worked with André Antoine and Lugné-Poe. Was the original Ubu (1896), director of the Théâtre National Ambulant (1911), of the Théâtre National Populaire (1920) and of the Théâtre de l'Odéon (1922–30). xiii, 4, 5, 37

GIDE, André (1869–1951) Novelist, poet and playwright. Nobel Prize for Literature (1947). Founder of the *Nouvelle Revue Française*. Translator of *Arden of Faversham*. Member of the Académie française. xxvii, 40, 72, 76–81, 83, 159–62, 201, 203

GILLES, Yvonne, a young painter whom AA met at Divonne-les-Bains in 1917. They corresponded until the early 20s. xiii, 5

GIRAUDOUX, Jean (1882–1944) Diplomat and writer. Successful playwright thanks to his collaboration with Louis Jouvet. 51, 53

GOGH, Vincent van (1853–90) Dutch painter. xvii, 209

GORKI, Maxim (1868–1936) Russian novelist and playwright. *The Mother* (1907), his most famous and most revolutionary novel, was

WATSON, Peter, editor of the literary journal *Horizon*, recipient of a very important letter from Artaud. 25, 194–200

WEBSTER, John (c. 1580–1624) Elizabethan/Jacobean dramatist. *The White Devil* (c. 1612), *The Duchess of Malfi* (c. 1614). 73, 76

WILDE, Oscar (1854–1900) Anglo-Irish playwright, poet, novelist and wit. 97

ZOLA, Émile (1840–1902) Naturalist writer. xix

Main Theatres Cited

ATELIER THÉÂTRE DE L', company founded by Charles Dullin in 1921–2. He then established himself at the Théâtre Montmartre (place Dancourt in Montmartre) which he renamed 'Théâtre de l'Atelier'.

BOULEVARD, THÉÂTRE DU, The name comes from the many theatres situated along the boulevard du Temple and the Grands Boulevards which specialize in melodramas, vaudevilles, operettas and commercial comedies.

CARTEL DES QUATRE, An organization linking four private arts theatres from 1924 to 1939: the Théâtre de l'Atelier (Dullin), the Comédie des Champs-Élysées (Jouvet), the Théâtre des Mathurins (Pitoëff) and the Studio des Champs-Élysées (Baty). The Cartel injected new life into French (Parisian) theatres between the wars, introduced many new French and foreign plays and playwrights, and reinterpreted the classics.

COMÉDIE-FRANÇAISE, LA, French national theatre founded by royal decree in 1680 when Louis XIV brought together Molière's 'comic' troupe and the 'tragic' actors of the theatres of the Hôtel de Bourgogne and Hôtel du Marais. Until recently the Comédie-Française performed almost exclusively the French classical repertoire.

ŒUVRE, THÉÂTRE DE L', Avant-garde theatre of the late nineteenth and early twentieth century founded by Lugné-Poe.

VIEUX-COLOMBIER, THÉÂTRE DU, Art theatre founded by Copeau in 1913.

LUGNÉ-POE, Aurélien-Marie (1869–1940) Actor and director. Founder of the Théâtre de l'Œuvre (1893), director of the original production of Jarry's *Ubu roi* (1896). xiii

MAETERLINCK, Maurice (1862–1949) Belgian poet, novelist and playwright. Chief exponent of French symbolist theatre. Nobel Prize for Literature (1911). *Pelléas et Mélisande* (1892), *L'Oiseau bleu* (The Blue Bird, 1908). 9–13

MANSON, Anne (Georgette), journalist, friend of AA. She met him in 1937, prior to his trip to Mexico. 177–8

MARAT, Jean-Paul (1743–93) Popular hero of the French Revolution. Murdered by Charlotte Corday. xix

MATISSE, Henri (1869–1954) French 'Fauvist' painter. xxxi

MEYERHOLD, Vsevolod Emilievich (1874–1942) Russian director. Started his career as an actor with Stanislavski. Revolutionized Russian theatrical art in the early years of the twentieth century. xxii, 16, 63

MIRBEAU, Octave (1848–1917) Novelist and playwright. 12

MNOUCHKINE, Ariane (born 1938) Director of the Théâtre De Soleil, Vincennes, Paris, heavily influenced by the forms of traditional Asian theatres. xxx, xxxiv, xxxvi

MOLIÈRE (Jean-Baptiste Poquelin, 1622–73) Playwright, actor, and director. *L'École des femmes* (School for Wives, 1664), *Don Juan* (1665), *Le Misanthrope* (1666). 6, 7, 13, 17, 87

MOSSÉ, Sonia, Jewish actress and painter. Acquaintance of AA. Murdered in Nazi gas chamber. 183–5

NERVAL, Gérard de (1808–55) Poet and novelist. Much admired by the surrealists. 187, 207

NIN, Anaïs (1903–77) American writer. Parisian socialite of the 30s. 131

NOVALIS (1772–1801) German poet and novelist. 10

OSTERWALD, Jean-Frédéric (1663–1747) Swiss theologian. Translated the Bible into French. In 1707 he published a 'Treatise Against Impurity'. 185

PABST, Georg Wilhelm (1885–1967) German film director. *The Threepenny Opera* (1931). xx

PAULHAN, Jean (1884–1968) Man of letters, director of the *Nouvelle Revue Française* (1925–40; 1953–68). Founded during the war the literary journal *Les Lettres Françaises* and the publishing house 'Les Éditions de Minuit'. Member of the Académie française. xxiv, 36, 64–5, 72, 79–83, 97, 118–9, 126, 152, 160

PIRANDELLO, Luigi (1867–1936) Italian playwright and novelist. *Six Characters in Search of an Author* (1921). Nobel Prize for Literature

(1934). Introduced to France by Pitoëff and Dullin. xiii, xviii, 8–9, 64

PISCATOR, Erwin (1893–1966) German theatre and film director. 63

PITOËFF, Georges (1884–1939) French actor and director of Russian origin. Disciple of Stanislavski and Meyerhold. With his wife Ludmilla, he opened a theatre in Geneva in 1915, but had little success in Switzerland. Director of the Théâtre des Mathurins (1924–39). Introduced a vast repertoire on the French stage: Chekhov, Gorki, O'Neill, Strindberg, Claudel, Anouilh, Pirandello. Member of the Cartel des Quatre. xiii, xviii, xxiv, 9, 37

PITOËFF, Ludmilla (1896–1951) French actress of Russian origin. Wife of Georges. Acted in most of her husband's productions. Scored her greatest success in Shaw's *Saint Joan*. 9

PIUS XII, Pope. 185

PLATO (428–348 BCE) Greek philosopher. 150, 165

POE, Edgar Allan (1809–49) American writer. xii, 3, 4, 5, 203, 207, 209

PORCHÉ, Wladimir, director of French broadcasting (Radiodiffusion française) in 1948, responsible for the ban on *Pour en finir avec le jugement de dieu*. 221, 228

POUEY, Fernand, Literary and dramatic producer on French radio. Commissioned *Pour en finir avec le jugement de dieu*. 220, 221

PUDOVKIN, Vsevolod (1893–1953) Russian film director. *The Mother* (1926), *Storm Over Asia* (1953). xiv, xix, 29, 46

PUGET, Claude-André (1910–75) Playwright. 183

RACINE, Jean (1639–99) Neo-classical dramatist. *Bérénice* (1670), *Phèdre* (1677). 13, 17, 87, 120

RIMBAUD, Arthur (1854–91) Poet. *Les Illuminations* (1886), *Une saison en enfer* (1873). Worshipped by the surrealists. 207, 209

ROBERT, Marthe, poet, literary critic. Friend of AA. 186, 233

ROBUR, Max, see Aron, Robert

ROLLAND DE RENÉVILLE, André (1903–62) Poet and thinker. Member of the surrealist splinter group 'Le grand jeu'. Corresponded with Breton and AA. 86, 119–120

RUYSBROEK, Jan van (1293–1381) Theologian and mystic from Brabant, much admired by Luther and Ignatius de Loyola. Stressed the importance of personal meditation. 10, 11

SADE, Donatien, Marquis de (1740–1814) Writer and philosopher. xv, xxx, 118

SAID, Edward (born 1935) Author of *Orientalism* (1978), the seminal text which challenged Western constructions of the Orient in the arts. xxxi

SALACROU, Armand (1899–1989) Playwright. 22

SCHLUMBERGER, Jean (1877–1968) Writer and co-founder of the *Nouvelle Revue Française*. 10

SENECA (4 BCE–CE 65) Roman philosopher and dramatist. Tutor to the future emperor Nero. *Thyestes, Phaedra, Oedipus, Medea*. xv, xxx, 82, 153–6

SHAKESPEARE, William (1564–1616) xv, xxxiv, 5, 6, 13, 14, 39, 77–81, 87, 118, 125

SHELLEY, Percy Bysshe (1792–1822) English romantic poet. *The Cenci* (1819), *Prometheus Unbound* (1819). xv, 69, 159, 163

SOPHOCLES (496–406 BCE) Greek dramatist. *Antigone* (442 BCE), *Oedipus Rex* (430 BCE). 13, 14, 125, 132

SPENGLER, Oswald (1880–1936) German philosopher and historian. 146

STANISLAVSKY, Konstantin Sergeyevich (1863–1938) Russian actor, director, producer. Founder of the Moscow Art Theatre (1898). Best known for his theory of 'Method' for realistic acting. xxxiv

STENDHAL (1783–1842) Novelist and diplomat. 159, 163

STRINDBERG, August (1849–1912) Swedish playwright and novelist. *A Dream Play* (1902), *The Ghost Sonata* (1907). xiii, xiv, xix, xxiv, xxvii, 29–30, 41–3, 51, 53

SUPERVIELLE, Jules (1884–1960) Poet, novelist and playwright. 109

THÉVENIN, Paule, Editor of AA's complete works. Friend of AA. xviii, 220, 227, 232–3

THIBAUDET, Albert (1874–1936) Philosopher, literary critic for the *Nouvelle Revue Française* from 1912 to 1934. 72

THOMAS, Colette, Actress and novelist. Friend of AA. x, 186, 187

TOLSTOY, Leo (1828–1910) Russian novelist and playwright. 5

TOULOUSE, Edouard, Dr, Psychiatrist. Looked after AA when he first moved to Paris in 1920. He and his wife remained life-long friends of AA. xiii, xxiii

TOURNEUR, Cyril (1575–1626) Elizabethan/Jacobean dramatist. *The Atheist's Tragedy* (c. 1606), *The Revenger's Tragedy* (1607). 40, 69, 63

UNAMUNO, Miguel de (1864–1936) Influential Spanish Republican philosopher, poet and playwright. 156

VILAR, Jean (1912–71) Actor and director of the Théâtre National Populaire (TNP, 1951–63). Founder of the Festival d'Avignon (1947). xi, xvii

VITRAC, Roger (1899–1952) Poet and playwright. Member of the surrealist group in the twenties. Co-founder of the Théâtre Alfred Jarry with AA and Aron. *Les Mystères de l'amour* (1927), *Victor ou les enfants au pouvoir* (1928), *Le Coup de Trafalgar* (1934). xiv, xix, xxiv, 29–31, 39, 43, 47–9

Main Theatres Cited